THE
1966 WORLD CUP FINAL
-MINUTE BY MINUTE-

Dear Chris,
Let's all hope a new edition
of this book is needed later
this year!! (Yes, I know....).
Thank you for being such a
wonderful member of Team M
since 2008.

Birdie x

Praise for *Titanic: Minute by Minute*:

'Reading Mayo is like watching a movie – the panorama starts breathtakingly wide, then suddenly you crash in on a single detail.'
– Jeremy Vine

'Compelling... There is something astonishing or heartbreaking on every page.' **– Daily Mail**

Praise for *Hitler's Last Day: Minute by Minute*:

'Compelling.' **– Radio Times**

'Beyond fascinating... this book brings to life a thousand different people in the most dramatic moment of the last century.' **– Jeremy Vine**

'Fascinating.' **– The Sun**

Praise for *D-Day: Minute by Minute*:

'Studded with extraordinary detail, it's the most joltingly vivid account ever written of the day the Allies gambled everything... Heartbreaking and thrilling by turns.' **– Daily Mail**

'This book creates a remarkably vivid picture of one of the most important days in modern history.' **– The Good Book Guide**

Praise for *The Assassination of JFK: Minute by Minute*:

'Reads like a pacey, page-turning, cold war political thriller.'
– Dermot O'Leary

'A blow-by-blow account of a moment that changed history... The pictures come thick and fast as the tragedy unfolds and some of the images painted are painfully powerful.' **– Radio Times**

'A gripping account of those blood-soaked few days in November 1963.' **– Daily Express**

THE 1966 WORLD CUP FINAL

-MINUTE BY MINUTE-

JONATHAN MAYO

First published in 2016 by Short Books
Unit 316, Screenworks
22 Highbury Grove
London N5 2ER

10 9 8 7 6 5 4 3 2 1

Copyright © Jonathan Mayo 2016

A CIP catalogue record for this book is available from the British Library.

ISBN 978-1-78072-280-1

Printed and bound in Great Britain by CPI Group (UK) Ltd, Croydon, CR0 4YY

Image credits:
Front Cover Photo
England captain Bobby Moore kisses the Jules Rimet World Cup trophy
Getty Images, © Central Press / Stringer

Back Cover Photo
Crowd at an England match at Wembley Stadium during
the 1966 World Cup Finals
Getty Images, © Bob Thomas / Popperfoto

Endpapers
England captain Bobby Moore holds the Jules Rimet trophy aloft,
surrounded by press and photographers
Getty Images, © Popperfoto

Page 31, team formations diagram by Short Books

Page 32 (Saturday 30th July 1966)
Some of the first supporters to arrive at Wembley Stadium
Getty Images, © A. Jones / Stringer

Page 272 (Sunday 31st July 1966)
Bobby Moore emerges from the Royal Garden Hotel and is
greeted by cheering fans
Alamy, © Trinity Mirror / Mirrorpix

Page 282 (After July 1966...)
Jack Charlton sinks to his knees as Geoff Hurst and Martin Peters celebrate
Getty Images, © Popperfoto

Where material has been quoted in this text, every effort has been made to contact copyright-holders and abide by 'fair use' guidelines. If you are a copyright-holder and wish to get in touch, please email info@shortbooks.co.uk

The 'Minute by Minute' format is applied to this publication with
the permission of TBI Media

TBI *
The Big Idea

As heard on BBC
BBC

For Hannah and Charlie and for my parents who took my sister, brother and me shopping on 30th July 1966 and wondered why the streets were so empty.

Contents

Introduction

It was 8.15pm on Friday 29th July 1966 and at the Hendon Odeon in north London, the comedy *Those Magnificent Men in Their Flying Machines* had just started. In a scene set in the office of newspaper proprietor Lord Rawnsley, a reporter asked Rawnsley, played by actor Robert Morley, about the size of the prize for winning his international air race.

'£10,000!'

'Most generous, sir! That should attract fliers from all over the world!'

'That's the idea – nevertheless, I shall expect the prize to be won by an Englishman...'

Sitting in the gloom of the upstairs balcony of the cinema were a group of 25 men – members of the England football squad, together with their trainers Les Cocker and Harold Shepherdson and their manager Alf Ramsey.

Ramsey loved going to see films. His family was so poor that he couldn't afford to go to the cinema until he was 14; since then he had made up for it. He once turned down the chance to go to the Bolshoi so he could see a screening of the film version of *Till Death Us Do Part* at the British Embassy.

A comedy about a pre-First World War air race was not Ramsey's first choice as he prefers westerns, but there were none on at the Odeon that week.

It had become a ritual that after training the England squad would hastily assemble in the foyer of the regular team hotel, Hendon Hall, and then follow Alf Ramsey down the hill to the Odeon, 'like some glorified school trip, struggling to keep up and putting coats on,' as former captain Jimmy Armfield said.

After the half dozen cinema trips the players had made in the previous seven weeks, this would be the last one they would make together. The art deco octagonal Odeon clocks either side of the screen were a constant reminder that it was less than 24 hours to kick-off at the Empire Stadium at Wembley for the World Cup final. In front of a predicted global television audience of 400 million, 11 of the men watching the film would be playing West Germany. Two of the team – Jimmy Greaves and Alan Ball – had no idea if they were playing or not. Greaves had passed a fitness test in the afternoon, but he expected the manager to stick with the team that won the semi-final. Whether he played was the big national talking point. Since he was about ten years old Greaves had never really had to look at a team sheet – he knew his name would always be there. Now, as Geoff Hurst said years later, he was wondering, 'Will I be chosen?'

Hurst already knew that he was in the team for the final. He had literally 'ached at the thought of not being in'. After their last training session that day Alf Ramsey had come up to him and said, 'I want you to know that you'll be playing tomorrow. But, Geoffrey, keep it to yourself. I won't be telling the others.'

For a moment Hurst thought about kissing his manager.

Martin Peters had only just been told. As they were coming through the foyer Alf Ramsey took him to one side.

'I don't want you to repeat this to anyone – I haven't told the others in the team, but I want you to know that you'll be playing tomorrow.'

Peters took a few deep breaths to contain his relief and elation.

Nobby Stiles had known for a few hours – Ramsey had told him after lunch.

'Nobby – are you ready for tomorrow?'

'I hope so...' said Stiles.

'You'd bloody better be,' Alf replied.

During their ten-minute walk to the cinema, the England squad had attracted some double-takes, and there were calls from passers-by wishing them 'good luck!' Car horns beeped in support.

1966 was a year when Britain was 'swinging'. British bands such as the Kinks, the Beatles and the Rolling Stones provided the soundtrack to the year; models such as Twiggy and Jean 'The Shrimp' Shrimpton provided the look and Carnaby Street the clothes. Even British films were cool – 60 million Americans saw *Thunderball* in 1966. The French magazine *L'Express* grudgingly admitted that England was where 'the wind of today blows most strongly'.

But that was not the whole picture. Not everyone was walking down Carnaby Street in velvet trousers with a skinny model on their arm. 1966 was a year beset by strikes and economic crises. In the days before the final, Prime Minister Harold Wilson had flown to Washington to urgently reassure a concerned President Johnson that the British economy was under control.

Many watched the swinging sixties from afar, untouched by the new clothes, music and attitudes. Britain was still an old-fashioned country, and old-fashioned formalities still held sway. Most men watching the football at Wembley on World Cup final day wore suits and ties; the players would never have dared to have a Beatles-style haircut, and at the post-final celebrations the Football Association (FA) kept their wives in a separate room as the banquet was thought to be no place for ladies.

England's victory meant so much to so many people because it was a revolution everyone could share in. It was the most unifying moment of the decade.

Even the sun shone that July afternoon. It was a day remembered by both the players and the fans with a sharpness and an affection that have remained undimmed after 50 years. The stories in this book reflect that emotion felt by all – from pop stars and Boy Scouts to Thames dockers.

The celebrity culture of the pop world had not yet overtaken football. The England of July 1966 had a kind of innocence: footballers lived as neighbours on the same modest housing estate and could simply walk to the cinema before the biggest match of their lives. Alan Ball said years later, 'I tell you what made us what we were – we had this wonderful feeling that we were still part of the people. Every street in England had a footballer living in it. We were ordinary, approachable people. You were welcome to walk the streets, you were patted on the back, you were touchable, reachable.'

Three weeks before the England squad's trip to the cinema to see *Those Magnificent Men in Their Flying Machines*, the chances of them running out onto the Wembley pitch on the 30th July had seemed slim. In the first game of the World Cup tournament – which took place immediately after the opening ceremony – they played Uruguay. Both teams were introduced to the Queen. The England captain Bobby Moore presented her with a bouquet of red, white and blue flowers. 'How happy, those are the right colours. I hope they bring you luck,' the Queen said.

The Wembley Stadium publicity officer Leonard Went had warned the public the game would be so popular that they should stay at home if they didn't have a ticket. In the end the stadium had 20,000 empty seats and the touts outside were left with fists full of tickets. World Cup fever had not yet gripped the nation.

After 90 minutes, the Hungarian referee signalled the end of a goalless draw with an apologetic spread of his hands. The England team were booed off the pitch – it was the first time since 1938 that England had failed to score at Wembley. Alan Ball, Jack Charlton, John Connelly, Roger Hunt and Jimmy Greaves all walked straight into their dressing room and FA officials had to persuade them to come out for the national anthems. Only Alan Ball returned to stand with the rest of the team and the Uruguayans.

'They had ten full-backs and a goalkeeper,' England's Ray Wilson complained of the Uruguay team with some justification, but the home nation had shown little bite in attack. 'England looked to the flair and opportunism of Jimmy Greaves or Bobby Charlton. They looked in vain,' wrote the *Sun*'s Peter Lorenzo. Under the headline: 'ANGRY, BAFFLED GOALLESS ENGLAND', Brian James of the *Daily Mail* declared: 'There is precious little time left to find the secret of destroying teams that have defence as their first and only priority.' The paper ran a cartoon of two men with scarves and England rosettes walking away from Wembley's twin towers; the caption read: 'I thought the bands and the opening ceremony were terrific.'

The joke was painfully true. On the train home, the *Observer*'s Hugh McIlvanney asked two young men wearing huge England rosettes what they thought of their team's performance.

'Rubbish.'

'And their chances of winning the World Cup?'

'Rubbish.'

Jimmy Hill, BBC pundit and Coventry City manager, expressed the nation's pessimism: 'It's not Alf's fault, nobody could win the World Cup with those players.'

Perhaps he was right.

I'm employed to win football matches, that is all.

Alf Ramsey

Q: What was Alf Ramsey like?
A: I don't know, I was only with him six years.

Jack Charlton

One man who still believed in the team was their manager Alf Ramsey. Despite the nation's doubts, he never lost faith in his team. In the dressing room after the goalless draw with Uruguay he surprised them with his reaction to their performance. 'You may not have won, but you didn't lose. And you didn't give away a goal, either. Wonderful, we didn't give them a kick. How many shots did you have to take, Gordon? Two? That's the stuff! Whatever anyone says, remember that you can still qualify, providing you keep a clean sheet and don't lose a game. We can win this cup without conceding a goal.'

'These were the words we wanted to hear,' said Ray Wilson.

The following day Alf Ramsey took the squad to Pinewood Studios, where they had a drink with Yul Brynner, Norman Wisdom, Cliff Richard and Sean Connery who was in the middle of filming *You Only Live Twice*. One scene had to be reshot as a tipsy Ray Wilson fell off his chair with a clatter. After filming was over Sean Connery told the players, 'I'm honoured to meet you and I know everyone should put their trust in you.' Buoyed up by meeting the stars (and in some cases by alcohol), the players went on to a civic reception at Hendon Town Hall to be honoured by the London Borough of Barnet. During a speech by the mayor of Barnet, a couple of the squad entertained themselves by slipping potato salad in the pockets of unsuspecting local councillors. The pre-Uruguay spirit was restored.

Alf Ramsey had consistently maintained his conviction that England would make the Jules Rimet trophy theirs. On 25th October 1962, the day he was appointed manager, he declared, 'We have a wonderful chance to win the World Cup.' By 21st August 1963 he was sounding even more confident: 'England will win the World Cup. We have the ability, the determination and the players to do it.' He kept repeating this message: on 28th August 1964 he said, 'England will succeed in 1966'; on 5th February 1965: 'I think England will certainly win the World Cup'; on 5th August 1965: 'If anything I am more confident than ever we will beat all comers.'

Once it had been announced by FIFA (Fédération Internationale de Football Association) that the 1966 World Cup was to be staged in England, the FA decided that England needed a new manager. Walter Winterbottom had looked after the side since 1946, with little World Cup success. In both 1950 in Brazil and 1958 in Sweden, they failed to get beyond the first round; in 1954 in Switzerland and 1962 in Chile, they were knocked out in the quarter-finals. Bobby Charlton said of Walter Winterbottom, 'I had a healthy respect for his knowledge and his desire. He had everything that you needed – but he just somehow didn't get that response from the players that you actually needed to win.'

The FA received 59 applications for the post of England manager, but they felt none were up to the job. In October

1962, they approached the manager of Ipswich Town who had taken the small East Anglian club, containing what Jimmy Greaves called 'honest journeymen and discards', from the Third Division South to First Division champions in only seven years. Being champions in their first season was a feat no other side had ever achieved. *The Times* wrote about Ipswich Town: 'They are not exciting, they do not make the pulses race; maybe after all there is a virtue in the honest labourer.'

Before managing Ipswich, Alf Ramsey had had a distinguished career as a full-back for Southampton, Spurs and England. When he took over the England managership from Walter Winterbottom in January 1963, he insisted that he picked the team himself, rather than the FA Selection Committee. Winterbottom was never able to pick his own team for key matches; instead the Selection Committee of 12 men voted on which players should represent their country, most often favouring players from their own clubs. Sir Stanley Rous, the FIFA president who had also been FA secretary between 1934 and 1962 said, 'They say of the camel that it looks so weird it could only have been designed by a committee, and some of our international teams were just as ill-balanced as a result of the system.'

It had taken Ramsey a while to find a winning formula for Ipswich Town and it took a while with England. He tried many permutations before he felt near to getting the squad he was after. His approach was summed up by two of the most experienced members of the final squad. 'The players didn't know best,' Bobby Charlton said. 'Alf was never influenced by any player. He was always after what made a team rather than individuals.' In the words of Jimmy Armfield, 'This was not going to be a team of celebrities.'

In the end the winning formula was discovered by accident.

In February 1965, two of England's wingers, Bobby Charlton and Peter Thompson, were prevented by their clubs from attending an England training camp. In an experiment which he admitted was 'a cruel trick', Alf Ramsey pitted the Under-23 team playing the standard Winterbottom 4-2-4 formation (two wingers and two centre forwards up front, two half-backs in midfield and in defence two centre-backs and two full-backs) against a senior team playing 4-3-3, a more defensive version of 4-2-4. In an attack two midfielders push forward with one dropping back to help the defence. 'The first team ran riot with the lads,' Alf Ramsey recalled.

Team formations are listed in numbers with the defenders listed first – the goalkeeper is never listed. The very first formation devised in the 1860s was 1-2-7; this was because forward passing wasn't allowed and so a large number of forwards attacked together, passing sideways.

Alf Ramsey proved that the new formation could work for England on the international stage in a friendly against Spain in Madrid in December 1965. England had never beaten Spain away from home. Ramsey explained to his players that they wouldn't have 'three players alone up front, but six in attack'. Once again the team ran riot, beating the hosts 2-0. Jack Charlton claimed it could have been 6-0 and an admiring press dubbed them 'wingless wonders'. Bookmakers made England second favourites to win the World Cup and for the first time the public began to believe Alf Ramsey's prediction of success.

Alf Ramsey was a complex man. He resented the football press and found interviews difficult, but he loved talking about the game with his players. Alan Ball hung on his every word. 'Everything I achieved in the game I owe to him. I loved Alf to death. My father said I was a rough diamond but Alf polished me.' Geoff Hurst was a latecomer to the squad – his debut for

England wasn't until February 1966, and he was immediately struck by the respect in which Alf was held, even though he could be a cold and remote figure.

Ramsey grew up in Essex in a cottage with no electricity; his father was a hay and straw dealer. It was rumoured that Alf had taken elocution lessons in the mid-fifties to lose his Essex accent, something he always denied. He did, however, once admit to listening to BBC radio announcers to copy their delivery. In a radio interview in the early 1960s he showed both his reluctance to acknowledge his past and an awkwardness that came from an obsession with choosing his words with care.

'Are your parents still alive, Mr Ramsey?'

'Oh, yes.'

'Where do they live?'

'In Dagenham, I believe.'

The day after the Uruguay match, when the squad were about to leave the set of *You Only Live Twice*, Alf Ramsey said a few words on behalf of the players and thanked 'Seen Connery'. Bobby Moore and Jimmy Greaves burst out laughing. 'Now I've SEEN everything,' Moore whispered to the team. But George Cohen didn't laugh. 'It's true Alf acquired a voice, but actually he'd come from Dagenham from the cloth-cap era and had come a long way. I admired him for that.'

The Tournament

The draw for the World Cup took place in the Royal Garden Hotel in Kensington on 6th January 1966. It divided the 16 teams taking part into four groups who would be based in London, the Midlands, the North West and the North East. England had automatically qualified as the host nation.

At the start of the qualification process, 70 teams had entered, but in the weeks that followed 19 withdrew. South Africa was excluded for breaking FIFA's anti-discrimination laws; Asian and African football associations protested at FIFA's decision to allow only one team to qualify from each continent and withdrew their teams; Syria had been drawn in a European qualifying group but pulled out in sympathy with the Asians and Africans; North Korea refused to withdraw from the Asian qualifying group so that meant they only had to beat Australia to win a place in the finals. They played Australia twice in the neutral venue of Phnom Penh, and following instructions from head of state Norodom Sihanouk, one half of the Cambodian crowd cheered for Australia and the other half for North Korea.

In August 1960, the FIFA congress met in Italy to decide who would host the 1966 World Cup. There were two contenders – England and West Germany. England was awarded the tournament by 34 votes to 27.

Almost immediately preparations began. Only Old Trafford and Wembley met the FIFA specifications for a pitch measuring 115 yards by 75 yards, so in Liverpool a whole row of Victorian terraced houses backing onto Everton's ground, Goodison Park, was demolished, all because the pitch was 12 feet too short; at Sheffield Wednesday's ground at Hillsborough, the Leppings Lane End was constructed (the scene of the 1989 tragedy).

Newcastle United were in dispute with the local council about the lease for St James's Park, so Third Division Middlesbrough found themselves hosting three Group 4 games. The official guide for foreign visitors declared: 'There is no shortage of entertainment of all types in Middlesbrough... it is the only urban centre ever to make the final of Britain in Bloom.' All grounds were adapted to seat 400 journalists in accordance with FIFA's stipulation that they needed 27 inches of work-space rather than the FA's standard 18 inches. At Everton alone £10,000 (about £200,000 today) was spent on new television cables and telephone lines.

Wembley Stadium's concrete stands were covered by a new roof made of aluminium and glass and a new press box was constructed.

The organisers had mixed fortunes when it came to marketing the tournament. They failed to find a single sponsor for their tickets or brochures, but the official mascot, World Cup Willie, the first of its kind, was more successful. The little lion was designed by commercial artist Reg Hoye, an illustrator of Enid Blyton's books. He gave Willie a Beatles-style moptop and a Union flag waistcoat; Willie appeared on a wide range of products from mugs to bottles of ale. Skiffle legend Lonnie Donegan recorded a single praising him: 'He's tough as a lion and never will give up / That's why Willie is favourite for the Cup.'

The original bearer of the name was the World Cup's chief administrative officer, E.K. 'World Cup Willie' Willson. This affectionate nickname from his staff was then passed on to the mascot.

Once the tournament was underway it had its fair share of surprises. The North Koreans, who arrived as underdogs and whose country was not even officially recognised by the British government, humiliated the Italians at Ayresome Park by beating them 1-0. When they eventually flew home to Genoa, the Italians were pelted with rotten tomatoes as they got off their plane.

The people of Middlesbrough took the Koreans to their hearts and 3000 travelled to Liverpool to see them lose 5-3 to Portugal in the quarter-finals.

Brazil were the reigning world champions and had been unbeaten in the World Cup in the previous 12 years, but were unprepared for the more physical European style of play that had developed in the past few years. The favourites were beaten 3-1 by Hungary and then 3-1 by Portugal. Pelé, believed by most people to be the finest player in the world, was on the receiving end of numerous vicious tackles and was carried off injured in the Portugal game. He threatened to retire from international football, saying, 'I don't want to finish my life as an invalid.'

During the three weeks of the tournament there were a number of cultural confusions. When the Brazilian fans arrived at London Airport (soon to be renamed Heathrow), their drums and tambourines were confiscated by suspicious customs officials, but fortunately returned to them just in time for the first game. The Brazilian players' ruling body refused the team permission to meet the Beatles because they said they would be 'a serious threat to the peace and security of the impressionable young men in their charge'. Many players were suspicious of British cuisine. Those 'impressionable young men' heard a rumour that the only meat their Chester hotel served was horse meat and so they only ate cabbage and potatoes. The Portuguese preferred to go into the kitchen of their Wilmslow hotel and cook their own food.

The Italians had expected to be quarter-finalists and so had booked Loyola Hall, a Jesuit retreat centre in Liverpool. The victorious North Koreans took over the booking after Italy's early exit (and inherited Brazil's team bus), but were disturbed by the large number of crucifixes on the walls and in the grounds, and by the fact that they each had their own room. They decided to sleep on each other's floors.

Show us a better team than the Germans and you'll have the World Cup winners.

Daily Mirror, 13th July 1966

The West Germans arrived in England on 8th July in a relaxed mood, having had three weeks off. Despite being ranked as 14-1 outsiders, they felt confident, having won all five of their warm-up matches. They made an immediate impact by crushing Switzerland 5-0 at Hillsborough. Switzerland were without two of their best players who had arrived late at the team hotel the night before, claiming they had got lost while sightseeing in Sheffield. Nonetheless, the *Observer* took the view that 'West Germany's opening statement was the most impressive of the first week'. The most disappointed fan at Hillsborough was Edward Hollinger, who had walked all the way from Zurich to watch the Swiss team, pushing his belongings in a pram.

The Germans faced tougher competition in their second game, which was against Argentina at Villa Park. Bizarrely, to ensure his team had a rest before the match, the West German manager Helmut Schön arranged for the team to have a sleep in the Dunlop tyre factory in Birmingham, after training at the company's sports centre. 'There were mattresses on the floor and the whole team had a sleep for about one hour and then we get up and go to the stadium – that's how it was in 1966,' Franz Beckenbauer recalled.

The West Germany v Argentina match was a bitter, aggressive, nil-nil contest. Wolfgang Overath and Willi Schulz committed numerous fouls but the South Americans were the worse offenders – half-back José Albrecht was sent off for kneeing

Wolfgang Weber in the groin. FIFA warned Argentina to 'play in a more sporting manner in future games'. The England team watched the match at the Hendon Hall Hotel on a television that had been installed at the request of Alf Ramsey to give a direct feed of BBC output. That meant the squad could watch any game, even those not broadcast live.

Returning to Villa Park, the West Germans had only to draw to qualify for the quarter-finals. Their fans unfurled a banner that read: 'The Beatles come from England, the World Cup Winners come from Germany.' That prediction was looking doubtful when, after 24 minutes, they were a goal down. The setback spurred the Germans to find their best form of the tournament so far, with captain Uwe Seeler (known as the Hamburg Torpedo) scoring the winning goal.

The quarter-final between West Germany and Uruguay was the angriest yet. In the second half, English referee James Finney annoyed the Uruguayans by dismissing their appeals for an obvious goal-line handball by Karl-Heinz Schnellinger which denied them the lead. A fight broke out – Lothar Emmerich kicked the Uruguay captain Horatio Troche, only for Troche to respond by kicking Emmerich in the stomach. Finney sent Troche off, and as he left the pitch he stopped to slap Uwe Seeler in the face, who simply burst out laughing. By the end of the game, the South Americans were down to nine men and had conceded four goals.

The semi-final was held at Goodison Park. This time West Germany's opponents were the Soviet Union. Helmut Haller and Franz Beckenbauer scored for West Germany in a 2-1 win. At the end of the game a large number of German fans invaded the pitch in celebration. The home fans responded by chanting: 'Go home, you bums, go home' and 'England! England!' But neither West Germany's fans nor their players had any intention of going home – they were in the final of the World Cup.

*

After the disappointing opening game against Uruguay, England faced Mexico at Wembley. For 36 agonising minutes, it seemed that England wouldn't give the white-coated men in charge of the Wembley scoreboards a chance to place any numbers next to their name. Then Roger Hunt passed the ball to Bobby Charlton near the centre circle. 'There's no one around me, so let's run and see what happens,' Charlton thought. While Hunt fooled the Mexican defence with a decoy run, Charlton didn't even look up as he blasted the ball 30 yards with his right foot. He would say later that it wasn't the best goal he ever scored for England, 'but I never felt more relieved or elated to see the ball smash the back of the net'.

It took another 40 minutes before Roger Hunt scored to settle the game. It was England's fourth win in 16 games in World Cup finals. Although the crowd confidently sang 'Oh, when the Whites go marching in', and England were leading their group, many in the press box were unconvinced by England's performance.

In England's final game in Group 1, their opponents France needed to win by two clear goals to progress to the quarter-finals (and keep England out). The match, watched in the drizzle by a near-capacity Wembley crowd of 96,000, was notable for two tackles. Joseph Bonnel slammed into Jimmy Greaves, dragging his studs down his shin and opening his leg up 'like a red rose towards the end of his bloom'. No substitutes were allowed in 1966 (they were allowed for the first time in the 1970 World Cup), so Greaves' leg was bandaged by the trainer Harold Shepherdson and he carried on playing. He needed 14 stitches after the game and was left with a scar still visible 50 years on.

Fifteen minutes from the end, Nobby Stiles tackled the French inside-left Jacques Simon viciously from behind. He admitted later, 'I was aware it was late, a terrible tackle. I knew it was bad.' As Simon lay in agony, Roger Hunt scored the second of his two goals.

Geoff Hurst, who hadn't played yet in the finals, watched from the stands with Judith, his wife. His frustration at not having a place in the team was exacerbated by a man in front of them insulting the efforts of his colleagues. Judith had to tug at her husband's sleeve to get him to 'shut up and sit down'. Hurst's mood changed when he arrived back at the Hendon Hall Hotel and saw the extent of Jimmy Greaves' injury. 'I knew at once I would play against Argentina in the quarter-finals.'

The FA demanded that Nobby Stiles be dropped. Alf Ramsey told them bluntly, 'If Stiles goes, I go.'

> **England's quarter-final with Argentina was not so much a football match as an international incident.**
>
> **Hugh McIlvanney, the Observer, 25th July 1966**

'Well, gentlemen, you know the sort of game you have on your hands this afternoon,' Alf Ramsey told his team on the morning of 23rd July.

The England players were worried already – the quarter-final was sudden-death and as Bobby Moore said later, 'We knew the public doubted we could do it, because we hadn't looked like scoring goals. We accepted in our guts it was going to be hard.'

From the outset, both sides were guilty of petty fouls and the German referee Rudolf Kreitlein wrote a long list of names in his notebook. 'One was reminded of a schoolboy collecting engine numbers,' wrote Brian Glanville in *The Sunday Times*. The match had its farcical moments. Nobby Stiles shouted at half-back Roberto Ferreiro, who promptly threw himself to the ground. As the Argentine cautions mounted up, their captain Antonio Rattin became more and more incensed. When Rudolf Kreitlein booked Rattin for tripping Bobby Charlton, the Argentinian spat on the ground in contempt. Kreitlein sent him off.

For ten minutes Rattin refused to move. The stand-off was complicated by the fact that the player and the referee didn't share a common language. The crowd slow hand-clapped and chanted 'Why are we waiting?' Ken Aston, who was in charge of 'referee's logistics' for FIFA, came onto the pitch and was finally able to persuade him to leave. Rattin was the first player ever to be sent off at Wembley.

Ten minutes from the end, Geoff Hurst scored with a glancing header. A small boy ran onto the pitch and forward Oscar Más was so irritated he smacked him around the head. At the final whistle, as the English celebrated, referee Rudolf Kreitlein had to be escorted to safety by two Wembley Stadium security guards and a policeman; his black shirt had been torn open by the Argentinian players.

A furious Alf Ramsey spotted George Cohen swapping shirts with an Argentinian player and rushed onto the pitch to put a stop to it. 'George, you are not changing shirts with that animal,' Ramsey shouted furiously.

The trouble continued off the pitch. An Argentine player urinated in the tunnel and a chair was thrown into the England dressing room.

'Send them in! Send them in! I'll fight them all!' Jack Charlton shouted. Some Argentinian players started kicking in the sides of the England bus. When a FIFA official tried to stop them, they pushed half an orange in his face. It was claimed the fourth official was hit.

Minutes later in the Wembley interview room, Alf Ramsey repeated his description of the Argentinians as acting like 'animals'. The anger in Argentina at the England manager's comments meant that the British ambassador, Sir Michael Cresswell, had to be given a police guard. After pressure from the FA, Alf Ramsey withdrew the comment.

(It was after this match that FIFA official Ken Aston – as he drove home, stopping at a set of traffic lights on Kensington High Street and watching them change – came up with the idea of red and yellow cards for referees.)

England's semi-final against Portugal was a very different affair – a feast of footballing genius. Alf Ramsey described the game to the press afterwards as 'England's greatest victory since I became manager'. After the brutality of so many of the preceding games, the Soviet news agency Tass described the style of football as being 'like a spring of clear water breaking through the sea of dirty football'. The first foul of the game wasn't until the 23rd minute.

Nobby Stiles contained Eusébio, the European Footballer of the Year, not by tackling him, but by backing off, intercepting and marking him out of the game. Alan Ball was a revelation, running non-stop, clearly enjoying every minute. Bobby Charlton scored twice – the first was from 15 yards, the ball ricocheting off goalkeeper Pereira's legs. The second was set up by a selfless Geoff Hurst who'd taken the ball into the box. 'I had little to do except hit it as crisply as I could,' Charlton said. It was an unstoppable shot and his 60th goal for England. The Portuguese players applauded him all the way back to the centre circle.

Jack Charlton, however, didn't enjoy himself as much. He was matched for height by Benfica's tall striker José Torres, who beat him repeatedly in the air. Ten minutes from the end, Torres headed a ball that was destined for the back of the England net, but Jack instinctively leapt and hit it away with his hand. It was a novelty for spectators to see 'Big Jack' looking guilty as the referee awarded a penalty. As Eusébio began his run-up, a white-coated member of the Wembley ground staff up by the scoreboard above the goal jumped up and down and waved his arms to put him off. 'What a good supporter!' a miserable Jack Charlton thought to himself. Despite the distraction, Eusébio scored, but England managed to hold onto their lead until the end. Charlton sank to his knees in relief; Eusébio left the pitch in tears. When the England team got to their dressing room, the rest of the squad had champagne and beer ready. 'England are so good,' Eusébio told the BBC afterwards, 'because they play as a family.'

At a Wembley Stadium full to capacity, the reception of the spectators had been the most enthusiastic of the tournament so far, and for the first time the England players felt that the country was truly behind them, glad to have a strong and skilful team to cheer on to the final.

The British economy was weak and the newspapers were dominated by headlines such as 'THE WORLD PUTS THE POUND UNDER SIEGE' and 'BRITAIN IS DEEPER IN THE RED', so success in the World Cup was providing a well-needed fillip. Television audiences for England games were increasing all the time.

It was three days after the Portugal game that the England squad were in the Hendon Odeon, watching *Those Magnificent Men in Their Flying Machines*. As the air race was about to begin, Robert Morley, playing Lord Rawnsley, walked towards the German bi-plane and declared: 'The trouble with these international affairs is that they attract foreigners...'

The timeline for this book was worked out by using the players' and fans' accounts, newspaper reports, television news, and archive of the final. Interesting events with little indication of when they took place, are given an approximate time.

West Germany

1. Hans *Tilkowski* (Borussia Dortmund), Goalkeeper, Age 31
2. Horst-Dieter *Höttges* (Werder Bremen), Full-back, Age 22
3. Karl-Heinz *Schnellinger* (AC Milan), Full-back, Age 27
4. Franz *Beckenbauer* (Bayern Munich), Half-back, Age 20
5. Willi *Schulz* (Hamburger SV), Centre-back, Age 27
6. Wolfgang *Weber* (1st FC Cologne), Centre-back, Age 27
8. Helmut *Haller* (FC Bologna), Forward, Age 26
9. Uwe *Seeler* (Hamburger FC), Forward, Age 29
10. Siegfried *Held* (Borussia Dortmund), Forward, Age 23
11. Lothar *Emmerich* (Borussia Dortmund), Forward, Age 24
12. Wolfgang *Overath* (1st FC Cologne), Forward, Age 22

England

1. Gordon *Banks* (Leicester City), Goalkeeper, Age 27
2. George *Cohen* (Fulham), Full-back, Age 26
3. Ramon *Wilson* (Everton), Full-back, Age 31
4. Norbert *Stiles* (Manchester United), Midfield, Age 23
5. John *Charlton* (Leeds United), Centre-back, Age 29
6. Robert *Moore* (West Ham United), Centre-back, Age 25
7. Alan *Ball* (Blackpool), Forward, Age 20
9. Robert *Charlton* (Manchester United), Midfield, Age 28
10. Geoffrey *Hurst* (West Ham United), Forward, Age 24
16. Martin *Peters* (West Ham United), Midfield, Age 22
21. Roger *Hunt* (Liverpool), Forward, Age 27

About 1.15pm, 30th July 1966. Some of the first supporters to arrive at Wembley Stadium.

Saturday 30th July 1966

'It is the diamond of my days.'
– Bobby Charlton

5.00am

The lawns and terraces around the Hendon Hall Hotel are
wet with overnight rain. The hotel is an attractive three-storey
ivy-clad Georgian stately home, built on land once owned
by the famous 18th-century actor David Garrick, and now
surrounded by suburban Hendon. A large portico with four
tall brick columns suggests an impressive interior, but its hall,
stairway and rooms are modest in size. In the 19th century,
Hendon Hall was a girls' school, and then an RAF conva-
lescent home in the Second World War. It's five miles from
Wembley and is now used by the England football squad whenever they're playing at the stadium. They have been staying
here since 7th July, four days before the opening match against
Uruguay.

Although Hendon Hall has the England squad under its
roof, the everyday business of the hotel carries on as normal.
There are plenty of other guests staying this weekend, and
later this afternoon there will be a wedding reception in the
banqueting hall.

As well as a television room to watch all the games, the

manager has given the footballers a temporary team room, now full of piles of mail from the public – requests for autographs and cards and letters wishing the players well.

When Alf Ramsey took the England job, one of his first decisions was to stop the practice of London-based players sleeping at home in the run-up to international fixtures. They would stay together from now on. Martin Peters reckons that Alf Ramsey likes it, as it keeps his players away from 'the temptations of the West End'.

Despite the fact that he doesn't normally sleep well in hotels, Alf Ramsey is enjoying a restful night at Hendon Hall. 'My own job was done. The responsibility was now theirs.'

6.15am

At Wembley Stadium fans have already started to arrive. A group who have just been dropped off by a coach look in vain for somewhere to have breakfast before flagging down a milk float passing the stadium car park.

In the small Staffordshire village of Hamstall Ridware, dairy farmers Reg and Philip Hodgskiss are milking their herd of 60 dairy cows in the dawn light on their farm. In a few hours they will be changing out of farming overalls and putting on suits and clambering into their Morris Oxford to head down the M1 to Wembley. They have to be back by 7pm for the evening milking. Philip was supposed to be going to a wedding in the next village this afternoon with his girlfriend Jean, but she understands that the World Cup final is more important.

Fifty-year-old Reg has been a dairy farmer all his life, like his father and grandfather before him; 24-year-old Philip is carrying on the family tradition. They have already been to Villa Park three times to see Group 2 matches – Spain v Argentina, Argentina v West Germany and Spain v West Germany.

Having seen the West Germans play twice, they know it's going to be a tough game for England.

In a terraced house in Middleton, near Rochdale, 16-year-old Anita Dunnington is exhausted – she's been pacing around all night with backache. Anita is nine months pregnant and she and her mother reckon that she's about to go into labour. Anita's married to 18-year-old Alan, but is still living at home with her parents. She and Alan met at the youth club next to her parents' house when Anita was 13. They were married in Oldham Registrar's Office in February.

Neither the football nor the arrival of a baby will disrupt the family's routine; Alan and Anita's father have to go into work this morning – they work at the same factory – and her mother has to stay behind to look after her youngest child. Even if she was free, they have no car, so Anita will be going to the hospital alone.

> *He woke me up every morning, clattering round, knocking into furniture... I just pulled the sheets over my head and said to myself, 'Thanks a lot, God. Please tell me this, too, will pass.'*
>
> *Alan Ball*

6.45am

Nobby Stiles is getting dressed as quietly as he can in his room on the top floor of Hendon Hall. Stiles is a Roman Catholic, and every day of the World Cup he has walked into Golders

Green to attend mass. Although today he is playing in the final, his routine remains the same.

As a schoolboy, Nobby Stiles would get up early seven days a week and set off for the convent chapel where he was an altar boy to assist with seven o'clock mass. 'The ritual became a big part of my life, my identity.'

Each night at the hotel Stiles wrestles with whether he should have a lie-in and get some well-needed rest or go to mass in the morning. He loves the rituals of church and always gives into the strong feeling that if he didn't make his morning pilgrimage he'd break England's successful run of games.

Nobby Stiles thinks his room-mate Alan Ball is asleep, but he has in fact woken him up, as he has every morning for the past seven weeks. Nobby is infamous for his clumsiness on and off the field, prompting sportswriter Hugh McIlvanney to claim that 'Inspector Clouseau was blessedly adroit' compared to the midfielder. 'Inspector Clouseau' has become Nobby Stiles' nickname.

Geoff Hurst describes Stiles and Ball (known as 'Bally') as 'the heart and soul of the team' – but they can also be mischievous. Responsible for picking the five-a-side teams at the end of training sessions, they always make sure that Jack Charlton is picked last. On more than one occasion he's shouted in mock anger, 'I'll kill one of you little bastards!' when they've got back to Hendon Hall.

In the spring of 1966, together with John Connelly, a veteran of the 1962 World Cup, Nobby Stiles and Alan Ball slipped out of the England training camp at the National Recreation Centre at Lilleshall in Shropshire and had a drink at a nearby golf course clubhouse. The players had nicknamed the tough training camp Stalag Lilleshall. They only managed a pint when, overcome by guilt, they returned to base. But they'd been spotted and were sent to the manager's room. Stiles and Ball couldn't look Alf Ramsey in the face.

'I didn't say you couldn't go to the bar, I didn't say you shouldn't go. I just expected you wouldn't go. We are here on serious business and I thought you all understood that. We are going to win the World Cup.'

The players, realising that their place in the team could be under threat, were very apologetic. John Connelly, however, had no intention of apologising.

'What are you two talking about!? We only had a pint, which isn't going to do us any harm after all the training we've been doing.'

Ramsey, initially won over by Stiles and Ball's remorse, exploded with rage. 'Get out of here, all of you! Get out of my sight!'

For days Stiles and Ball worried their escapade had blown their chances of playing in the biggest football tournament on the planet, and knowing how angry their families would be if they found out what they'd risked, they agreed to never mention it to them. Their wives only found out in 2002 when Alan Ball let the story slip when the two couples were eating out together.

Ramsey demands 100% commitment. Jack Charlton's wife Pat is expecting a baby at any moment and Nobby Stiles' wife Kay gave birth to a boy a few weeks ago. Neither player has asked to go home even for one night, as they know it would seriously jeopardise their chances of playing for England.

Bobby Charlton discovered this in June 1964 at the end of Brazil's Jubilee Tournament, which was nicknamed 'The Little World Cup'. When they were sitting in a restaurant, Ramsey asked him, 'What did you think about the tour?'

Charlton told him that it was the best he had ever known and that the team was in great shape for the World Cup in two years' time. Then Charlton added, 'But of course, Alf, it's been a very long *tour and I have really missed my wife and daughter and I will be glad to see them.'*

Alf Ramsey leaned forward. 'If I thought that was your attitude, I wouldn't have brought you on this trip.'

Bobby Charlton never fully understood why he'd responded so harshly but concluded, 'You take the best of him and learned to live with the rest.'

Alf Ramsey is strict, but not unbending. On Tuesday evening, after they beat Portugal in the semi-final, he stood in the bar of the Hendon Hall Hotel and told the team, 'You have done well for yourselves and for your country. But tonight I want you to have just two pints. After the Argentina game you were, well, how shall I put it, rat-arsed. But not tonight, gentlemen, just two pints because we have a World Cup to win on Saturday. When you do it, I will make sure you are then, and for quite some time, permanently pissed.'

A few floors below Nobby Stiles and Alan Ball is an immaculate room that the England captain Bobby Moore shares with Jimmy Greaves. Moore is the one who likes to keep everything neat – he travels with his own travel iron to press his handkerchiefs and, Alan Ball claims, even bank notes. His trousers are lying flat under the mattress.

Moore never starts a game without a neatly ironed kit. His mother used to cut small 'Vs' in the side of his shorts to give him greater room for movement, a job his wife Tina took over for a while – until a pair split during a match. Moore even hangs his jumpers in wardrobes so that they range neatly from dark to light – a habit he's had since childhood. In football dressing rooms he always stands on a bench when getting changed so the bottom of his trousers don't get wet.

Twenty-five-year-old Bobby Moore ('Mooro' to his team-mates) is English football's first pin-up. In 1962, the photographer Terry O'Neill took pictures of the West Ham star surrounded by girls; since then he's advertised Brylcreem (despite the fact that it doesn't work in his curly hair); he has a column in Titbits *magazine, and most recently he's modelled Hardy Amies suits for the* Daily Express. *Ford has given him and his wife Tina a white Escort car with a picture of World Cup Willie on each side.*

Moore has led West Ham to victory in both the 1964 FA Cup final and the European Cup Winners' Cup final the following year and has captained England 24 times. He's admired for his calm authority on the pitch and an uncanny ability to predict play.

In the words of Alf Ramsey: 'Bobby was the heartbeat of the England team, the king of the castle, my representative on the field... I could easily overlook his indiscretions, his thirst for the good life, because he was the supreme professional, the best I ever worked with.'

Nonetheless, Alf Ramsey can be irritated by Bobby Moore and his room-mate Jimmy Greaves. He believes they have been disruptive influences over the past three years. In May 1964, the night before flying out to a friendly in Portugal, Bobby Moore, Jimmy Greaves, Johnny Byrne, George Eastham, Gordon Banks, Ray Wilson and Bobby Charlton slipped out of the team hotel in Lancaster Gate, breaking a curfew, and headed to a bar called the Beachcomber, where Jimmy Greaves says they 'got stuck into a drink called a Zombie, rum-based with a real kick'.

When the seven returned to the hotel at 1am, they discovered Alf Ramsey had placed their passports on their pillows. As Jimmy Greaves said, 'It was his way of saying, "Any more of this and you won't be travelling with England."' Ramsey was furious, but waited two days before saying to his squad after training in Portugal, 'You may all go and get changed now, except, that is, those players who I believe would like to stay and talk with me.' The seven stayed behind and were told, 'If there had been enough players in this squad, I would have sent you all home when back in London.'

A fortnight later, Bobby Moore and Jimmy Greaves pushed their luck further, this time in New York on the eve of a friendly against the USA, by going to see Ella Fitzgerald perform when they should have been asleep in bed. According to the football reporter Ken Jones, Alf Ramsey said to him as the two players giggled at the back of the coach, 'I'll win the World Cup without either of those two.'

In the two months before the World Cup, it looked like Ramsey might be serious. In May 1966 he replaced Moore with Jimmy Armfield as captain for a game against Yugoslavia and dropped him again in June against Finland. Ramsey suggested to reporters that he was thinking about leaving Moore out of his World Cup squad. His plan worked. 'It made me sit up,' Moore said later. 'I never expected to be in the England squad until the letter from the FA arrived through the letter box.'

But Moore still didn't toe the line completely. When the football reporter Nigel Clarke visited Hendon Hall to interview the players a few days before the final, Bobby Moore and Alan Ball showed him six crates of lager cooling in Moore's bath.

6.55am

Nobby Stiles comes downstairs and finds George Cohen in the lobby. Cohen hasn't slept well, partly because of the impending match but also because he fell asleep reading a Dennis Wheatley occult thriller.

'You'll sleep like a baby when the battle's over, you'll have the dreams of a winner, I can feel it in my bones,' Stiles reassures him.

7.15am

The pavements are damp as Nobby Stiles walks down Brent Street to church. He enjoys these early-morning walks; they give him time to think about the game ahead.

'Good luck, Nobby. You're going to do it, mate!' a passer-by shouts.

'Thanks, I think you're right,' Stiles replies.

> **We were tough then – you had to be tough. Nobody shouted 'pain relief! Gas and air!' My mum's attitude was 'you've made your bed, you've got to lie in it'.**
>
> **Anita Dunnington**

7.20am

It's clear that Anita Dunnington is in labour. Her mother runs up the road to the nearest phone box to call an ambulance.

7.30am

Nobby Stiles takes his regular place in the back pew of the Golders Green Catholic church. 'It was a day when anything was possible, and there was nothing desperate about my prayers...' he recalled.

The England training camp at Lilleshall in Shropshire was so tough that the Catholic players were envied for their trips to mass on Sundays. The squad suddenly became full of Anglicans very keen to attend the local parish church. Alf Ramsey nipped their religious fervour in the bud by saying that the warden of Lilleshall was a lay preacher and he was more than happy to hold a service for them at the camp.

Mr McElroy, one of the oldest members of the Wembley ground staff, is walking up the steps in front of the main gates, with his Saturday paper under his arm. As he's done many times before, he gets out his keys and opens up.

Until the Metropolitan Railway bought Wembley Park in 1890 for £32,000, it was no more than 'a few broad acres... watered by many streams'. The Metropolitan Railway's chairman, Sir Edward Watkin MP, wanted to turn the site into a massive amusement park with a huge tower as its main attraction. Visitors to the tower would be brought by train to a new station called Wembley Park.

Gustave Eiffel turned down the commission as he felt it would be unpatriotic for a Frenchman to build such a structure. The French people 'would not think me so good a Frenchman as I hope I am'. So a competition was launched, stating that all entries had to be at least 46 metres taller than the Eiffel Tower.

The winning design was an eight-legged metal structure, 48 metres higher than the Eiffel Tower. To cut costs the design was modified to have only four legs, and work began in June 1893; at the same time a cricket pitch and boating lake were laid out.

The tower never rose higher than its 47-metre first stage, as it began to sink into those 'acres... watered by many streams'. It was christened 'Watkin's Folly' and dynamited in 1907. But by then Wembley Park had become a popular sporting venue, with facilities for football, cricket, cycling, rowing and athletics. The site was chosen as the location for the 1924 British Empire Exhibition – 'a family party to which every part of the Empire is invited'. The exhibition's pavilions were to be located along an avenue called Kingsway (later nicknamed Wembley Way) that ran from Wembley Park Station to a new stadium for 125,000 spectators built on the foundations of Watkin's Folly.

The Empire Stadium was built in 300 days and in April 1923 hosted its first FA Cup final – the notorious 'White Horse' final when 200,000 fans filled the stadium and overflowed onto the pitch and had to be cleared by PC George Scorey on his horse Billie.

The stadium's 100-foot concrete Twin Towers facing Kingsway and modelled on Sir Edward Lutyens' New Delhi, were designed by architect Owen Williams, and soon became iconic symbols both of Wembley and English football.

Between the wars, greyhound racing and speedway were introduced to Wembley to help make it financially viable. At the end of FA Cup finals, 20,000 seats and the two goalposts were speedily removed, in readiness for the dogs. In 1966 they were still essential for Wembley's survival – the Group 1 game between Uruguay and France was moved to White City Stadium as Wembley's owners refused to cancel the evening's greyhound race.

7.45am

Alf Ramsey is having his breakfast in the restaurant at Hendon Hall. He's keeping his distance from Jimmy Greaves, who has recovered from his injury, but still hasn't heard if he's playing today. Greaves takes it as a bad sign that the manager isn't catching his eye.

7.55am

Outside the hotel, photographers are getting shots of Nobby Stiles walking back from mass.

8.00am

The West Germans are having breakfast at the Homestead Court Hotel in Welwyn Garden City in Hertfordshire. The

French squad had stayed there, as had the Argentinians – but only after a stand-up row with their manager Juan Carlos Lorenzo because they had expected to stay in a smart West End hotel.

The West German team is popular in Welwyn. They are polite to autograph hunters and the press, and have given the staff of the hotel ten free tickets for the final and arranged transport for them.

Nobby Stiles is back from church. His room-mate Alan Ball, who still doesn't know if he's playing in the final, asks him if he's heard anything. Stiles has heard nothing.

> *Last night the phone rang in their room – it was Alan Ball Senior.*
> *'Has he picked you, lad?'*
> *'I don't know, Dad.'*
> *'You don't know?'*
> *'Dad, I don't know.'*
> *'Well, I don't know if I can afford to come down there if you're not playing, son.'*
> *'Dad, as soon as I know I'll let you know.'*
> *'Alright son, good night. God Bless, you go to bed.'*

Alan Ball Senior had a career in the lower leagues; his greatest achievement was playing for Birmingham City Reserves. By 1966 he had become a foreman joiner at a firm in Warrington, while managing Nantwich Town part-time. Alan Ball Senior has single-mindedly guided his son's career, refusing to see his slight stature as a barrier to football greatness. He encouraged him to box when he was a teenager, and instead of getting him a bike for his paper round, he told him to run with the bag on his back. 'The faster you run the lighter it will become and the fitter you will be.' The young Ball was so determined to succeed as a footballer that he never squeezed the spots on his face – 'to be repulsive and keep the girls away.'

Like Alan Ball, Nobby Stiles has a father who plays a huge part in his life. Once, when his son was walking down the players' tunnel at Old Trafford after being booked for losing his temper, Charlie Stiles shouted 'Norbert!' and then proceeded to give him a dress-ing-down in public for his disgraceful behaviour while wearing a Manchester United shirt.

Anita Dunnington is in an ambulance on her way to the Royal Oldham Hospital. She is going to the hospital by herself.

> **It was the biggest disappointment of my life... and I hope it always will be. I don't want another.**
>
> **Jimmy Greaves**

8.30am

Martin Peters and his room-mate Geoff Hurst are having breakfast in their hotel room at Hendon Hall. Peters has his usual cereal, toast and tea. They can get more privacy up in their room, as the restaurant is full of other hotel guests.

The two men are reading the morning papers, and it's not England's footballers that dominate the front pages of the tabloids, but their wives. Reporters have discovered that the players' wives haven't been invited to the FIFA banquet this evening to honour the top four teams. The *Daily Mail* has a front-page picture of Tina Moore holding a parcel containing 'a mimosa-yellow silk short dress with a flared skirt, deco-rated with a bugle and topaz heading' (the shop's owner had tipped off photographers that Tina would be there). The paper says she won't be wearing the dress in the banqueting hall of the Royal Garden Hotel, but in a restaurant upstairs called the Chophouse. 'ENGLAND WIVES LEFT OUT OF PARTY' is the *Mail*'s headline. The hotel manager is quoted as saying, 'I don't think an extra 30 guests would put us out.'

The *Sun* headline is: 'ENGLAND WIVES BARRED: FA WON'T INVITE WORLD CUP "WIDOWS" TO CELEBRATIONS.'

Until a few months ago, neither Martin Peters nor Geoff Hurst would have dreamed that they'd be in the squad of 22, let alone playing in the World Cup final. Before the tournament they only had eight caps between them. Martin Peters was so convinced that he wouldn't be involved that he and his wife Kathy decided to move house in July from the estate in Hornchurch, where they lived next door to Judith and Geoff Hurst, to nearby Barkingside. Yesterday Kathy moved house single-handedly. She was so tired she missed the trip organised by the FA for the players' wives and families to see the Black and White Minstrel Show at the Victoria Palace Theatre. (As a tribute to their special guests, the show opened with the song that had been adapted as a football chant 'When the Saints Go Marching In'.)

The sports pages of all the papers discuss whether Alf Ramsey will go for Geoff Hurst or Jimmy Greaves. Brian James, the *Daily Mail*'s football correspondent, writes:

Alf Ramsey, the England manager, last night slept with his secret at the team's headquarters a short coach drive from Wembley, where his final decisions must be put to the test. No one should envy him that decision. For three years he has held down the loneliest job in sport.

Geoff Hurst has the satisfaction of knowing Alf Ramsey's secret.

Jimmy Greaves thinks he knows what the manager has decided. Bobby Moore is waking up to find his room-mate packing his bags.

'What on earth are you doing?'

'It's all over for me, mate. I'm just getting ready for a quick getaway once the final is over,' Greaves says.

Moore knows that his friend is right – Alf Ramsey is unlikely to pick him.

'You can do that tomorrow morning. We'll all enjoy a few bevvies tonight, together, to celebrate us winning the World Cup.'

8.40am

As shops open up around the country, Saturday staff are hanging bunting and Union flags in the windows. In the John Collier's department store in Kingston, Surrey, Malcolm Stock, the manager of the Television and Radio Department, is putting out half a dozen televisions in a semicircle for any customers who want to watch the final. If he's lucky, Malcolm thinks, he may get some sales.

In Morecambe, 17-year-old Brian Bowker is in a phone box at the end of his road dialling the number for Littlewood's department store in the town centre. He is phoning in sick. For the past month Brian has had a temporary job in their stockroom to raise money for teacher training college next year.

Brian isn't ill – he's perfectly well, but he's desperate to watch the final this afternoon.

Last night he told his mother Jane that he wasn't going in to work. Jane, who works in Littlewood's cafeteria and who persuaded the the store manageress to give him the job, wasn't impressed.

47

'What do you mean you're not going into work tomorrow?' his mother said.

'I'm watching the World Cup final – England may never get that far again!'

'You've got to – it's a job, you've made a commitment. There will be millions of others who want to watch the game – like bus drivers, train drivers, airline pilots – they can't just change their schedule!'

Brian reluctantly agreed to go to work in the morning, but today he woke up with fresh resolve. When his mother set off for work Brian told her he'd see her there. But as soon as she was safely on her way, he headed to the local phone box.

Brian is put through to the manageress of Littlewood's.

'I'm not feeling very well…' he begins.

'That's fine, Brian, thanks for letting me know.'

He can hear by the tone of her voice that she's not convinced by his excuse, but perhaps understands.

In Hendon, it's starting to rain. Geoff Hurst and Martin Peters decide that they'll wear boots with long nylon screw-in studs that give better grip on soft surfaces than the usual boots with moulded rubber studs. The loss of speed caused by the screw-in studs is preferable to slipping all over Wembley's pitch in front of the thousands of fans in the stadium and the millions watching on television.

'Don't dare come back beat.'

About 8.45am

Alan Ball finally comes down to breakfast. Alf Ramsey walks straight over to him.

'Jimmy Greaves isn't a fit young man. I'm keeping the same team that beat the Portuguese; you'll play right side of Bobby Charlton.'

Ball dashes to his room to call his father.

Jimmy Greaves still doesn't know for certain he's not playing.

Alan Ball is on the phone.

'Dad – he's picked me!'

'Brilliant, son! I'll fill the Morris Minor up and I'll get down.'

'What advice can you give me today?'

'Son, this is the greatest day of your life, but I'll tell you what, lad, you've got to enjoy it. You've got to puff your chest out, and look around and smile. Take everything in and love every minute of it, because before you know where you are, you'll be sat in that bath, you will, and if you've not done yourself justice, you'll never forgive yourself for the rest of your life!'

'Thanks a lot, Dad, I was all right until you said that...'

'Good luck, son!'

'Thanks, Dad'

'Son?'

'Yes, Dad.'

'Don't dare come back beat.'

9.00am

At Paddington Green Police Station in the office of 'the Governor', the superintendent in charge, 21-year-old PC Peter Weston is being briefed alongside two more experienced constables about the day ahead. Weston has been an officer for only six months after his 13 weeks' training at Hendon Police College. The three constables have been seconded to Q-Division, a team

49

of officers looking after security at Wembley Stadium during the World Cup.

'You are to go to the Football Association at 22 Lancaster Gate,' the superintendent begins. 'Once there, report to the FA secretary, Denis Follows. There is a car waiting for you downstairs – your call sign is Delta 101.'

Weston wonders what on earth the three of them are going to be assigned to do on World Cup final day.

The old brick Paddington Green Police Station is well known to BBC TV viewers as the setting of the police drama Dixon of Dock Green. *In 1966, after over a decade on screen, the series can still attract 11 million viewers on a Saturday night.*

England full-back Ray Wilson is on the phone in his hotel room trying to get the exhaust on his Ford Zephyr fixed. His wife Pat drove down with Bobby Charlton's wife Norma yesterday, and the exhaust went, halfway down the M1. She managed to drive the car ('What a noise it made. Oh my God!') to the Royal Garden Hotel in Kensington where most of the players' wives are staying, and then told Ray that he'd have to sort it. This is not what he expected to be doing this morning.

9.15am

A car pulls into a reserved area of the Wembley Stadium car park. A middle-aged man gets out and walks towards the BBC broadcast vehicles. He is a veteran pilot from RAF Bomber Command who won the Distinguished Flying Cross for carrying out exactly 100 missions over Germany and Occupied Europe; when he flew his last mission he was only 23. Now he is the BBC's main football commentator. Kenneth Wolstenholme likes to be early so he's not caught out by unexpected roadworks or traffic jams. For today's commentary he is being paid £60, the same at the players' match fee.

Since August 1964, Wolstenholme has presented BBC2's Match of the Day *highlights programme. Its early editions achieved low audiences but it was seen as a worthwhile exercise to give BBC cameramen the chance to rehearse for the World Cup finals. In fact, the first* Match of the Day *on 22nd August 1964 had an audience of only 20,000 – less than half the attendance at the match at Anfield they were covering.*

Today the BBC has seven cameras around the stadium. Cameras 1 and 2 are on the television gantry high up under the roof opposite the royal box, Camera 3 is by Exit 37 to the west, Camera 4 is in a hole dug in the side of the pitch called 'The Pit' and Camera 5 is in front of the scoreboard by the giant orange Radio Times advertisement: 'Look and Listen. Radio Times. BBC TV and Radio' (the only advertising allowed at Wembley); behind the goals are Cameras 6 and 7. There are three additional cameras outside the stadium. Each camera weighs 280 pounds and it has taken four men to carry them into position in the days before the opening ceremony.

The BBC also has 19 'effects' microphones around the pitch and suspended above the terraces.

The BBC team of 54 cameramen and engineers is led by producer Alec Weeks, who has already been on site for a couple of hours checking the equipment. Weeks (also ex-RAF) insists that all his team stay at the Hilton Hotel at Wembley away from wives and husbands – he doesn't want anyone late or distracted by domestic concerns.

ITV and the BBC have divided the coverage of the World Cup games between them, but both networks are covering the final.

Each has a new piece of equipment – a slow-motion stop-action machine, the only ones in the country.

In 1964, the broadcasters told the government that colour transmissions of the tournament would be both possible and desirable, but the television manufacturers argued that they couldn't produce enough colour sets in time. There is a suspicion that the delay is really due to the manufacturers wanting to sell all their black-and-white models before introducing colour ones.

In March, the BBC announced that it would be the first broadcaster to offer a regular service in colour, starting with an initial four hours of colour programmes on BBC2, rising to ten hours in 1968. A new colour television set is expected to cost £250 and would incur a supplement to the licence fee. David Attenborough, the controller for BBC2, is overseeing the changes.

About 9.20am

At Hendon Hall, Alf Ramsey takes Jimmy Greaves to one side. He keeps it brief.

'I'm going with an unchanged team, Jim, and I hope you can understand my reasons why.'

'Sure, Alf. They'll win it for you and England.'

'I think so.'

He knew it was coming, but as the manager walks off, Jimmy Greaves is choked with disappointment.

Alf Ramsey made up his mind after 'days of anguish'. He said later, 'Jim was England's leading goalscorer, he loved the big occasions and he was a lethal finisher, but the team had performed magnificently in his absence. After a lot of thought, I decided to leave well alone. I felt sorry for Jim.'

At the Homestead Court Hotel in Welwyn Garden City, a

German fan arrives dressed as a chimneysweep in a black top hat – a symbol of good luck in Germany. On his back he has sewn on his prediction for a West German win: 2-1. He poses for a photograph with the German chief press officer, who gives a thumbs-up.

'Welcome, George... just settle in and enjoy the experience. I'm sure you'll do well. Just keep working hard, as you have been doing for so long.'

9.30am

In his room, Jack Charlton can't stop himself thinking about all the things that could go wrong this afternoon, such as an injury or an accidental deflection.

Right-back George Cohen has had a walk around the garden at Hendon Hall and is now calling his wife Daphne at their home in Chessington for what he calls 'a family team talk'. Each England player is given two tickets for each match and Daphne has gone to every one. Her father and George's mother have taken turns to use the other ticket. Because she's going with George's mother, Daphne tells him, 'Today is Ladies' Day and I'm sure it's going to be a joyful one!'

George Cohen has played for Fulham for ten years. Although he helped them win promotion to the First Division in 1959, since then Fulham has been a club untroubled by success. Most of the games Cohen's played for them in the 1960s have been to keep the club from being relegated. In 1966, they've performed a minor miracle. At the end of February they had only 15 points from 29 matches and were bottom of the league. But in their last 13 games they lost only once and reached safety. Alf Ramsey appreciates the spirit of the club and its athletic full-back George Cohen. 'I wasn't a natural footballer, but I recognised my greatest asset was my strength and my speed.'

Jimmy Armfield had been England's captain and first-choice full-back for many years, but a bad pass across goal that led to a Scottish victory 'signed his death warrant', in George Cohen's words. 'After that pass, any time he spent on an international field was on borrowed time.' In September 1963, the FA called Fulham to tell them that Cohen had been selected for England. Alf Ramsey met him in the lobby of the Hendon Hall Hotel. 'Welcome, George. I'm sure you know a lot of the players. Just settle in and enjoy the experience. I'm sure you'll do well. Just keep working hard, as you have been doing for so long.'

Nobby Stiles has gone back to bed to try and get some sleep. Alan Ball tells him that he's going to the room of Jim Terris, the representative of the sportswear company Adidas (the company prefers the lower case 'adidas') to tell him that they'll both be wearing Adidas boots for the final and to collect their payment of £1000 each. It is a considerable sum, considering their match fee is £60.

Jim Terris is an easy-going Scotsman, who calls everyone 'son', even his female secretary. It is extremely important for Adidas that at 3pm this afternoon, 22 players run onto the pitch at Wembley wearing boots with their distinctive three white stripes. Horst Dassler, the son of the company's founder Adolph 'Adi' Dassler, has been based with his team in a hotel in Bayswater since early June, with the intention of making the tournament an Adidas-dominated competition. So far they have been very successful; only about a quarter of the players have worn the boots of their rival, Puma, the company founded by Adi Dassler's brother Rudolph. Rudolph has sent his son Armin to England to fight the Puma cause.

Initially Adi and Rudolph worked together. Adidas began life as the Gebrüder Dassler Schuhfabrik (Dassler Brothers Shoe Factory) in their mother's laundry room in the small town of Herzogenaurach. By the 1930s, the brothers were supplying shoes to leading athletes such as Jesse Owens, who wore their track shoes when he won four gold medals at the 1936 Berlin Olympics.

But success brought tension to the brother's relationship, and during the war Adi and Rudolph fell out. One cause of the rift was said to be a misunderstanding during an Allied bombing raid on Herzogenaurach in 1943. Adi and his wife joined Rudolph and his wife in an air-raid shelter. 'The dirty bastards are back again,' said Adi, referring to the bombers, but Rudolph thought his brother was insulting his family. When Rudolph was arrested by the Americans in 1945 for working for the Gestapo, he was convinced (correctly) that it was Adi who had informed on him.

In 1948, Rudolph formed his own sportswear company, which he christened Ruda, then changed to Puma. He built his factory in Herzogenaurach on the other side of the river to his brother's. It is still a town of divided loyalties, nicknamed 'the town of bent necks', as people often look down at what a person is wearing before deciding to speak to them.

Jim Terris and Horst Dassler don't have to worry about the West German team – they will all be wearing Adidas boots this afternoon. Ever since the 1950s, the squad has had close ties to the company. Indeed, the relationship is so close that a spare seat is kept free on the team coach for Adi Dassler.

In his room at the Hendon Hall Hotel, Jim Terris hands over £2000 to Alan Ball. He's relieved that two more players have agreed. Most of the England team have taken his money over the past few weeks – but not all. Gordon Banks and Ray Wilson have agreed to wear Puma, and Jack Charlton has got so irritated by Adidas and Puma men badgering him that he's threatened to wear one boot from each company in the final.

Puma's failure was due in part to bad luck. They knew that the key to the England team was Bobby Moore. In March 1966, Puma representative Derek Ibbotson asked Moore to tell his team-mates when they met to play Scotland the following month that the company would pay them each a significant amount for wearing Puma boots.

As a back-up, Ibbotson approached defender Ray Wilson and promised him £100 for every game he played for Everton and England. Wilson agreed and said that he'd recommend the Puma offer to the team. But Wilson was injured and never made it to Scotland, and Moore had already made his mind up. 'Moore just told the others that Adidas wanted the whole team and he didn't bother to give them the Puma offer,' said Ibbotson.

Everywhere we went, everybody was saying: 'Bobby! Bobby Charlton! Look! And who's that little bugger with him?'

Ray Wilson

About 9.40am

Jimmy Greaves knocks on Geoff Hurst's door and wishes him 'the best of luck'.

9.45am

Alan Ball comes back to his hotel room. Nobby Stiles is still lying in bed. Ball throws £2000 worth of notes into the air.

'They all came down like confetti. We laughed like kids,' he said later.

It's a great deal of money for putting on a pair of boots they would have worn anyway.

Room-mates Ray Wilson and Bobby Charlton are walking out of the hotel entrance and onto Parson Street, which will take them down to Hendon. Charlton wants to change a shirt he bought a few days ago and to get away from the hotel for a while. Wilson braces himself for the usual double-takes that he knows are not for him, but for his friend. Before he was roomed with him, Wilson preferred to stay in bed as long as possible 'killing time by trying to keep it nice and easy'. That's not Bobby Charlton's style.

Thirty-one-year-old Wilson is part of the Everton team who in May came from two goals down to beat Sheffield Wednesday in the FA Cup final. They were the first club in 63 years to have reached the final without conceding a goal – a tribute to Wilson's abilities as a defender. He won his first cap for England in 1960, making him one of the team's most experienced players. England reserve Ian Callaghan said of him, 'He was a quiet lad until he'd had a few beers. But on the field you never got a moment's peace – he was relentless.' He was also focused and efficient; as George Cohen said, 'He was that neat a player, I always felt he could go out there and do his job in a collar and tie.'

Wilson's background was a tough one. His father was a miner who was forced to give up work after he was injured; his mother died when he was 15.

She had named him Ramon after her favourite film star Ramon Novarro, but he always called himself Ray. 'It's not easy growing up in a Derbyshire mining village full of hairy-arsed miners with a name like that.'

Wilson was repairing wagons on the railways when one of his former schoolteachers recommended him to a talent scout from Second Division Huddersfield Town. He continued to work on the wagons at night and to train with Huddersfield by day. He was with the club for 12 years before joining Everton. Wilson's a very self-controlled player and in over 400 league appearances he has never had his name taken.

Bobby and Jack Charlton have a similar background to Ray Wilson's – they too are from a mining family, but from a village in Northumberland. Their father Bob won the money to buy their mother Cissie a wedding ring by winning a bare-knuckled fight. Bob still works as a miner and turned down the chance to watch England play Portugal at Wembley last Tuesday because he had to work a shift underground at the Linton colliery and was worried about losing a day's pay. The BBC's David Coleman arranged with the Coal Board for Bob to be shown a special recording of the match in the colliery office. Boxing and pigeon fancying are his preferred sports.

Jack trained to be a miner after leaving school, but he'd been appalled at the conditions underground; the explosions to extract the coal made him want to run for the lift to take him back to the surface. One day he asked to see the pit manager.

'I want to resign – I'm not coming back any more,' he told him.

'You can't do that! We've just spent a fortune training you! If you walk away now, I'll see that you'll never get another job in a pit – anywhere.'

'I don't want another job in the pit. I've seen it. I've done it and I've had enough. I don't know what I'm going to do with the rest of my life, but it won't be that.'

Soon after, a scout from Leeds United who had seen Jack play football for Ashington YMCA offered him a job as a ground staff boy. This meant sweeping the terraces, boot cleaning, pitch weeding, painting and oiling the turnstiles, cleaning toilets, re-seeding the pitch, and cleaning and re-studding the boots of the senior players.

The closest that Jack Charlton's younger brother Bobby ever got to being a miner was going with his father to the pit every Friday to collect his wages. 'I'd see all these fellas coming up from the shaft and the ones that were black were all smiling because the shift was over, and the ones that were going in were all miserable. And they had this up and down every day, and I thought, not for me, if I can help it.'

Bobby also managed to escape being a ground staff boy at Old Trafford by enrolling as an apprentice electrical engineer. At 17, he lodged in a house with seven other young talented Manchester United players, dubbed the 'Busby Babes' – it was one of the happiest times of his life. The Babes would attract huge crowds – 30,000 turned up to see Manchester United play in the 1954 Youth Cup final against Wolves.

At an early age Bobby found that football came easily to him. 'I didn't have any difficulty with the running, with controlling the ball, with passing, and you saw others who found it unbelievably difficult. When I was a little lad, me and our Jack used to go to the park on a Sunday. There were two or three pitches, and the big lads all wanted me to play for them. There were matches that started about 8am and they would continue till 8pm. It just went on forever.'

Nobby Stiles, Ray Wilson and George Cohen also worked as ground staff boys. George Cohen joined the Fulham ground staff at 17. 'I got £20 for my signing-on fee, £28 for my monthly wage, and we had a couple of good results where I got another £8 in bonuses, so in the end I took home £50. I said to my dad, 'Look at that, Dad, I got £50 this month', and I could have bitten my tongue. My father was earning £10-12 gross for a 40-hour week.

Here was a little twit coming home saying I've earned £50 after tax. My father just looked at me and smiled. I can see the smile now. It haunts me.'

10am/11am Spanish Time

In a café in a small village on the Spanish island of Ibiza, a tall, thin Englishman is ordering a beer. If there were any other English people in the café, they might well recognise him as John Cleese, from *The Frost Report*, which began on BBC1 in March. Cleese has rented a villa nearby with his writing partner Graham Chapman. They have come up with an idea for a film about a political pollster who becomes prime minister. David Frost liked the idea so much he gave them £2000 to write it. They have used some of the fee to pay for the villa. Cleese works indoors at the typewriter, fleshing out the ideas and dialogue, while Chapman, who has recently finished medical exams, sunbathes on the balcony.

The plan was that they would write the first draft of the screenplay in five weeks and then Cleese, a big football fan, would return home in time for the start of the World Cup. He had tickets for all the England games, and a ticket for the final.

But things didn't work out. The screenplay wasn't written in time, so Cleese left Chapman in Ibiza and flew home to watch England's first game, against Uruguay. Depressed by the dull 0-0 draw, and convinced that England would never make it to the final, he decided to book a flight back to Ibiza and gave his ticket to his friend Bill Oddie. Cleese saw England beat Portugal on the day of his flight but it was too late to change his plans. He returned to Chapman and their screenplay and Oddie kept the Wembley ticket.

The café has a television. John Cleese finds himself a good seat, and settles down to enjoy the beer and the excitement of knowing his country is in the World Cup final.

'Nothing at all went wrong with our security. The cup just got stolen.'

About 10.15am

The phone is ringing in the home of Manchester businessman John Hogan. Hogan answers – it's his old friend Denis Law of Manchester United and Scotland.

'You said "a return match any day, you name it". I will name it now: today,' Law says.

Hogan's face falls.

'But it's the World Cup final today!'

'Well, you said it,' Law replies, unmoved.

A few weeks ago, the two friends had played a round of golf together and despite the fact that Denis Law was the better golfer, by some miracle John Hogan had won. Rubbing it in, Hogan had crowed, 'Any time you want a return game, just give me a shout.'

Denis Law is having his revenge.

The United player has had a bad few months. In April, they were knocked out of the European Cup by Partizan Belgrade, and three days later they were knocked out of the FA Cup by Everton. An old knee injury has returned and to make matters worse, in early July, Law was transfer-listed by United manager Matt Busby after he asked for a pay rise. 'No player will hold this club to ransom – no player,' Busby told journalists. Law went into hiding for a while, as the press interest was so intense. In the end, the dispute was settled – Law secretly getting the extra £10 a week he was after – but it left a bitter taste. Now he has to endure the prospect of England in the World Cup final, the culmination of a tournament in which he's convinced Scotland would have done well – in their qualifying group, they were runners up to Italy, who beat them in the last and deciding game.

Denis Law has no intention of watching the final on television.

Hogan and Law arrange to meet at the golf club that afternoon. Law bets him £25 that this time he will win.

In the Hendon Hall Hotel, Martin Peters is sitting in the lounge, 'chatting with anyone who wanted to talk'. Every now and then Alf Ramsey wanders in and out.

PC Peter Weston and two other constables from Q-Division are standing in the office of the FA secretary, Denis Follows, at Lancaster Gate.

Denis Follows' printed signature is on every ticket for the final, described as 'World Championship 1966 Jules Rimet Cup FINAL TIE'.

'What you're going to do today must be done in the strictest confidence. You are to take these two wooden boxes to Wembley.'

The three officers look inside the boxes on the desk in front of them, open-mouthed. In one box is a gold statue of a winged goddess with her arms raised, and on the marble base at her feet they can see the words 'Germany, Uruguay, Brazil'. It is the World Cup. In the other box is an identical statue.

Denis Follows explains that one is the real Jules Rimet trophy and the other is a perfect copy. The policemen's job, once the Queen has presented the trophy to the winning team, is to switch the real one for the replica. He emphasises that they must tell no one what they are about to do – not even their families.

The trophy is named after FIFA's third president and represents the Goddess of Victory. It was made from solid silver and gold plate by the French sculptor Abel Lafleur. It is not the first time that the trophy has been concealed in a box. It survived the Second World War hidden from the Nazis in a shoebox under the bed of the Italian vice-president of FIFA (Italy had won the World Cup in 1938).

The FA has good reason to be worried about security. On 20th March, the Jules Rimet trophy was stolen from the Methodist Central Hall in Westminster where it had been on display in a glass case as part of a stamp exhibition. It had been a fairly straightforward robbery – the security guard whose job it was to sit next to the trophy had the day off as it was a Sunday, and the other guards were on a tea break. A Sunday school teacher had spotted a man near the men's toilets looking suspicious, and so the police concluded they were looking for a single suspect. 'Nothing at all went wrong with our security. The cup just got stolen,' said an FA official.

Soon after the theft, the then FA chairman Joe Mears received a ransom note from a man who called himself 'Jackson'. 'Dear Joe Kno [sic] no doubt you view with very much concern the loss of the world cup... to me it is only so much scrap gold. If I don't hear from you by Thursday or Friday at the latest I assume it's one for the POT.'

As requested, Mears put an advert in the Evening News *saying, 'Willing to do business, Joe.'*

Detective Inspector Len Buggy from the Metropolitan Police's Flying Squad, pretending to be Joe Mears' assistant, met 'Jackson' in Battersea Park. The £15,000 ransom Buggy had with him was in fact £500 bulked out with pieces of cut-up newspaper. 'Jackson' spotted a Transit van with Buggy's back-up team in it and tried to make a run for it, but was caught. There was no sign of the World Cup. 'Jackson' turned out to be 46-year-old former soldier and petty thief Edward Betchley. Betchley claimed that he was merely the middleman and was working for someone known as 'The Pole'. 'Whatever my sentence is, I hope that England wins the World Cup,' Betchley said before his trial.

A few weeks after the theft, Denis Follows met with London silversmith George Bird to ask him to make a perfect replica of the trophy. He told Bird never to speak about the replica. Very few people know about Bird's work, not even FIFA's president, Sir Stanley Rous.

About 10.30am

The phone rings at the Hendon Odeon. It's Nobby Stiles. Last night he left a cardigan on his seat and he's very keen to have it back – it's his lucky cardigan that he wears before every big game. The Odeon staff check, but are apologetic, nothing has been handed in.

A white Jaguar is on the hard shoulder of the southbound side of the M1; a policeman is talking to the driver he's just stopped for speeding. The policeman takes the driver's details but doesn't recognise the name, despite the fact that 20-year-old George Best is one of the most famous players in the country. In the passenger seat is another footballer, Mike Summerbee. Best plays for Manchester United and Summerbee for Manchester City, but they are still friends. They are running late, but hope to make it to Wembley before kick-off.

The two met last year in a coffee shop in Manchester city centre and hit it off straightaway. They go to watch Stockport County play every other Friday evening, hang out in after-hours drinking clubs such as Phyllis's in Moss Side (run by Phyllis Lynott, mother of 17-year-old Phil) and stand in the audience of Top of the Pops *in the BBC studio in Rusholme.*

Life had changed for George Best on 9th March 1966, when Manchester United became the first foreign team to beat Benfica in Lisbon. George scored twice and played so well and looked so striking with his long hair that he was dubbed 'El Beatle'. Two days later, when Best and Summerbee tried to walk to the coffee shop that by now had become their regular haunt, everyone wanted Best's autograph and picture.

In the royal box, rugs are being draped over the backs of a line of blue wicker chairs. The Queen and the Duke of Edinburgh have plain chairs with scarlet cushions. Name cards are placed on each seat.

At Luton Airport, the sound of hunting horns is heard across the runway tarmac as the German fans, the vast majority male and wearing suits, disembark from their planes.

Earlier, FIFA announced in a press release that of the 15 visiting teams, West Germany has brought the most away supporters to England over the past three weeks.

The history of football in Germany is very different from that of Britain.

The violent football played in British streets since medieval times was adopted as a team sport by public schools in the 19th century, as a way to encourage discipline and fair play. Each school developed their own rules, which made inter-school matches confusing. To resolve this, a group of former public-school boys representing 12 London clubs met on 26th October 1863 at the Freemasons' Tavern in Lincoln's Inn Fields to agree the laws of the game. At the end of the afternoon, they announced: 'the clubs represented at this meeting now form themselves into an association to be called the Football Association.'

Thirteen rules were soon agreed upon, and probably the most significant was Rule 9: 'No player shall carry the ball.' Those that disagreed with the decision went on to create rugby union. Rule 13 sought to make the game safer by regulating the footwear worn: 'No player shall wear projecting nails, iron plates, or gutta percha [glue] on the soles or heels of his boots.'

Different types of teams grew up, based around pubs, churches, towns and factories. In 1888, the first national football league was established, comprising 12 teams. The game was starting to spread beyond Britain – in 1889, Denmark formed its own league; in 1893, Argentina started a national championship and, in 1894, Genoa became the first Italian football club.

Germany was slow to take to football; in the 19th century, gymnastics was the most popular sport. There were scores of sports associations named after the year of their founding, such as Munich 1860, but football was not encouraged – in fact, it was hard for football players to even find space for a pitch and their game was considered un-German.

However, by 1900 there were enough amateur clubs for an association to be formed, the Deutscher Fußball-Bund (DFB). By 1932, Germany had a million amateur football players.

Under the Nazis, any player who wanted to join a DFB club had to provide two non-Marxist sponsors, and Jews were purged from all sports organisations. As Germany invaded other countries, their football teams were incorporated into the German football leagues or Gauliga. The Luftwaffe and SS sponsored teams.

In the early years of the war, it became increasingly difficult for the manager of the national team, Sepp Herberger, to assemble his squad as so many were fighting at the front. To take advantage of the rule that anyone in the armed forces who was decorated was given home leave, Herberger forged documents awarding the Iron Cross to his best players in order to bring them back.

Immediately after the war, Germany was divided into zones, each with different rules about the place of football. The Soviets closed down the clubs in their zones and confiscated their property; any football match in the French zone had to be officially approved; the British response was confused – they closed down some clubs (and ordered their kit to be burnt) while allowing British Army teams to join local leagues. It was the Americans, who knew least about association football, who did the most to promote it, encouraging the formation of the South German FA.

Food and fuel were scarce in post-war Germany so winning teams were rewarded with coal and produce. One club used gravestones to replace broken steps in its stands, with the inscriptions face down.

Cloth was also in short supply. Many teams played in red strips made from Nazi banners with the swastikas removed.

In 1949, FIFA allowed West German clubs to play friendlies against foreign sides, and the English FA, led by its secretary, Sir Stanley Rous, encouraged youth fixtures between England and West Germany (he was later awarded a Grand Cross of the Order of Merit for his services to German football).

Meanwhile, the intrepid Sepp Herberger was building a successful international squad. In the 1954 World Cup final in Switzerland, the so-called 'Miracle of Bern', his amateur players beat the favourites Hungary 3-2.

The reaction of German radio commentator Herbert Zimmermann when the West German team scored the winning goal six minutes from time made the former 14th Panzer Division major a legend in Germany.

'Rahn shoots! Goal! Goal! Goal! Goal! ...Goal for Germany!' Then Zimmermann stayed silent for a full eight seconds, overcome with emotion. 'Germany lead 3-2,' he eventually screamed. 'Call me mad! Call me crazy!'

The German historian Joachim Fest wrote about the victory: 'It was a kind of liberation for the Germans from all the things that weighed down upon them after the Second World War. July

4, 1954 is in certain aspects the founding day of the German Republic.'

Yet a section of West German society was alarmed by the celebrations after the 1954 World Cup victory, which seemed too nationalistic. 'Well now, celebrate the players, but let's become sober again; the game is over, and it was just a game,' said the newspaper Süddeutsche Zeitung.

Herbert Zimmermann is in the press box at Wembley, once again commentating for German radio. He's hoping that his side (now all professionals) can produce a second stunning World Cup victory.

> **People are aghast when I tell them my story – but I've never regretted it.**
>
> **Jim Tucker**

The Charlton brothers' parents have arrived at the Hendon Hall Hotel to see them. Cissie does most of the talking while Bob listens. 'We knew each other so well that we could read one another like books; instead of passing on the tension, we relied upon each other for a bit of morale-boosting,' she said later.

Cissie Charlton comes from a footballing family. Her father 'Tanner' Milburn played in goal for Ashington FC; all four of her brothers played league football and her cousin is Newcastle and England legend Jackie Milburn, who won 13 England caps and the FA Cup three times for Newcastle United. On summer evenings, Cissie would join in her sons' football games in the street, and she coached the local team when Jack and Bobby left home.

Twenty-four-year-old Jim Tucker is sitting on a Metropolitan Line Tube train on his way up to Wembley. In his jacket pocket is a ticket for the final.

Jim is a devoted England and Chelsea fan. Last year he hitchhiked all the way to Barcelona to watch Chelsea play at the Camp Nou stadium in the Fairs Cup, even though he didn't have a ticket. The Chelsea Supporters Club told him that he should find the team hotel in Barcelona and ask Chelsea's manager Tommy Docherty for a ticket.

Jim knocked on Docherty's door. He answered the door wearing only a pair of boxer shorts. 'His willy was hanging out – I do remember that...'

'Hello, Mr Docherty, I've been told I can pick up a ticket. I've hitchhiked from London to see the game,' Jim said.

'My God, you deserve a ticket if anybody does, son,' Docherty said and disappeared into his vast carpeted suite, returning with a ticket. Jim watched the match with the Chelsea squad. Sadly, Chelsea lost 5-1.

For the duration of the World Cup, Jim has got a job as a delivery driver for a wholesale grocer in his home town of Dorking because the hours are perfect for him. They need him to start work early and finish early – allowing plenty of time to get home to see every match on television.

Jim's parents had managed to get a ticket for each of England's qualifying games at Wembley, and for the quarter-final, the semi-final and the final itself. Either his mother or his father would go to the game; the ticket was always for the same seat. On the day of the quarter-final against Argentina, Jim had to drive his parents to Gatwick Airport as they were flying to the United States for a holiday, so he missed the game. For the first time in the tournament their seat at Wembley was empty.

Before they left for the States, his parents gave him the tickets for the semi-final and the final. On Tuesday, Jim went to Wembley for the game against Portugal. The seat was about six rows back from a corner flag. Jim was not impressed. He could see play in only the quarter of the pitch closest to him – the rest of the time he wondered what on earth was going on. A Portuguese fan shouting 'Portugal! Portugal!' in his ear the whole time didn't improve the experience.

'I can't be doing with this,' Jim thought. 'I've got to see the final on television.'

So today, Jim isn't travelling to Wembley Stadium to see the World Cup final – he's going there to sell his ticket to a tout. He doesn't want to make money; he just feels it would be wrong for it to be wasted.

About 10.45am

George Cohen is reading some of the mail that's piled up in the team room and answering some of the correspondence. 'It was one of the chores Alf expected of us.'

Ray Wilson and Bobby Charlton have returned from their shopping trip in Hendon town centre. Charlton has changed his shirt and bought some cuff links for his friend, the Portuguese winger José Augusto, who he'll see at tonight's FIFA banquet. Wilson has bought some shoes to wear.

The shopping trip was a revelation for Bobby Charlton. 'People kept wishing us good luck, almost shyly, as though not wanting to unsettle us. Even the shop girls were full of England and the desire to win the World Cup. It was then that I realised how much the game meant to the nation. It was the greatest day that had ever dawned for the English game.'

11.00am

There is a clap of thunder over Wembley Stadium and hail starts to fall. Percy Young, the Wembley groundsman for over 30 years, and his five technicians stop their work marking out the white lines, and make their way up into the stands and watch the pitch go whiter and whiter as the hail tumbles out of the sky. It's hard to believe that it was 100 degrees on the pitch a week ago during the England–Argentina quarter-final. Roof panels above the stands had to be removed to improve ventilation in the stadium.

As PC Peter Weston is driven to Wembley in an old black Wolseley police car, he's trying to work out how he is going to switch the real trophy for the fake. Both are in the boot of the car.

Anita Dunnington has arrived safely at Royal Oldham Hospital. There is a lull in her contractions and she's asleep in a maternity ward.

11.10am

Ten miles east of Wembley, in Barnet, 20-year-old Cathy Baker is in a chauffer-driven car on her way to her wedding. Back at home, her mother Ethel is dealing with the caterers and arranging for television sets to be in every downstairs room, so guests won't miss any of the final.

Cathy turns to her stepfather sitting next to her in the back of the car.

'I don't think that I want to do this'.

'Cathy, you don't have to, if you don't want to,' he says.

'But Mum's gone to all the trouble sorting out the catering...'

Cathy looks out of the window and tries to think about what would be the right thing to do.

> *She is marrying Joe Matos, a New York Puerto Rican. They met in Majorca, where they both work for the airline TACA – Cathy is a stewardess, Joe a pilot. She was swept off her feet by the good-looking American. 'I was your absolute virgin personified. I couldn't have been more innocent.'*
>
> *However, Cathy grew tired of Joe's womanising and fled the island last month and returned home. Joe followed her, driving all the way to Barnet in his Alfa Romeo. They made up and surprised everyone by deciding to get married in just three weeks time. When Cathy asked her old friend Pat Rigby to be best man, he went pale – he had tickets for Wembley that day. She had no idea what final he was talking about.*

Cathy is not sure she trusts Joe.

About 11.30am

Jim Tucker has found a ticket tout who's offering him the face value of £5 for his ticket. Jim doesn't bother haggling – he's keen to get to his mate Colin's house in Reigate to watch the game on television.

In the restaurant at the Hendon Hall Hotel, the England squad are sitting down for an early lunch. Geoff Hurst is having his usual pre-match meal of a pot of tea and baked beans on toast. Everyone else is having chicken. The team doctor Alan Bass believes three hours is enough time for food to be properly digested before a match. No one is eating very much.

During the pre-tournament training at the National Recreation Centre at Lilleshall, Dr Bass monitored their diet and even showed them the best way to cut their toenails. Under the guidance of Alf Ramsey and trainers Les Cocker and Harold Shepherdson, their day began at 9am and ended at 9pm and comprised of practice matches, intensive training, sports such as indoor cricket and badminton, and films of their opponents to identify their strengths and weaknesses.

This was in stark contrast to England's preparations for the last World Cup in Chile under Walter Winterbottom. The squad flew out without even a team doctor. 'We ploughed on quite happily with immovable faith in our trainer's magic sponge,' Ray Wilson remembered. 'We were in a pretty backward state – we used to laugh at the entourage with the Brazilian team.'

The sound of a marching band is echoing around the empty Wembley Stadium. On the pitch, the hail has melted and Her Majesty's Royal Marines Band are rehearsing their half-time performance. There are 50 musicians, some who arrived an hour ago by coach from Portsmouth, the rest from Deal. The Royal Marines are dressed in their Number 2 uniform – blue suit, white belt and blue peaked cap. Bringing up the rear is the bandmaster Michael Hutton, a veteran of many sporting events at White City Stadium, Olympia and at the FA Cup Final at Wembley, where the Royal Marines play the traditional hymn 'Abide with Me'.

This rehearsal is essential to get a feel for the space and a reminder of the stadium's acoustics. Hutton knows from experience that it will sound very different once it's full of 97,000 people.

Michael Hutton joined the Royal Marines Band Service aged 16. His job is the organisational side of the band, as well as being in charge of all the rehearsals, so he can hand over to the director of music to 'wiggle his stick' during the final performance.

The goalposts have been erected and the goal nets have been hung.

One of the rules established in 1863 was that goalposts should be eight yards apart, and that is still the case. Another rule to survive is the coin toss to decide ends. Rules that have been modified over the years include: changing ends after every goal; throw-ins should be taken by the player who touches the ball after it has gone out of play; no crossbar for the goalposts and no pitch markings.

Outside Wembley, 250 car park attendants are getting ready to deal with an expected 3,500 cars and 2,000 coaches.

11.35am

Cathy Baker has decided to banish her doubts and go through with her wedding – the service at Monken Hadley church just outside Barnet has just started. Cathy looks stunning in her wedding dress and Joe looks impressive in his pilot's uniform. About a dozen of Cathy's friends have tickets for the final in their pockets – they are heading to Wembley as soon as the service is over.

Nine-year-old Gary Bradley is hanging around outside the entrance of the Hendon Hall Hotel clutching an autograph book. He's walked up with his father Geoffrey from their house in Golders Green hoping to see the England players. Bobby Charlton spots them, introduces himself and asks if they'd like to come in and meet the team. Gary can't believe his luck.

Midday

Grandstand starts on BBC1, presented from Wembley by Kenneth Wolstenholme, David Coleman, Frank Bough and Alan Weeks. Their studio guests are the former England manager Walter Winterbottom, Leeds United manager Don Revie and West Ham manager Ron Greenwood.

It's three hours to kick-off and already a queue of chartered coaches and cars is making its slow progress up Wembley Way and into the car park surrounding the stadium. Hundreds of people are spilling out onto the road from the pavements on either side. Some supporters are wearing England rosettes and carrying rattles; most of the men are wearing jackets and ties.

The FA releases Alf Ramsey's team selection to the press.

'Have either one of you got a dog?'

12.30pm

A maroon Mark 1 Mini is parked outside the Birmingham Municipal Bank in Kings Heath. In the driver's seat is 24-year-old Graham Saunders, who is waiting for his wife Sally to finish work at the bank. In the car with him are two friends – Alan and Sandra Morris, neighbours from their housing estate.

In January, Graham suggested they all went to the Royal Tournament at Earls Court on 30th July. He had no idea that the World Cup final was on the same day. So he's arranged for them all to watch the match at his aunt and uncle's house in Ascot.

Graham looks at his watch. Sally is running late at the bank, as there is a discrepancy with the figures. They should have set off for Ascot over an hour ago.

Alf Ramsey gathers his team for a brief meeting at Hendon Hall. He's watched footage of the ten most recent West Germany games. He runs through the tactics he's been drilling into them for the past few days.

> *Yesterday he told Bobby Charlton he wanted him to 'stick on Franz Beckenbauer every minute of the match', adding, 'This boy is the only German player who can beat us.'*
>
> *Charlton was stunned. 'I had never been asked to man-mark in my life. Ever.' He had imagined he'd have his usual attacking role. His two electrifying goals against Portugal had put England in the final.*

Alf Ramsey tells them they have done their work well and should now collect their rewards. He turns to Nobby Stiles and Alan Ball.

'Lads, may I ask you a question?'

'Yes, Alf,' they say.

'Have either one of you got a dog?'

'I've got one, Alf,' says Alan Ball.

'Do you take it for walks?'

'Yes, Alf.'

'Do you take a ball with you or a stick?'

'I take a ball, Alf.'

'What do you do with it?'

'I throw the ball.'

'What does the dog do?'

'Alf – all dogs chase a ball, mine chases it, brings it back to me and I throw it over there, he goes over and gets it, and sometimes he brings it back and drops it at me feet.'

'I'm glad you said that, young man, because that's what you two have got to do for Bobby Charlton.'

Alf Ramsey knows Bobby Charlton well. Charlton once said, 'My philosophy of the game was always as an out-and-out forward. I never put my foot in – getting the ball was other players' work.'

12.45pm

Along Wembley Way, spectators are buying England scarves, World Cup posters, Union flags and rosettes from display boards ten feet high. Some of the products are FIFA approved, but most are unofficial.

Sunday Express football reporter James Mossop is walking up Wembley Way. He spots some elderly buskers playing 'There'll Always Be an England'. James loves their innocent patriotism. By now the queues of people lining up outside Wembley's turnstiles are hundreds of yards long.

The coach carrying the players' wives who stayed at the Royal Garden Hotel in Kensington last night is making slow progress past the vendors.

Travelling separately is George Cohen's wife Daphne. She's on a bus from Chessington in Surrey with her mother-in-law Catherine. Daphne is wearing a navy-and-cream dress and jacket that she bought especially for the game from a friend's boutique. With her she has a suitcase containing a black cocktail dress for the evening event at the Royal Garden Hotel.

Eighteen-year-old John Nutkins has seen all the England games at Wembley but each time he's missed the first five minutes.

John is a Rover Scout, part of the 4th Edgware pack raising money to send one of their number to Idaho for the 1967 Scout International Jamboree by selling drinks to fans. British Rail has allowed them to sell cartons of Jubbly Orange Drink at Wembley Hill Station (originally called the Exhibition Station) close to the stadium. John Nutkins helps himself to a box of Jubblys from the pile stacked up by the station and starts selling them.

On the afternoon of the opening game between England and Uruguay, the Scouts soon discovered that they could sell more drinks if they moved closer to the stadium. When the game started, ticket touts came up to the Scouts and offered them tickets. They said they couldn't afford them, but the touts gave them to them for free. Since then, the Scouts from 4th Edgware have been given free tickets as the whistle was blown for kick-off for every England game.

They have decided that this piece of extraordinary good fortune is something that they should keep to themselves.

'It's bloody electric!'

12.55pm/1.55pm Spanish Time

ITV's *World of Sport* is just beginning, presented from Wembley by Eamonn Andrews. In the studio with him are the Liverpool manager Bill Shankly, the Celtic manager Jock Stein and Welsh international Phil Woosnam.

At the microphone providing the commentary for the match will be Hugh Johns, only recently recruited by ITV.

Like Kenneth Wolstenholme, Hugh Johns was a Second World War pilot. He went on to become a newspaper sports reporter and an occasional commentator for Cardiff City matches for the local ITV company Television Wales and West. Johns' producer sent a tape of him commentating to ITV and at the audition that followed they liked his broadcasting philosophy of 'homework, identification, no waffle, go-with-the-flow'.

All the ITV networks will be showing the final, except Channel TV in the Channel Islands, which will be broadcasting an old movie.

Prime Minister Harold Wilson's RAF Comet lands at London Airport. He's been in Washington for talks with President Johnson about Labour's prices and wage freeze plan as laid out in the Price and Incomes Bill. Johnson has been concerned about the stability of the British economy for some time and had pressed for the freeze. Never one to miss a photo opportunity, Wilson has rushed back to be in time for the final.

There had been reports in the press that prior to the talks, American officials had provided President Johnson with a gloomy assessment of the modern British character. 'They are unwilling to roll up their sleeves and really work... there is a dwindling of the old spirit of resolution in time of adversity.' The Daily Express *and other papers see the World Cup final as 'a chance to set the record straight'.*

Wilson has spent much of July abroad. Earlier in the month, he was in Moscow to attend a trade fair and to have talks about the war in Vietnam.

In the café on Ibiza, John Cleese is tucking into a delicious rabbit stew. Although the film script is taking rather longer to write than planned, he is enjoying his time on the island. His girlfriend Connie Booth often flies out to stay, as well as friends such as Marty Feldman and Tim Brooke-Taylor. In his spare time John has learned how to ride a bike and how to water-ski (he arranged for his first lesson to be early in the morning to avoid public humiliation).

The café is beginning to fill up.

1.00pm/2.00pm Spanish Time

The gates are opening at the Empire Stadium and the fans are pouring in, waving Union flags and rattles. Hugh McIlvanney of the *Observer* wrote later: 'the people hurrying and jostling and laughing nervously inside had a flushed, supercharged look… "It's bloody electric!" said one of the doormen.'

Seventy-four-year-old doorman Tom Sawyer is on the lookout for forged tickets at the turnstiles – there have been rumours that thousands have been printed.

'I can spot a shyster a mile off,' he assured reporters earlier.

> **Schön possesses a greater number of first-class players than England and if one looks at the two sides on paper one's optimism as a German grows.**
>
> **Ulrich Kaiser, sports journalist, 29th July 1966**

> **I knew it was my day.**
>
> **Alan Ball**

1.10pm

ITV's *World of Sport* has left its Wembley coverage to show wrestling.

On the BBC Home Service, *Round the Horne* starring Kenneth Horne and Kenneth Williams is just beginning.

1.15pm

Fans on the pavement bang on the sides of the coach carrying the England squad as it pulls away from the Hendon House Hotel. The players have a police motorcycle escort to take them on a back route to the stadium, avoiding the traffic on the North Circular Road.

In the dining room at the hotel, banqueting manager Victor Bianchi and his staff are preparing for the wedding reception later this afternoon.

The leader of the Conservative Party, Ted Heath, has just arrived in the stadium car park and is signing autographs for the fans.

1.20pm

The England coach is passing the Hendon Fire Station. Bobby Charlton looks out of the coach window and is impressed by the newly cleaned and polished engines out in front; their bells are ringing in tribute to the England team.

This is Bobby Charlton's third World Cup. He knows well the feeling of responsibility it brings. Playing for Manchester United is a 'personal thing' but playing for your country is 'a duty, and if you play for England then something special is expected'. A few days ago he was told by a Herefordshire farmer, 'Bobby, you and your team-mates are playing for all of us. You will win games and collect the trophy, but all over the country, in towns and villages, amateur

> *players like me will be able to puff out their chests and say, "We are the champions of the world!"'*

In his brother Jack's kit bag are his boots and some money – silver for luck.

> *Earlier a reporter said to Jack, 'There's been a lot of conjecture about what you might call your new baby...'*
> *'Well, it won't be called Willie...' he said with a smile.*

As the coach makes its way through Hendon, Alan Ball is thoughtful; he has a feeling everything is going to go well for him today. The entire squad is fond of Ball – he's normally like a chatty kid brother, so those around him notice his silence.

Next to him, Nobby Stiles is wearing his match-day attire: the same suit, shirt and underpants. But no lucky cardigan.

> **Performing was just a bloody chore. No one was interested in us. We were totally in the background. We all hated it.**
>
> **Michael Hutton**

1.30pm

On BBC1, *Grandstand* is showing a pre-recorded film about both teams' progress to the World Cup final called 'How they got there'.

At Wembley, in full uniform, Her Majesty's Royal Marines Band march onto the pitch to provide a programme of music from each of the 16 nations represented in the tournament. North Korea had posed a problem, but the director of music settled upon the piece 'Oriental Patrol'.

Marching behind them is bandleader Michael Hutton, in front is the director of music. The musicians have changed out of their Number 2 uniform and into their Number 1 uniform – full ceremonial dress of red tunics and white helmets. None of the bandsmen enjoy playing at Wembley – they know no one has come to hear them, but as always, they give their best.

Prime Minister Harold Wilson is talking to reporters at London Airport about his meeting with President Johnson.

'The Price and Incomes Bill will create very great difficulties for industry but we believe them to be in the national interest. Our aim is to improve the balance of payments by £300 million.'

The prime minister is wearing a World Cup Willie tie.

1.40pm

One hundred feet up on one of Wembley's famous towers, a member of the ground staff is poised to 'break' the Royal Standard as soon as the Queen enters the stadium.

The fans entering the stadium are walking past notices pasted on every gate telling them in English, German and French to retain their ticket stub in case there's a replay.

The game will be played on Tuesday if there is a tie after extra time.

Almost all the houses around the stadium have Union flags hanging from their windows.

'Don't worry, if one single person tries to get over this small wall and onto the pitch, I'll have them!'

About 1.40pm

The light-blue West German team coach is arriving at Wembley with a motorcycle escort and a policeman on a white horse. It is cheered by both English and German fans.

Travelling as the West German team's attaché is a German who speaks English with a Lancastrian accent – Bert Trautmann, the former goalkeeper for Manchester City. Wembley is a stadium Trautmann knows well as he played in two consecutive FA Cup finals in 1955 and 1956 with City. He was voted Footballer of the Year in 1956.

Bert (born Bernd but the British find it hard to pronounce) Trautmann is a football legend. He is famous for playing the last quarter of an hour of the 1956 FA Cup final with a broken neck, after being briefly knocked unconscious. Two days later, he was at the celebrations in Manchester city centre with his head leaning to one side. Only later that day did he go to hospital and find out how serious his injury was.

Trautmann is a former prisoner of war who was captured in Belgium towards the end of the war by a British soldier whose first words to him were: 'Hello Fritz, fancy a cup of tea?' He was moved to a POW camp in Cheshire where, when he wasn't working on local farms, he played football. At the end of the war, he decided to stay in England and gained a reputation as a talented goalkeeper for non-league St Helens. In October 1949, he signed for First Division Manchester City. Perhaps inevitably, Trautmann is friends with Adi Dassler and was the first player in Britain to wear his boots. He retired in 1964, aged 42. Trautmann is currently Stockport County's manager.

Martin Peters played against Trautmann towards the end of the German's playing career when West Ham beat Manchester City 6-1. After he conceded a fifth goal, Trautmann was so incensed that the referee Keith Stokes hadn't given offside, that he ran to the halfway line and kicked the ball into Stokes' back, who immediately sent him off.

Asked a few weeks ago who would win the tournament, Trautmann said without hesitation, 'England.'

Trautmann is one of Gordon Banks' heroes. 'I used to marvel at his anticipation, courage and agility.' He also taught Banks an invaluable lesson. To improve his chances of catching a ball when not wearing gloves – Banks only wears them if the pitch is very wet – Trautmann advised him to suck on a couple of pieces of gum and then, just before cracking the shell on the gum, spit on his hands and smooth the spit over his palms. Whenever the opposition was attacking once the spit had worn off, he should lick his palms.

England trainer Harold Shepherdson always puts a packet of chewing gum out for Gordon Banks on the massage table in the dressing room. However, last Tuesday, just before the semi-final with Portugal, there wasn't a packet there.

'I've got to have it, Harold, you know how greasy a ball gets out there at night,' Banks said.

Alf Ramsey looked at Shepherdson, who went bright red and confessed he'd forgotten it. Two minutes later the England trainer was running down Wembley Way looking for a newsagent that was open late.

The two teams lined up in the tunnel while Gordon Banks stayed in the dressing room. He heard Alf Ramsey say to Bobby Moore, 'Delay the referee!'

Banks opened an exit door and he could see, among the crowds still hoping for a ticket, Harold Shepherdson running at full pelt. The out-of-breath but triumphant trainer pressed a packet of gum into his hand and Banks took his place in the line just in time.

The BBC's Kenneth Wolstenholme is walking around the stadium, soaking up the atmosphere. This is the eleventh game of the tournament he's commentated on.

A policeman standing by the pitch wishes Wolstenholme luck and, looking towards the excited fans, says, 'Don't worry, if one single person tries to get over this small wall and onto the pitch, I'll have them!'

The South American teams were amazed that the English fans were trusted not to rush onto the pitches. Pelé said, 'I have played in countries where a moat, a fence, a battalion of crack troops could not prevent a crowd expressing a personal opinion of a referee's decision in physical fashion, and Britain was a pleasant exception to those experiences.'

1.42pm/2.42pm Spanish Time

On the island of Ibiza, the café where John Cleese has chosen to watch a match he would later describe as 'the most important event since the Crucifixion' is slowly filling up with Germans. '*Guten Tag! Ich liebe Deutschland!*' he says in his schoolboy German, as a friendly greeting.

The coach carrying the England squad is making a slow journey up Wembley Way. Some fans are banging on the sides of the vehicle and others are cheering as they pass.

Nearby, the Jubblys are selling well. John Nutkins has been

back to Wembley Hill Station a few times to get a fresh box. The Scouts are selling them for sixpence – a penny halfpenny from each goes towards the Jamboree fund.

'Be magic little man.'

1.45pm

The England players make their way up the cool, whitewashed Wembley tunnel and turn right into their dressing room. Gordon Banks' yellow goalkeeper's shirt and ten red England shirts are hanging from wire hangers all around the room.

'Why aren't we wearing white?' asks Geoff Hurst. George Cohen explains that Wembley is a neutral venue so a toss of the coin has decided that West Germany get to wear their home strip of white shirts.

By their kit, some of the players have telegrams waiting for them. Alan Ball has one from his father: 'You're there. Don't miss a minute of it. Be magic little man.'

1.47pm

The players walk out onto the pitch to test it and are instantly recognised by the crowd and are given a rousing cheer.

The pitch at Wembley is Cumberland turf, and is famous for being soft and moss-like; it's now soft and slippy after the morning's rain and hail.

1.55pm

Walking up Wembley Way are two couples – Bill and Winnie Harrison and John and Jill Andrews. John Andrews has a spare ticket in his hand and he is trying to sell it, but having no success.

'How much do you want for it?' someone says.

'You can have it at face value,' John replies.

'Are you kidding? Only face value? It must be a fake!'

John begins to wonder if they'll ever get rid of it.

The two couples met on holiday in Italy last year and it's been easy to stay in touch – the Harrisons run a pub called the Lord Derby in Ashton-under-Lyne and the Andrews live only ten miles away in Cheadle. The Harrisons' two daughters, Sue, nine, and Janet, five, are at home upstairs in the pub, being looked after by their grandmother. Winnie wants to find a phone box so she can call her mother to see if the girls are all right. It's a long time since they left the house this morning to catch the bus to Stockport railway station.

2.00pm

In the England dressing room, the 11 members of the squad not playing, known as the reserves, wish their team-mates well and walk out into the stadium. Bobby Moore's predecessor as captain, Jimmy Armfield, feels awkward: 'Footballers want to play, not watch. No more matches; this was it and we weren't on the field.' They find their seats up in the stands.

Armfield is wearing a red jumper. Not normally superstitious, this is the jumper he'd worn at the opening ceremony and then during every game of the tournament. He isn't the only one in the squad to have a lucky piece of clothing; Norman Hunter, the tough tackler from Leeds United, has brought a mackintosh to every game to ensure victory. Like Jimmy Armfield, he hasn't kicked a ball in the finals.

'I know you haven't played, Norman, but thank you for coming,' Alf Ramsey would say to him at the end of every game.

A member of the FA committee is walking around the England dressing room wishing everyone luck. He goes up to Ray Wilson.

'All the best, George.'

Nobby Stiles is killing himself laughing. 'Ray had been playing for England for years, and I thought, "how could he do that – mistake him for George Cohen?"'

For many years Bobby Moore was called 'Ron' by a member of the FA Selection Committee who mistook him for another fair-haired midfield player called Ron Flowers.

England was a good place for a young boy to be in 1966.

Terence Stamp

2.05pm

Tina Moore and Judith Hurst are taking their seats in the rows allocated for the players' wives. They spot actor Terence Stamp and his girlfriend, the model Jean Shrimpton, who two years ago left the photographer David Bailey for him. Tina can't take her eyes off 'The Shrimp' as she looks so glamorous.

Terence Stamp is one of Britain's hottest young actors, Oscar-nominated for his role as the hero of Billy Budd; *his latest film* Modesty Blaise *opened last month.*

Jean Shrimpton later said of their relationship: 'We were two pretty people wandering around thinking we were important. Night after night we'd go out for dinner, to the best restaurants, but just so that we could be seen. It was boring. I felt like a bit part in a movie about Terence Stamp.'

Tina Moore knows that she and Bobby are lucky to be here. He has a secret that he's kept from Alf and his fellow players.

In November 1964, Bobby Moore was diagnosed with testicular cancer. For a year he had suffered the pain in silence, ignoring the testicle which had become so swollen it was obvious to others in the dressing room. One day, the West Ham full-back Eddie Presland spotted it.

'Mooro – that's taken a few overs hasn't it!'

Tina, pregnant with their first baby, read up all she could on the cancer, but Bobby found it hard to talk about. 'Don't tell anyone what I'm here for,' he told his wife when he was admitted to the London Hospital in Whitechapel to have the testicle removed. He didn't play football for three months. The press and West Ham were told that he had a severe groin injury.

When Moore was wearing shorts on holiday after the operation, he was convinced that people could tell something was wrong. In Tina's words, 'he didn't feel whole'. During the radiotherapy that followed, blue crosses were drawn on his back to show the radio-therapist the location of his kidneys. When back at West Ham and playing for England, to hide the blue crosses, Moore made sure no one saw him get in or out of the communal baths.

Always a poor sleeper, his anxiety about cancer made his insomnia worse and since his diagnosis he's been drinking more heavily.

After West Ham's victory in the 1965 European Cup final, the Moores wanted to say thank you to their GP who had been so helpful to them, so they gave him one of Bobby's England shirts. Dr Kennedy is a lay preacher and held up the shirt the next time he gave a sermon. He asked from the pulpit, 'Does anyone know what this is?'

'It's an England shirt,' a small boy called out.

'And do you know who wore this shirt?'

'Bobby Moore!' the boy replied.

Later in the sermon, Dr Kennedy asked, 'Do you know who God is?'

'Bobby Moore!' the boy called out again.

[Bobby Moore was] a bit like a messiah... out of the gloom of the fifties and the debt and everything, and our sports history wasn't very great and he just came, like a gleam of light.

Michael Caine

To us, he was the governor. Everybody loved him, everybody who came into contact with him wanted Bobby as a friend. You couldn't help it.

Harry Redknapp

2.15pm

The England dressing room is teeming with about 100 people – members of the FA, television crews and photographers. Alf Ramsey is giving last-minute quotes to reporters. A cameraman films George Cohen putting on his England shirt – he looks anxious. The Wembley tea man is walking around asking the players for their autographs. The noise is magnified by the dressing room's high ceiling.

'Have you counted the number of people in here?' Bobby Moore says to Geoff Hurst as they try and collect their thoughts. Hurst agrees that it's unlike Alf Ramsey to allow such chaos. But what's uppermost in his mind is the thought 'Am I really part of all this?' Only a week ago he was in here getting ready for his first game of the tournament, the quarter-final against Argentina.

Alan Ball is getting ready and trying to ignore the chaos. He was silent in the coach and he barely says a word here. The 20-year-old is keen to get on the pitch and play. Karl-Heinz Schnellinger may be one of the world's greatest full-backs and earned the nickname 'Volkswagen' because of his reliability, but Ball knows he can run rings around him.

Ball's earliest memory is the smell of sweat, liniment and dubbin in the Southport dressing room where his father was a player. As a teenager he told his father, 'Dad, I will play for England before I am 20'; he played for England three days before his 20th birthday.

Nobby Stiles' eyes are watering as he puts in contact lenses, which are large enough to cover the entire surface of his eyes and come with a small sucker to pull them out again.

It was the Manchester United goalkeeper Harry Gregg who spotted that Nobby Stiles was finding it hard to judge the ball properly during his debut in 1960. The club sent him to a specialist who recommended contact lenses for severe myopia. They helped his game but have not been completely effective.

'You've gotta stay within a 15-yard range of me, 'cos that's as far as I can see,' he once told Bobby Charlton.

In May 1965, when he forgot his contact lens solution for an England game against Sweden, Alf Ramsey called Denis Follows, the secretary of the FA, asking him to find someone to buy the correct solution and put it on a flight to Gothenburg. Stiles got his solution.

Stiles puts in his lenses for matches but takes out his false teeth. As a child he was terrified of the dentist and his front teeth rotted away. Today he's given his false teeth, wrapped in a handkerchief, to reserve player Ian Callaghan to look after. Callaghan has them in his pocket.

Martin Peters is using shoe whitener to enhance the three white stripes on his Adidas boots. Others are painting the three stripes on their favourite old boots made by other companies – the £1000 from Adidas has also been offered to those who merely make their boots look like Adidas boots. Peters has a sip of tea from a white British Rail mug. He has a pre-match ritual that takes about an hour. His kit has to go on in a specific order, with his shorts going on last. The ritual is not his own idea.

At West Ham, Bobby Moore is so revered that the younger players, such as Peters (who always calls his captain 'Robert') and Harry Redknapp, copy his way of doing things. Bobby Moore always puts his shorts on last and likes to hang a small keyring on a gold chain from his trouser belt. 'Soon everyone had one of those,' says Redknapp.

Alan Ball also idolises his captain. 'I wanted to be a better player so he'd respect me for that. I wanted to be great so he'd be proud of me.' After one international match, Ball asked shyly if he could join him out on the town that evening. Bobby Moore smiled, turned round, held out the back of his jacket and told him to grab hold of it. He was going to show him London.

The dressing room was in a positive mood. Within the squad the atmosphere has always been very positive. We've always had a lot of fun. We'd reached the final, and well, we wanted to win it, of course.

Siggi Held

2.20pm/3.20pm Spanish Time

On the other side of the players' tunnel, the West German dressing room is quieter. Helmut Schön, who has been the West German manager for 16 years, is giving his players last-minute advice and encouragement. Schön is particularly concerned about his goalkeeper, Hans Tilkowski, who injured his shoulder in the semi-final against the Soviet Union and has since bruised his ribs in training. He has little choice but to play him as his two reserve keepers – Günther Bernhard and Sepp Maier – are too inexperienced for a World Cup final.

Helmut Schön reminds Franz Beckenbauer of his main task – to mark the English player Schön fears the most.

'Stick on Charlton, stick on Charlton... It's very important because you're fast enough to stay with him, to control him.'

Beckenbauer is daunted by his task – for him, 28-year-old Bobby Charlton is the best midfielder in the world. But he agrees to do what Schön asks.

'I will do whatever you want me to do – you're the boss.'

Beckenbauer has been single-mindedly dedicated to football since he was a small boy, using every spare hour to kick a ball in the streets of Munich. His family was so poor he used to practise in old leather ski boots. 'There was a cobbler who lived on the ground floor beneath us. He just sawed off the soles and hammered some cleats [studs] into them... I wasn't interested in the usual 1960s things – politics, the student movements of the time and so on. I was always football, football, football.' He admires Helmut Schön – the manager is like a father to him.

Schön is in many ways similar to Alf Ramsey – not always popular with the press but appreciated by the players. 'He gave us the ball and we just started to play – we played our own game,' Franz Beckenbauer said.

Yesterday, Helmut Schön was asked by Gerald Seymour of ITN which England player he was most worried about.

'Eleven men,' the manager replied.

Like Alf Ramsey, Helmut Schön played for his country. He was extremely fast and dangerous in front of goal, scoring 17 times in 16 international matches. His father was a dealer in fine art and had wanted his musically gifted and opera-obsessed son to become a doctor. Instead, young Helmut followed his passion for football. Schön became the manager of Saarland – a small corner of West Germany that was part of the French occupied zone and an independent football nation between 1948 and 1956. Saarland entered the 1952 Olympics and the 1954 World Cup where they lost each time to West Germany.

However, the performance of Schön's team prompted Sepp Herberger, the West German coach, to hire him as his assistant. Then in November 1964, after 28 years in charge, Herberger stepped down and named Schön as his successor. At six foot one, Schön is nicknamed 'The Tall One'; West German captain Uwe Seeler said that in his one-to-ones with the manager, 'I would have liked a stool to stand on.'

Sepp Herberger has been travelling with the German squad for the past few weeks and is at Wembley today.

Helmut Schön has made only one change to the team that won the semi-final – Friedel Lutz has been dropped in defence for Horst-Dieter Höttges. Goalkeeper Hans Tilkowski doesn't think that's such a good idea – on a purely physical level, the tall Lutz would be a better match for Geoff Hurst. Tilkowski played against Hurst only three months ago when West Ham United met Borussia Dortmund in the European Cup semi-final and twice Hurst beat him in the air.

To the players in both dressing rooms, the muffled sound of the crowd in the stadium is getting louder with every minute.

John Cleese is realising that he has chosen the wrong café

to watch the final. He is the only Englishman there – almost everyone else is a German tourist. He just wants to watch the game in peace without attracting any hostility. Since his initial greetings in German he's spoken English, so his only hope now is passing as a Canadian or a Rhodesian watching the game 'out of curiousity'.

John Andrews has had enough of trying to sell his spare ticket at face value. The game is going to start soon and he wants to find his seat. He spots a boy walking away from the stadium.

'Are you going to the match?'

'No.'

'Would you like to go?'

'Yes, please!'

'Well, here's a free ticket.'

> *In the houses in our street there was only one wall socket. During the World Cup you could always tell if people were watching the games because they were going around with creased shirts, because you could either watch TV or get your shirt ironed – but you couldn't do both.*
>
> *Carl Gillwood*

2.22pm

For the eight boys who live in the terraced houses along Clarence Grove in Liverpool, the World Cup is the centre of their lives. When Group 3 games were played at Goodison Park, they shot down to the stadium just before half-time and 'bunked in'. They've watched all the televised games at Georgie 'Buster' Marsden's house as his dad, who's a docker, has the best telly.

The boys, all ten years old, play football endlessly on the

cobbles, sometimes with the tougher 'Debris Lads' from the end of the street that was bombed in the war. They even have their own replica Jules Rimet trophy made from cardboard that they place on the ground when they play outside, or bring indoors when there's a match on.

The goalie is always David Lomas, who wears leg irons and bottle-end glasses and can't see a thing with or without them. 'He just stood in goal with his arms outstretched. If he got hit with the ball he would just fall over like a duck in a shooting gallery,' remembers Carl Gillwood.

The friends plan to watch the final at Georgie's house; he has said they can use his new leather football for a kickabout afterwards. The boys are confident of an England victory – after all they have Gordon Banks, Bobby Moore and of course the great Jimmy Greaves.

The boys arrive at Georgie's house. He opens the door, revealing a red face streaked with tears.

'Jimmy Greaves isn't playing! It's some fella called Geoff Hurst!'

The bad news doesn't end there.

'And our telly caught fire last night...'

Disappointed, they all agree to watch the match in their own homes and meet up after to replay the game. Carl Gillwood takes the cardboard trophy back to his house at Number 20 with its small but reliable Radio Rentals television.

In the England dressing room, Geoff Hurst is only too aware of the job he has to do to impress disappointed fans like the boys in Clarence Grove. 'Not too many people agreed with Alf on the morning of the match. I had to astonish half of Britain that afternoon, just to stop them wanting to string Alf up for leaving Jimmy on the bench.'

Gordon Banks is in the dressing-room toilets going through his pre-match ritual of stretches and toe-touches.

Ray Wilson is applying Vick's VapoRub around his nostrils and on the front of his red shirt.

Jackie Charlton is putting Vaseline on his eyebrows so the sweat doesn't run into them.

George Cohen is reading the souvenir match programme, on sale at 2/6.

> *The programme is full of adverts for alcohol and cigarettes – 'Player's No.6 – the cigarettes that give you guaranteed quality'; Mobil Oil has an advert in the form of a competition: 'Where was the first World Cup played? Clue: You could get there and back from London in a Mini on 4 gallons of Mobil Special – plus a 7500-mile boat trip!'; FA secretary Denis Follows is pictured in his office modelling a new suit: 'All the suits worn by the 200 officials responsible for the smooth running of this year's World Cup were made to measure by Burton Tailoring.'*

Bobby Moore has had enough of the crowded, noisy dressing room.

'Aren't we supposed to be getting ready for a big match!?' he shouts irritably.

He said later: 'If I'd had my way, I would have cooperated until two o'clock, but then cleared the decks because the job still had to be done.'

2.25pm/3.25pm Spanish Time

In the main hotel in Calella, a Spanish seaside town on the Costa del Maresme, north-east of Barcelona, the television lounge is packed with English and West German guests. They are all seated as close as possible to a small black and white television. It's a hot day and the bar at the back of the room is doing good business.

The hotel manager has placed a large brandy glass on top of the television and next to it a Union flag and the West German flag. He explains that each time a team scores their flag should be placed in the glass.

One German tourist declares loudly that he promises he will shave his head if West Germany lose.

2.30pm

Alf Ramsey is wearing his blue England tracksuit, white socks and black brogues. He's in the England changing room giving each of his players last-minute words of advice. He reminds Bobby Charlton of the danger that Franz Beckenbauer poses – a player eight years his junior. He tells Martin Peters to make sure he attacks the near post of the German goal every time there's a free kick.

Roger Hunt is instructed to stick to defender Willi Schulz.

Having finally got rid of their spare ticket, Bill and Winnie Harrison and John and Jill Andrews take their places in the stadium, and they're good seats, close to the pitch and level with the centre spot. John Andrews realises that the row of suited young men next to him are the team England defeated in the semi-final here on Tuesday – Portugal. Winnie passes her match programme along the row for some autographs. João Lourenço and Joaquim Carvalho oblige.

Meanwhile, upstairs in the Lord Derby pub in Ashton-under-Lyne, Winnie's daughter Sue is upset. Although only nine, she is a big football fan and went to Old Trafford to see a Group 3 match with her mum. Just before they went into Wembley, Winnie rang her mother to check on Sue and her younger sister. Sue has just found out about the spare ticket.

2.35pm

Nineteen-year-old John Janes and his friends Roger Halle and Fred Munt had feared they would miss the biggest game of their lives – but it looks like the passenger in their car has saved the day. John, Roger and Fred have been camping near Ryde on the Isle of Wight for the past two days, and at lunchtime went into a local pub hoping it had a television, or to find somewhere they could watch the final. They got talking to a girl about their age who said they could watch the game at her house.

Fred is driving them in his Ford Zephyr through the outskirts of Newport, heading north on the A3020. The girl tells them to turn left. In front of them is an imposing brick wall and a sign saying 'HMP Parkhurst'.

'Where are you taking us?' John asks her.

'This is where I live. My father's a prison officer.'

Their car is waved through the main gate and the girl points out a brick terraced house.

The three friends are going to watch the final inside one of Britain's most notorious prisons. In the newly opened maximum-security block nearby, six of the Great Train Robbers are serving their sentence.

2.37pm

Room-mates Ray Wilson and Bobby Charlton have their own pre-match ritual. Their kit is in the same bag, always brought from the hotel by Wilson. He hands Charlton his boots one at a time, then an ammonia inhaler (it has to be the same one with a broken top) for him to clear his nose.

Gordon Banks is tying his laces for the third time. The knot has to be at the side of the boot and not over the lace holes – he doesn't want to feel it when he kicks the ball.

Martin Peters is waiting for his captain to put his shorts on – his pre-match ritual dictates that he must be the last to do so. Moore puts his shorts on, then Peters does the same. But Moore has a plan.

2.40pm

In Tenby in South Wales, a man known by his work colleagues as 'The German Scouser' is making his way towards a cottage at the top of the hill above the town. Forty-three-year-old Heinz Kurt-Doerr is on a camping holiday with his wife Joan and their sons Eric and Kenneth. Ever since West Germany reached the final, Heinz has been desperate to find somewhere to watch the game. All they have with them in their tent is a Decca radio.

Heinz has been told by the lady who runs the campsite shop that the family in the cottage on the hill have a television, and she was sure they would be happy for him to join them. 'However,' she said, 'you'd better not let them know you're German.'

Heinz Kurt-Doerr was a 21-year-old petty officer in the German navy – the Kriegsmarine – when he surrendered to US forces in Bordeaux in August 1944. He was taken as a POW to England. Like Bert Trautmann, he was put to work on the land. While on a farm on the Wirral, looking after the tractors, Heinz met a 17-year-old Land Girl named Joan. She and the other Land Girls were terrified of the German POWs at first, but soon she fell in love with the handsome sailor. After breaking up with him three times, because other people disapproved of her courting a German, Joan and Heinz were married in 1946, in a village outside Frankfurt.

But they both missed England and moved back to the Wirral, and Heinz got a job in the engine shop at the Cammell Laird shipyard in Birkenhead.

They don't have much money, so every summer they go camping with their two sons in an old but sturdy ex-British army tent. Usually they just camp in a farmer's field, but this is their first time on a proper campsite.

Heinz wonders what sort of reception he will get at the cottage on the hill. He decides to keep his mouth shut if possible. Back at the campsite, everyone who has a radio has it on; those with car radios have their doors open.

A buzzer goes in the England and West German dressing rooms. Five minutes until the players must leave and head out into the tunnel.

Bobby Moore takes his shorts off, knowing full well that this will upset Martin Peters' pre-match routine. Someone has to be last to put them back on – and it's going to be him.

2.42pm

Standing in the tunnel at Wembley, close to the dressing rooms, is PC Peter Weston. The real World Cup has been put safely into the hands of Wembley's head of security. The copy is in the boot of their police car, parked at the car park end of the tunnel. PC Weston still hasn't worked out how he is going to switch trophies.

Weston is a big football fan, and a semi-professional player. He turns out for the Metropolitan Police Team, the Divisional Team, Paddington Green Police Station and for Croydon Amateurs. Now he is at the heart of the biggest football match England has ever seen.

Gordon Banks is pummelling a practice ball against the wall of the dressing room until his hands are used to the feel of the leather. He is following Bert Trautmann's chewing-gum advice: he tucks the ball under his arm and spits into his hands.

Alf Ramsey goes round to each of his players, shakes their hand and wishes them good luck.

2.44pm

In the Wembley dressing rooms the buzzer sounds again. One minute to go. The noise goes right through a nervous George Cohen. Bobby Charlton and Ray Wilson shake hands – the final part of their pre-match ritual.

> *Believe you me, if I could wish something for you all, it would be to experience that feeling when you crest that rise and what you saw at Wembley was just fantastic– the colours, the noise, the banners and that strip of green is waiting for you and you've got your shirt on – it's the most fantastic feeling of all time.*
>
> *Alan Ball, after dinner speech*

2.45pm

'Come on! Come on! Let's go!!'

The England dressing-room door opens, and the players file out into the tunnel. The noise from the crowd is extraordinary. Bobby Moore is carrying his shorts.

Whether playing for Leeds or England, Jack Charlton always makes sure he is at the back of line when they walk onto the pitch. Martin Peters also likes to be last, but as Jack is the more senior, he doesn't want to challenge him and slots in third from the back in front of Nobby Stiles. His superstitious routine has been broken for a second time.

The England team shake their legs with nervous energy. Bobby Moore finally puts on his shorts – they are, of course, immaculate and still have an ironed crease on them.

The West Germans emerge from their dressing room and line up alongside the English players. For Martin Peters it is 'a chilling moment' as he looks along the opponents' line.

Bobby Charlton looks over at Hans Tilkowski, the West German goalkeeper, whose face is expressionless.

'Are you a man of iron or just a hell of a good actor?' the Englishman wonders. For Tilkowski, like Bobby Charlton, this is his third World Cup – he played in 1958, and was the reserve keeper in 1962. He is a formidable talent – as goalkeeper for Borussia Dortmund, he was voted German Footballer of the Year.

Tilkowski holds out his hand to Gordon Banks, who wipes his on his shirt to get rid of the chewing-gum spit before he shakes.

Hans Tilkowski had been desperate to play in this World Cup. He was distraught when he didn't get to play in Chile in 1962. Just before they left for South America, goalkeeper Wolfgang Fahrian impressed everyone when – in Tilkowski's words – he 'performed an air show between his goalposts' in Hamburg against Uruguay.

In the build-up to the 1966 finals, Tilkowski had played well and his place seemed assured, then on the way back from the cinema on the eve of their last warm-up game, a fixture against Yugoslavia, a member of the squad accidently hit Tilkowski on the nose. He was panic-stricken. Tilkowski was taken to a specialist who assured him there was no lasting damage. But he has a permanent souvenir from that cinema trip – a slightly crooked nose.

Tilkowski loves writing postcards and almost every day during his time in England he has spent his daily allowance from the Deutscher Fußball-Bund (ten marks a day abroad, five marks at home) on buying and posting them. So far he has sent about 500 postcards.

The Wembley crowd is getting impatient to see both teams. The hunting horns brought by some of the German fans are being blown with force.

For Hans Tilkowski, there is only one way to avoid being overwhelmed by the occasion: 'Have tunnel vision – you must neither look to the right, nor to the left, and ignore everything and everyone – even if the Queen walks past you.'

Siggi Held is aware of the crowd, but he's so focused on the matter in hand it's as if he's hearing them 'through a wall'.

Waiting at the mouth of the tunnel are the Swiss referee, Gottfried Dienst, and his two linesmen, grey-haired Tofik Bakhramov from the Soviet Union and Dr Karol Galba from Czechoslovakia.

> *Gottfried Dienst is a postman who used to play for FC Basel in the Swiss First Division until a knee injury ended his career. He's overseen several important games including the 1961 and 1965 European Cup finals. In the 1961 final between Benfica and Barcelona when the score was 1-1, the Barcelona goalkeeper Antonio Ramallets pushed a mistimed defensive header against the crossbar and the ball bounced twice along the goal line and out onto the pitch. Amid protests from the Barcelona players, Dienst awarded the goal.*
>
> *Tofik Bakhramov was a linesman for England's opening game. He is repeatedly called 'Russian' by commentators because his home country of Azerbaijan is controlled by the Soviet Union.*

Dienst, holding the orange match ball in his left hand, turns to the players and raises his right hand to signal that they are heading onto the pitch. Bobby Moore nods at Uwe Seeler. The two columns start to move, the sound of their studs echoing in the concrete tunnel.

The television audience gets their first view of the players.

2.46pm

Gordon Banks keeps his eyes down as he comes out onto the pitch, bouncing the practice ball like a basketball. Ray Wilson tucks his shirt into his shorts. Geoff Hurst bounces a ball in front of a television camera. Jackie Charlton holds back, keeping a few paces behind everyone else. Alongside him, head down, is Horst-Dieter Höttges, nicknamed 'Iron Foot', the last of the Germans to file out.

There are shallow puddles of rain on the concrete.

The familiar rhythmic clapping, followed by a chant of 'Eng-land!', accompanies the players as they walk across the dog track.

The chant has been adapted from the Brazilian fans' war cry at the 1962 World Cup in Chile.

Martin Peters is thinking about his wife Kathy as he jogs out.

When they first met, Kathy asked him, 'What do you do?'
'I play football,' he replied.
'But what do you do for a job?'

Nobby Stiles remembers his father's advice when he first started his career: 'Look around, enjoy all of it because you might not pass that way again.'

'I love this. This is for me!' Alan Ball thinks. He looks for his parents and 19-year-old girlfriend Lesley Newton sitting with the team's wives behind the royal box. He can't see them.

Gordon Banks is looking in the same direction, trying to catch a glimpse of his wife Ursula and their son Robert. Ursula is German and they met when he was doing his national service in Germany. Yesterday, a journalist asked her who she thought would win.

'I wouldn't like to say. But out of loyalty to Gordon, I hope it's England.'

As they touch the Wembley turf, both teams break into a jog and start to line up behind the bandsmen across the centre circle. The referee stands over the centre spot, the ball at his feet. Bobby Moore's cheeks puff out as he exhales.

'Here we are,' thinks Ray Wilson. 'We've arrived.'

Geoff Hurst spots a banner that says: 'Nobby Stiles for Prime Minister.'

Bobby Charlton loves playing at Wembley. He first walked onto the pitch at 15 when he played for England schoolboys. 'Wembley was so beautiful. It was just made for me. I used to love passing the ball, and it used to go where you meant it to go. True as anything. It was like a billiard table.'

George Cohen is telling himself not to panic at the level of noise from the crowd. He remembers telling himself the same thing during a game at Anfield when, dazzled by the flood-lights and deafened by the noise of the Kop, he couldn't hear the familiar boot-on-leather sound and judge how Liverpool's Tommy Smith had struck a cross towards Fulham's goal. He'd forced himself to keep calm.

'Don't bugger things up, George, not now when the job is so nearly done.'

Alf Ramsey and Helmut Schön, together with their trainers, take their places on the green team benches.

2.47pm

The two teams line up facing the tunnel and the royal box. Jack Charlton looks at the scoreboard to his right.

England 0 Germany W 0

'I wonder what it will read in another hour and a half?' he thinks.

Apart from Gordon Banks and Ray Wilson who are wearing Puma boots, all the players have Adidas stripes on their boots.

The sound of a single Brazilian drum can be heard reverberating around the stadium.

There are plenty of banners among the West German spectators, bringing greetings from their home towns: '*Delmold grüßt London*'; '*Bottrop grüßt England*'.

The Queen and the Duke of Edinburgh arrive in the royal box, escorted by Sir Stanley Rous, the president of FIFA. The Queen is wearing a yellow hat and coat and a pair of white gloves. The prime minister is two seats to her right. Wilson occasionally exchanges a few words with the chancellor of the exchequer, Jim Callaghan, who is seated behind him.

The Queen, who is the patron of the FA, will present the trophy to the winners from the safety of the royal box. Lessons have been learned from previous World Cup finals. In 1958, the king of Sweden was pulled into the team photos by the victorious Brazilians, and 17-year-old Pelé, who had scored twice, wept on his shoulder. Then in 1962, at the end of the final in Santiago, Sir Stanley Rous was almost knocked over by photographers keen to get shots of the Brazilian team.

To many of those [supporters] who'd lived through the war, defeat by the Germans in a football match would have been a devastating humiliation.

Martin Peters

English football was at its strongest then because we were children of the war and as youngsters we had been deprived a lot of what are called life's good things.

Jimmy Armfield

From the perspective of the television gantry opposite the royal box, the view from which much of the memorable action footage will be recorded, England will begin the first half playing right to left.

2.49pm

Everyone stands silently as the band plays the British national anthem. On one of the twin towers the Royal Standard is flapping in the strong breeze.

As well as the Royal Standard, the flags of all the 16 countries that have taken part in the tournament are displayed on 25-foot steel flagpoles around the roof of the stadium. At the opening ceremony, wooden ice cream sticks were placed in each of the lanyards to give a satisfactory snap when the flags were unfurled.

About 80,000 England fans are singing 'God Save the Queen' as everyone in the royal box stands to attention. Gordon Banks is singing at the top of his voice.

There's applause when the anthem finishes. The West German squad bounce on the spot to relieve the tension, stopping as their anthem starts.

Between 1945 and 1950, no national anthem was sung when West Germany played. Then the old anthem was reintroduced but the strongly nationalistic first verse was dropped ('Deutschland, Deutschland über alles / Über alles in der Welt'; 'Germany,

Germany above all else / Above all else in the world') and only the inoffensive third verse was used ('Unity and justice and freedom / For the German fatherland! / Let us all strive for this purpose / Brotherly with heart and hand!')

However, at the 1954 World Cup presentation ceremony, large sections of the German crowd sang the banned first verse. Swiss and East German radio pulled the plug on their broadcasts until the anthem was over.

The English players are well aware that the match has added significance because their opponents are German. 'There was a lot more emotion from my father-in-law that afternoon who'd been a paratrooper, than just because we were playing a football match,' Geoff Hurst said later.

In front of the BBC commentary position is a Union flag, placed there earlier by a commentator from a country occupied by the Germans in the war. 'You mustn't lose this one...' he said to Kenneth Wolstenholme.

Martin Peters' father-in-law lost his parents, three sisters and their husbands who were home on leave when a bomb hit their home. He was the only survivor. The three sisters were called Kathleen, Doris and Winifred, and Martin Peters' wife is named Kathleen Doris Winifred in their memory.

The players were aware, Peters said later 'of an added responsibility'.

Nobby Stiles was born in a cellar in Manchester as the Luftwaffe bombed a factory a few hundred yards away. His mother had been too frightened to leave the house to go to an air-raid shelter down the road. Neighbours acted as midwives.

111

Jack Charlton can remember hiding under the stairs of their home in Ashington when the sirens sounded and hearing the bombs dropping on Newcastle. 'We waged a war for six years against Germany and now we were preparing to do battle on the football field,' he wrote later.

Robert Frederick Chelsea Moore was only four days old when the Luftwaffe targeted Barking power station, where his father Bob worked. Bob and his wife Doris (known as Doss) took their baby son in the mayor of Barking's car (commandeered for emergencies) to the house of one of Doss's sisters, where the future England captain spent the night in a drawer pulled out from a chest. They didn't go home for six weeks.

For the German manager Helmut Schön, the war was a painful experience.

On 13th February 1945, he was on duty as an air-raid warden at a factory outside Dresden when British and American bombers attacked the city. 'This is the death of Dresden,' a colleague said, as flames lit up the sky. Schön's wife and his 87-year-old father were in the city. Schön found a lorry to take him into Dresden and searched desperately for them. His wife was safe in an air-raid shelter. It took him five days to find his father.

The West German anthem ends, and hundreds of flags are waved by their supporters. The teams break – the Germans to the left, the English to the right. Both sides test out the pitch and the atmosphere, passing and trying gentle shots on goal.

In Tenby, Heinz Kurt-Doerr arrives at the cottage on the hill. The door is open and the television is on, and the front room is full of locals and English holidaymakers. He's waved in and finds himself a seat. Heinz doesn't say a word.

2.50pm

In Royal Oldham Hospital, Anita Dunnington is being wheeled into the delivery room. Neither her husband nor her family know she's about to give birth.

2.53pm

As the teams warm up, they can immediately tell that the pitch is greasy and soft.

Gordon Banks presses a divot in with his boot. He has let in only one goal in 450 minutes of World Cup football, and that was a penalty. The pitch is wetter than he thought it would be – so he's going to have to wear gloves after all. Banks puts them on and wipes them on the grass. He calls to his back four to give him plenty of crosses as practice.

Nobby Stiles is retying the shoelace on his right boot.
    'Let's hope Nobby Stiles isn't going to have trouble with his boots all afternoon,' Kenneth Wolstenholme says, up high in his position on the television gantry.

> *In January 1965, Wolstenholme suffered a heart attack and has since lost weight and given up smoking. His medication is close at hand.*

Bobby Moore waves to Tina in the crowd. He stretches his arms over his head, and spits.

Martin Peters feels a twinge of regret. After their semi-final victory, each of the team were given two complimentary tickets for the final. Most of the players have been approached by touts in the last few days. A young tout named 'Fat' Stan Flashman approached Peters. Flashman is one of the richest touts in London, although he dislikes the word 'tout' – he prefers 'entertainment broker'. Peters immediately agreed to sell the tickets – he has just bought a new house and has a wife and baby daughter to support. The £100 a week he gets at West Ham doesn't go very far.

He has Flashman's money, but his mother and father are watching the final at home on their black and white television set, rather than at Wembley with the other players' families.

Stan Flashman bought many of the complimentary tickets given to the West Ham players for the 1964 FA Cup final. Doss Moore queued up with the rest of the fans for a ticket as her son had sold his quota.

In the stands, Cissie and Bob Charlton watch their sons warm up.

As part of his routine before kick-off, Jack has to score. His first shot goes over the bar. He finds a second and sends it flying into the net. Relief.

There are three orange match balls at Wembley, each handmade at Slazenger from 25 high-quality leather panels by a craftsman named Malcolm Wainwright. The players are surprised by the colour of the balls, as they normally only play with an orange ball in the snow. The spares are being kept by the fourth official (the reserve to the referee and the two linesmen). Both ITV and the BBC would have preferred a white ball as that shows up much better on a black and white television set.

At the 1962 World Cup in Chile, match balls of the correct size and weight (27–28-inch circumference; weight 14–16 ounces) couldn't be found, so they had to be especially flown in at the last minute.

To prevent the same thing happening again, FIFA invited manu-facturers well ahead of the 1966 finals to submit balls for consid-eration by an official panel who met at the Olympic Restaurant at White City Stadium in May 1965, watched by members of the press. Of the 111 footballs supplied by nine different manufacturers, Slazenger of Croydon won the competition. They have supplied 400 balls to FIFA in three colours – orange, white and lemon.

2.57pm

At the centre spot, first Uwe Seeler and then Bobby Moore shake hands with the three officials; then with a nod and a smile, the two captains shake hands with each other and exchange banners.

The referee tosses a coin, and Bobby Moore wins. He indicates to Seeler by pointing to his side of the pitch that England will stay at the right-hand end.

Hugh Johns is making a faltering start on ITV: 'From those curious signals I would suggest that England won the Cup, er… won the toss – ha ha! That is probably anticipating things! They've won the toss anyway – that's a start!'

2.58pm/3.58pm Italian Time

With their pre-match performance over, Michael Hutton and the 50 members of the Her Majesty's Royal Marines Band under his command are being shown to their seats in the stands.

Sixteen-year-old Christina Stark is watching the final in Rome in a room full of boisterous Italians – mostly men and boys, some lying on the floor, others sitting on the backs of sofas. She is at the home of Paolo, the fiancé of her friend Susan Medway. The only part of the television coverage she has understood so far is when the commentator says 'Bob-by Charl-ton!' The Italians are not supporting either side – they are simply looking forward to an exciting game.

Earlier this month, Christina turned down the chance to see some World Cup games close up.

Christina is a schoolgirl halfway through her A-levels, but also works as a model. She got a job publicising milk for the Milk Marketing Board at all the World Cup games held at Sheffield Wednesday's ground, Hillsborough. The Milk Girls, as they were known, were supplied with white T-shirts but had to bring their own tennis skirts. They would hand out cartons of milk before the games.

'Remember, girls, you'll be on the pitch so everyone will be a long way away from you,' Miss Myra Needham, the boss of the model agency, had told them at a briefing meeting, 'so wear lots of make-up!'

When Christina told Miss Needham that she wasn't going to be a Milk Girl after all, but was going to Rome as a chaperone for a friend, Miss Needham was furious and said, 'I'll make sure you'll never work again!' Watching the final in Rome, with the prospect of an exciting summer ahead, Christina has no regrets.

2.59pm

Thirty-two million Britons are watching the final on television. Only 15 million homes have television sets, so most people are watching with others. Forty-eight countries around the world are taking the final live – all using the BBC's pictures.

For those thousands unable to watch the game, Brian Moore

and Alan Clarke are providing the commentary on BBC Radio. Alan Clarke is an old hand and has been commentating for the BBC since 1947. Brian Moore is a newcomer. He had hoped that he'd be part of the BBC TV commentary team. Six months ago, the corporation approached him, but his fierce agent Teddy Sommerfield refused their offer of £2750 declaring that Moore wouldn't accept anything less than £3000. This wasn't the case. 'I would have snatched their hands off had it been left to me.'

The final is not sold out. There are 96,924 spectators in Wembley Stadium, just below the 97,000 capacity. Outside, John Nutkins and half a dozen other Scouts are once again being given free tickets by touts.

> **Since Mr Ramsey doesn't much like speaking, the England team will try to say what he means.**
>
> **Bobby Moore**

3.00pm

Referee Gottfried Dienst blows his whistle.

Kenneth Wolstenholme says, 'The rain has stopped, the excitement is intense. The ground in many places is soft and the 1966 World Cup final is underway!'

Centre forward Siggi Held taps the ball left to Wolfgang Overath, who kicks it towards Helmut Haller on the right wing – but it's too far in front of him and the ball spins out of touch.

Martin Peters knows Wolfgang Overath, having first played against

117

him at Wembley seven years earlier in a schoolboys' international and later in an Under-23 match.

Peters, playing left-side midfield, takes the throw-in quickly – a short one to his West Ham team-mate Bobby Moore, who passes it to Geoff Hurst – but Willi Schulz dives in front of the Englishman's raised boot and intercepts it. The first boos of the day echo around the stadium.

Free kick to England.

Martin Peters played six times for England schoolboys and was part of the team in 1959 that beat West Germany 2-0 in front of a crowd of 95,000 at Wembley. He performed so well that day that in the dressing room at the end of the game he received telegrams from clubs asking if he'd be interested in joining them. Peters finally settled on West Ham, but his father William had needed some persuasion. He was a Thames lighterman and he had hoped his son would end up working on the barges as he had done.

Ray Wilson sends a short pass to Bobby Moore by the touch-line, who passes back. Martin Peters and Geoff Hurst take it forward and Nobby Stiles, who has space, shoots. It's deflected to Cohen, who loses the ball to Lothar Emmerich (known as 'Emma' to his team-mates). The first England attack is over.

3.01pm

About 20 yards out, Martin Peters' shot is deflected by the stocky West German captain Uwe Seeler. It comes back to the West Ham striker, who hits it with the top of his boot towards the right-hand corner flag. There are groans and whistles from the crowd. Peters, chewing gum, runs back to midfield.

Martin Peters is concentrating on 'doing the simple things well... and not to make any mistakes'.

Uwe Seeler is the team's most popular player. At home the crowd often shout not for West Germany but 'U-we!'. It caused a national upset when the Italian club Inter Milan offered Seeler the huge sum of 1.2 million marks to leave Hamburger FC to join them. Adi Dassler called Seeler up and reminded him that he was at heart a man of Hamburg 'with his feet on the ground'. He also offered him a lucrative position as an Adidas representative. Seeler stayed in Germany.

In 1965, Seeler's career seemed to be over. He was tackled by Frankfurt's inside-right Georg Lechner and the supporters in the stands heard a sound just like a whip cracking. Seeler felt as if he'd been 'hacked down by an elephant'. Lechner hadn't touched him – Seeler's Achilles tendon had torn. Few players recover from such an injury. West Germany's coach, Helmut Schön, was 'mortally shattered' at the news – Uwe Seeler was vital for West Germany's World Cup qualification campaign.

To get fit for an away match in Sweden that the West Germans had to win to qualify, Uwe Seeler endured intensive training, including running on sandy beaches to help rebuild his leg muscles. Adi Dassler designed a special Adidas boot called the Achilles, with extra padding at the heel to help support Seeler's damaged ankle.

For the first time in his career, Helmut Schön had a good-luck charm in his pocket as he sat on the bench in Stockholm. The charm or the training paid off – ten minutes into the second half, Seeler stuck the Achilles in front of a cross from Peter Grosser and scored the winning goal that sent his team to England. 'Seeler is the ideal captain; he never gives in,' Helmut Schön said.

Watching Seeler's performance with particular interest in the

Wembley crowd is 66-year-old Adi Dassler. As well as providing the boots for the players, Dassler has provided financial assistance. The German FA had said that they couldn't afford to bring assistant coach Udo Lattek over to England, much to the players' disappointment. Dassler stepped in and has paid his expenses.

Back in Dassler's hotel room is a souvenir he is particularly delighted to have. He visited the German squad at their team hotel in Derbyshire during their qualifying round and in nearby Ashbourne bought an old, battered football boot used in the traditional Ashbourne Shrove Tuesday football match. Dassler is going to give the boot pride of place in his private museum.

In Ashbourne today there are divided loyalties. The West German team made many friends during their stay; they were always happy to oblige with autographs and pose for photographs (it's a German football tradition that the public can watch their teams train) and local girls fell in love with young Franz Beckenbauer. Ashbourne was nicknamed 'Little Deutschland'. Not everyone was won over; an elderly resident was asked if he was going to watch the Germans train on the local field. 'No thanks, I've seen them on two fields already and that was quite enough for me.'

3.02pm

There is a rush of people in the Wembley stands as the hot-dog vendors, programme sellers and turnstile attendants try to find places now their job is done – at least for 45 minutes.

Brian Bowker, who should be working in the stockroom at Littlewood's in Morecambe, but has phoned in sick, is watching the game at his girlfriend Avril Roberts' house. Her parents run a bed and breakfast and the lounge is decorated with Union flags and full of guests.

Meanwhile, Brian's mother is hard at work in Littlewood's cafeteria, and she is seething. She's heard that the stockroom is a person short.

Alan Ball passes to George Cohen, who nervously flicks it to no one. The crowd groan.

Throw-in to West Germany.

Bobby Charlton recalled that although his friend George Cohen was a terrific defender, 'the quality of his final delivery was not something that prompted huge optimism'. Bobby Robson said of him, 'George hit more photographers than Frank Sinatra.'

West German full-back Karl-Heinz Schnellinger throws the ball to Willi Schulz who kicks a high, long ball towards the England penalty area. Bobby Moore heads it, Lothar Emmerich collects it and passes to an unmarked Siggi Held. Bobby and Jackie Charlton are either side of him but too far away to do anything. Held stops it with his thigh, turns and smacks it well to the right of the England post. A photographer sticks his foot out to stop the ball.

Siggi Held stands motionless for a moment, furious at the missed opportunity.

Goal kick.

Most of the photographers are behind Gordon Banks' goal, anticipating that Germany will take the lead.

Twenty-seven photographers are allowed around the pitch at Wembley today and during the game they must stay in marked-out areas behind the goals. In previous World Cups, they'd been free

*to roam the touchlines. Another new restriction is that the team
dressing rooms are out of bounds after the games.*

It has been frustrating for the *Daily Mirror* photographer Kent
Gavin; he hasn't got a press pass giving access to the pitch
so he's stuck in the stands. Lots of his shots so far have been
spoiled by the arms and heads of spectators.

Alan Ball passes too far in front of Bobby Charlton, who slaps
his hands against his legs in irritation.

It's taking the players time to get used to the pace of the damp
pitch.

3.03pm

Franz Beckenbauer and Bobby Charlton are never far from
each other. They exchange glances. Charlton realises they
both know their managers are taking a dangerous gamble by
making the same decision – to neutralise their opponents' most
creative and unpredictable player. Beckenbauer has played as a
sweeper (a *libero* as the West Germans call the role) for Bayern
since 1964, so is finding the man-to-man marking restrictive –
he likes to have more influence on the game, 'instead of a duel
against a single opponent'.

> For the 20-year-old, playing at Wembley is his dream. 'England
> was the motherland of football… Wembley was the Mecca. In
> Germany at this time we played in front of 15,000 maximum, but it
> was 100,000 – they made a big noise!' he said later.
>   Franz Beckenbauer is fortunate to be playing. He had received
> his second booking of the tournament in Monday's semi-final
> against the Soviet Union and it should have meant an immediate

one-match suspension. The West German management's argument that the whole incident was a case of mistaken identity – the referee must have intended to book Beckenbauer's fellow midfielder Wolfgang Overath – wasn't necessary. FIFA had recently put in place a system that meant that any booking by a referee had to be 'confirmed' by them – they would decide if any disciplinary action was necessary.

Sceptics concluded that when FIFA refused to 'confirm' the referee's booking of Franz Beckenbauer but 'confirmed' the sending-off of the Russian Igor Chislenko in the same match, the governing body simply didn't want to exclude a player who'd scored four times in five games and was the new star of the West German team.

Three-quarters of the way down the pitch and two yards from the touchline, Lothar Emmerich, the Bundesliga's top scorer last season, hits a perfect ball into the centre of the England penalty area to Uwe Seeler, but Ray Wilson, (expertly carrying out his job to man-mark the West German captain) slides across the wet grass and makes a successful interception. The ball spins out for a West German throw-in close to the England corner flag.

> **[At the start] there was a lot of control and push, control and push. Not a lot of running with the ball.**
>
> **Gordon Banks**

3.04pm

Jackie Charlton has yet to touch the ball. 'I'm never going to get a kick in this game,' he thinks.

Geoff Hurst realises that Horst-Dieter Höttges has been given the job of marking him, and reckons he stands a good chance of beating the German in the air. He also decides that as Höttges is a full-back used to marking wingers, he will feel uncomfortable if Hurst makes the centre of the pitch his own.

Helmut Schön watches from the bench, worried about Höttges' fitness – he missed the semi-final against the Soviet Union at Goodison Park because of an injured ankle. In fact, Höttges has been injured in each of the four games he's played. The manager knows that Höttges is not technically gifted but he is 'a fighter – not dirty, a fighter who was clean'.

It's clear that England aren't playing a 4-3-3 formation but instead a 4-1-3-2 formation with Nobby Stiles in front of George Cohen, Jack Charlton, Bobby Moore and Ray Wilson.

3.05pm

Eighteen year-old Scout John Nutkins takes his seat on a bench in the stadium. He has with him a box of Jubbly drinks that he managed to bring through the turnstiles. In his Rover Scout uniform, John stands out among the hundreds of German fans he finds himself with.

> *Once more, I get a taste of how English strikers deal with goalkeepers...*
>
> *Hans Tilkowski*

3.07pm/4.07pm German Time

In the German town of Uhingen, five-year-old Jürgen Dudek is watching the match with his parents Hubert and Irmengard. With them are close relatives Walter, Friedel and Richard Fischer, who have made the 90 minute journey from their home in Augsberg because they don't have a television and the Dudeks have a large one, something of a rarity in 1966. The German forward Helmut Haller is from Augsberg, so the Fischers are watching his progress with particular attention. They are so proud that a local boy who progressed from Third Division Augsberg to play for FC Bologna is now in the national team.

The *Daily Mail* described Haller in this morning's edition as 'unpredictable – but his blonde head has appeared in the right spot for four World Cup goals'.

It's a corner to West Germany on the far side. The soft ground in the England goal area is already badly cut up. Helmut Haller sweeps it in, but centre-back 'Big Jack' Charlton coolly heads it away to Alan Ball.

Hurst.

Hunt.

Stiles chips the ball into the West German penalty area, but it goes over Roger Hunt's head and goalkeeper Hans Tilkowski punches it away with two hands. Bobby Charlton collects it and chips it back in, to where Geoff Hurst in now waiting. Hurst and Tilkowski jump together – Hurst accidently hits Tilkowski in the jaw, Tilkowski accidently punches Hurst in the right eye. The keeper tumbles and lies face down.

Play carries on until referee Gottfried Dienst sees the injured Tilkowski and blows his whistle.

The West German trainer jogs onto the pitch to look at the keeper. He sponges Tilkowski's face with water.

Years later, Franz Beckenbauer said to Bobby Charlton as they watched a recording of the game, 'We were very angry at the time.'

'That's the way we play.'

125

> *'Yes, but Tilkowski had badly hurt his ribs in training. Didn't you know that?'*
>
> *Charlton said they didn't.*

The referee awards a free kick, not for the injury to Tilkowski, but for a foul outside the West German penalty area. Tilkowski spits some blood out onto the grass, rubs his jaw, but is otherwise OK.

'He's probably saying to himself, "Well, I knew Muhammad Ali, Cassius Clay was here, but I didn't think he was on the field",' Kenneth Wolstenholme says cheerily.

> *Muhammad Ali is indeed in the crowd at Wembley to publicise his fight at Earls Court next Saturday against the English boxer Brian London. Three years ago, Ali fought Henry Cooper in Wembley Stadium and Cooper downed him in the fourth round with his trademark left hook, but after being revived by his trainer Angelo Dundee with the use of (prohibited) smelling salts, the American went on to win.*
>
> *Ali knocked out Brian London after one minute and 40 seconds in the third round with a sharp short right to the jaw.*

What's actually on Hans Tilkowski's mind is that their team should be a credit to the republic. 'The main thing was that we left a good impression. Back in 1966, the appearance and behaviour of the team was essential.' This is something that Helmut Schön has told his players repeatedly.

3.10pm

'Turn that thing off!' a woman hisses in the United Reformed Church on Richmond Green in south-west London. Not everyone is concentrating on the wedding of Doris David and Ken Smith.

Dotted throughout the congregation are men with earpieces attached to small transistor radios. They are standing up and sitting down when they are supposed to, but clearly not paying attention. Their wives are getting irritated.

Nineteen-year-old Ann Marshall is there with her parents Dorothy and Ted. The bride rents a bedsit below their flat on Richmond Hill and they were delighted to be invited to the wedding. Ann watches her mother purse her lips in disapproval at the men with the earpieces. Neither Ann nor her mother has any idea what the men are listening to.

Jack Charlton plays a tidy one-two with Alan Ball, who passes the ball to Martin Peters on the far side of the pitch, who, after one touch, shoots with his left foot. Hans Tilkowski dives across the goal, prompting the biggest roar from the crowd so far. Both sides are less nervous, more confident. The game has had an exciting start.

One evening, leaning on the bar at the Hendon Hall Hotel, Jack Charlton asked Alf Ramsey why he'd chosen him to play for England. 'You see, Jack, I pick the players I think will do the job I want them to do. They may not be the best players available, but they are the players who will do the job I give them.' Jack had the strong feeling that he was among those he considered 'not the best players'.

'I used to say to Alf: "Can I have a few headers at Banksy? Just me?"'

'No.'

'We did a free kick at Elland Road last week where someone rolled it back, you flick it up, someone volleys it because the ball's coming down, you dip it over the wall. It's quite good. Can I show you?'

'No.'

127

Royal Marines bandmaster Michael Hutton gets a signal from the drum major that the band have to leave their seats, with their excellent view of the action, and line up in the tunnel to get ready for their half-time performance. This is much sooner than they expected. There is some grumbling from the Marines as they make their way to the steps.

At the campsite in Tenby, the sound of about 30 radios tuned into the BBC Radio commentary echoes around the little valley.

> *It was a Third Division ball in… and I'm playing a guy Haller, who would have never challenged me in the air; there were nothing there to be frightened of. I got up too early and I got no weight on it.*
> *It bothers me more now than it did then.*
>
> **Ray Wilson speaking in 1999**

3.13pm/4.13pm Spanish and German Time

Close to the far touchline, Ray Wilson slides with both feet into Uwe Seeler's ankles. Helmut Haller takes the free kick quickly.

Seeler.

Schnellinger.

Siggi Held pauses, looks up and kicks a high, speculative ball into the far side of the England penalty area.

'Leave it!' Gordon Banks shouts to Ray Wilson.

But Wilson, unthreatened by any German attacker, instead of heading the ball safely away, heads it weakly down to the feet of Haller, who controls it neatly and with his right foot sends it low past Bobby Moore, Ray Wilson and Jack Charlton.

Banks sees it too late.

The orange ball smacks the far left-hand corner of the net.

England 0 West Germany 1

Helmut Haller turns and runs back towards the West German half, acknowledging the German fans' applause with a wave.

In Uhingen, five-year-old Jurgen Dudek watches open-mouthed as his parents and their relatives from Helmut Haller's hometown leap for joy. Richard Fischer jumps from the couch and punches the air, smashing a lampshade hanging from the ceiling.

In Tenby, Heinz Kurt-Doerr does his best to stifle a cheer. The people around him groan in disappointment. At the campsite down the road, his two sons Eric and Kenneth cycle up to a parked car with the radio on and its doors open to hear who's scored.

In the television lounge in the hotel in Calella, Spain, a West German guest leaps up and places his country's flag in the large brandy glass on top of the television. His fellow West Germans yell in delight.

'Oh, well played Germany!' John Cleese exclaims in the café in Ibiza, trying not to aggravate anyone in a room filled with Germans. He's decided to take the role of 'the ultra-sporting, frightfully decent Upper-Class Twit'.

'*U-we! U-we! U-we!*' the German supporters chant, despite the fact that it's Haller who scored, which baffles some of the England fans.

Banks is furious with Charlton for straying into the six-yard box. 'I never ever wanted people to do that – he really should have known that. He's in an area that's really close to me. By the time he's now left it for me, it's now going past me. Had he been three yards further forward, which he should have been, I might have saved it.'

Jack Charlton scowls at Ray Wilson, but gets on with the game.

'Jack can be an argumentative bugger in a crisis, but on this occasion he shrugged his shoulders and accepted it was just one of those things,' Gordon Banks said.

Ray Wilson has been marking Uwe Seeler, who is usually a centre forward but has switched to playing wide on the right. In the last few minutes he's changed places with Helmut Haller. Wilson doesn't fear him as much so, as he said later, 'I was a bit casual going for the ball. It came, and I was on me back feet, and tried to jump – but it just dropped down 'cause I couldn't get any power on it at all.'

Years later Ray would to say to the other England players, 'Well, I set you going, because when we were 1-0 down, we started playing then...'

'Bloody hell, that's not like Ray. But heck, it's early enough, still time,' Bobby Charlton thinks.

Centre forward Siggi Held knows that there's everything still to play for. 'Of course, it's nice to score and be ahead but nothing had been won at that point. That much was clear,' he said later.

To his left, Alf Ramsey is impassive. 'I was not particularly worried when they scored their first. It was a bad goal defensively – but these things do happen.'

This is the first goal England has conceded in the tournament in open play and the first time they have fallen behind.

'That's never very world cupp-y, is it, my son?

Back at the centre circle to restart the game, Bobby Charlton thinks, 'The world hasn't ended – but we have to score quickly.'

On the gantries behind the two giant scoreboards at either end of the stadium, the white-coated Wembley ground staff remove the blank board next to 'Germany W' and insert a three-foot high number 1.

Lord Harewood, the president of the FA, is sitting next to the Queen in the royal box. He can see that she looks a little disappointed that England are a goal down, 'as if she thought that was that for the game'. Harewood decides to reassure her.

'Well, the legend is that the side that scores first in the World Cup never wins it,' he says.

The Queen smiles.

Kenneth Wolstenholme has had the same thought. He tells his viewers: 'Let me tell you that this is the fourth World Cup final I've seen and in the previous three, the team that scored first lost.'

Kenneth Wolstenholme's words are some comfort to 26-year-old Dave Corbett watching in his garden flat in Norwood, south London. With Dave is his wife Jean and a photographer from the *Daily Express* named John Downing. Downing isn't here to get photographs of the Corbetts; his editor wants shots of their five-year old collie-Labrador cross called Pickles. Pickles is the most famous dog in the world.

One Sunday evening, 27th March 1966, Dave Corbett, who works at the London docks as a lighterman, wanted to phone his brother, whose wife was expecting a baby at any moment. He didn't have a phone at home so, still in his slippers, he headed out to the phone box across the road, taking Pickles with him to give him a bit of exercise. Before he could get him on the lead, Pickles started sniffing around the back of a neighbour's car.

'C'mon Pics!' Dave called, and went to get him. Pickles was sniffing at a package wrapped in newspaper and tightly bound in string.

Dave picked up the package. It was heavy, and as there had recently been IRA bomb threats he quickly put it back on the ground. He decided to carefully loosen the string and tear a piece of the newspaper away. When he saw the words 'Uruguay', 'Brazil', 'West Germany' engraved on metal shields at the base, he tore at the paper at the top and found himself looking at a gold angel with her arms raised, holding a shallow dish.

He grabbed Pickles and ran inside to his wife shouting, 'I've found the World Cup! I've found the World Cup!'

'What World Cup?' she replied.

'The football World Cup!'

Pickles had found the trophy stolen a week earlier from Westminster Central Hall by petty thief Edward Betchley.

Dave drove to the Gypsy Hill police station, ran through the double doors and thumped the trophy on the desk in front of the sergeant on duty, who took a step back in surprise. He looked at the small gold figure dubiously.

'That's never very world cupp-y, is it, my son?' the sergeant said.

A detective was summoned, who compared the trophy with colour photographs and measurements issued to all police stations; he also gave Dave some whisky from his police locker to calm him down.

At 1am on the Monday morning, Dave was then driven, still in his slippers, to Cannon Row police station in Westminster – and taken in through a back door as there were already reporters outside.

Questioned by senior detectives until nearly 3am, Dave soon realised that he was the prime suspect. 'I wondered if I should've chucked the cup back in the road. I was up at six the next day for work.'

For three weeks they brought him in for questioning, sometimes showing him criminals with the same surname; 'Is this a relative of yours – this Corbett?' they'd ask. Dave was told by the police that the thief or thieves were under such pressure they decided to get rid of the trophy and threw it over the hedge in front of his flat, just to get rid of it.

Since the robbery, Pickles has become a media star – he has an agent called George Skinner; he has opened Coventry Zoo and numerous restaurants (one owner gave Pickles a steak and begged, 'Please, Pickles, make Italy win the World Cup!'); he even got to meet the West German team as they trained at Ashbourne Town Football Club. George Skinner works for Associated British Films and has promised Dave that Pickles will appear in a new movie written by Ray Galton and Alan Simpson called The Spy With a Cold Nose. The money that Pickles is bringing in is very welcome to Dave and Jean, as work on the docks has been slowly drying up.

Although the theft was a huge embarrassment for the FA, it

also generated a great deal of publicity for the tournament. The FA report on the incident declared: 'An atomic explosion could scarcely have been given more coverage.'

In the Corbetts' flat, *Daily Express* photographer John Downing takes a picture of Pickles watching the final on Dave's lap. He asks Dave to turn and smile for the camera.

Back at Wembley, Siggi Held, on the left wing, is shouting for the ball. On getting it, he sends a weak cross into the penalty area – Jack Charlton clears it easily.

'Jack Charlton is as impenetrable as the Tower of London,' thinks Hans Tilkowski.

Schulz.

Beckenbauer.

The Germans have a greater momentum now. Roger Hunt has hardly kicked the ball and he's getting plenty of stick from the Wembley crowd – most of whom would prefer Tottenham's Jimmy Greaves to Hunt, a Liverpool player.

'I was in another world for the first 20 minutes of play – it was such a big occasion,' he admitted later.

Roger Hunt started his professional career later than the rest of the team – but is one of the most successful. He was 21 when a scout for Second Division Liverpool spotted him playing for an amateur team. 'The Blonde Bomber' became a key member of manager Bill Shankly's squad, scoring 41 times in 41 games in the 1961/62 season that saw them become Second Division champions. Two years later, they were First Division champions, and then in 1965 FA Cup winners – Roger Hunt scoring the first of Liverpool's two extra-time goals against Leeds. Liverpool are the current First Division champions.

In Maidstone Fire Station in Kent, 19-year-old fireman Clive Bradburn and his colleagues are in the mess room watching the final on an old black and white television. They're fed up that they have to be on duty today, but so far it's been quiet and they're enjoying the drama of the game.

Suddenly the alarm bells go off. They leap up and run for the poles that take them down to the fire engines. The officer in charge is told by the control room that there's a chimney fire in a house just over a mile away on South Park Road. 'Who has an open fire in July?' the crew wonder. There is plenty of cursing.

> **You'd look at Nobby Stiles and think, 'He's never an England player,' but at what he did, he was the best. And my brother was a very, very effective player. They didn't look elegant players, but if you have 11 elegant players – you win nothing.**
>
> **Bobby Charlton**

3.14pm

FC Bologna's Helmut Haller has the ball. Nobby Stiles tackles him, landing a kick on the German's shins. Referee Dienst blows his whistle.

Stiles curses at the decision. Haller makes the most of it. He has been accused in previous matches of being a 'leading actor'.

> *When the England players returned to the dressing room victorious at the end of the semi-final against Portugal, Alf Ramsey did an uncharacteristic thing – he asked for a round of applause for Nobby Stiles. Stiles had done a supreme job marking Eusébio – the European Footballer of the Year.*

In February 1965, Alf Ramsey picked Nobby Stiles for the England international against Scotland. This posed a dilemma for Nobby. Matt Busby, his manager at Manchester United, had made it clear he wanted him to play for the club on the Tuesday before the England game. Stiles was torn – United had taken him on when he was only 15 and nurtured his talent, yet Alf Ramsey was offering him a chance to become part of his World Cup squad. Stiles phoned Matt Busby and said, 'Boss, I've decided I would like to play for England.'

There was a pause.

'OK,' Busby said, and hung up.

During the match against Scotland, Stiles showed how tough he could be – and just how bad his eyesight was. At half-time Alf Ramsey asked him to put the Scottish winger Charlie Cooke 'out of the game'. Stiles tackled Cooke so hard he flew into the air. Norman Hunter, one of today's reserves for the final, took him to one side and asked him what he was doing.

'Doing what Alf asked me to do, taking Charlie Cooke out of the game.'

'I think you'd better look again, you stupid bastard.'

'What are you talking about?'

'You didn't do Charlie, you did Billy Bremner!'

Stiles was horrified: Billy Bremner was one of the hardest men in a tough team. He had forgotten his contact lens solution and so was playing half blind.

On another occasion, Stiles lost the rest of the England team during a post-match meal at the Café Royal in London and ended up at a wedding reception.

3.15pm

Enjoying the final are John Allison and his 14-year-old daughter Eileen. They are huge football fans who never miss a

Hartlepool United home game. They are on their way back to the north-east after a holiday in Devon.

The rest of the Allison family is not far away. John's wife Moira with their three other children, 13-year-old Susan, ten-year-old Lorraine and five-year-old John Junior, are sitting in their estate car in a section of the Wembley car park in between the twin towers and just feet away from the stadium. They could get only two tickets in advance and so Moira's stuck in a hot car with the younger children, who are fidgety and tired. It's been a long day – they left Devon early this morning. They can hear the roar of the crowd amplified by the bowl of the stadium through the open car windows. Seconds later, the same roar comes out of the car radio's tinny speaker.

To the left of the car are some steps leading up to what looks like a VIP entrance to the stadium that's shaded by a green and yellow striped tarpaulin. Some boys in shorts and England hats are hanging around the steps hoping to see someone famous.

Suddenly Moira sees three black men in dark suits and dark ties coming down the steps. A few paces behind them and only a few feet away from the car is a familiar slim, broad-shouldered figure. The boys stare. Moira, a keen photographer, has her camera with her in the front of the car. She grabs it and captures an image of one of the most famous sportsmen in the world.

'I think that was Muhammad Ali!' Moira exclaims once he's walked past.

At least that moment is some compensation for being left behind in a stifling hot car with three children while her husband enjoys the final.

Bobby Charlton, in space in midfield, kicks a long ball that bounces just outside the West German penalty area – Wolfgang

Weber is just a split second faster than Roger Hunt, and, sliding, kicks it out of touch on the far side.

3.16pm

Halfway inside his own half, England Number 2 George Cohen sends a long, hopeful ball, and challenged by Martin Peters, Wolfgang Weber gives away a throw-in. Still chewing gum, Peters yells 'Come on!' to get George Cohen and Jack Charlton closer. Cohen loses the ball almost immediately. Nothing is working for England, and the only noise is coming from the German fans.

Alan Ball robs Wolfgang Overath of the ball, and as he runs away, Wolfgang Overath trips him. Free kick to England.

As they run back into position, the two men shake hands.

There's a traffic policeman standing at the junction of St Michael's Avenue and Harrow Road in Wembley. Harrow Road is one of the main routes to the Empire Stadium and he's been directing coaches and cars all afternoon.

Bert Kirby is watching the final with his wife and daughter in their house on St Michael's Avenue. Bert opens his front door and calls out to the policeman, 'Fancy a cup of tea?'

He gladly takes up the offer. And stays for the whole match.

3.18pm/4.18pm Ibiza Time

Hans Tilkowski kicks the ball halfway into the England half – the two captains Moore and Seeler jump for it – Moore wins it but it's picked up by the tall number 4, Franz Beckenbauer – the 'revelation of the tournament', as more than one British paper has described him.

Far from hanging back to defend their lead, the West Germans are keen for another goal.

Bobby Charlton skips over a challenge from his white shadow Beckenbauer, and passes the ball to Bobby Moore, who's moving swiftly up the pitch. Moore's heel is clipped by Wolfgang Overath, and the England captain is brought down 15 yards outside the German penalty area.

Always a quick reader of the game, Bobby Moore gets up and sees Geoff Hurst unmarked in front of goal. This is an opportunity for a move straight out of the West Ham manual. Hurst knows exactly what Moore is going to do.

Moore doesn't wait for the referee's whistle – he kicks a high 40-yard ball. Hurst runs – makes a small jump – and heads it sweetly into the back of the net.

A stunned Hans Tilkowski stands behind the line, pointing at the spot where Hurst had been seconds before. It takes the Englishman a second to realise that he's scored.

England 1 West Germany 1

Hugh Johns on ITV is triumphant: 'It's there! It's there! What a great moment for the young Geoff Hurst of West Ham!'

Now Geoff Hurst is leaping for joy. Roger Hunt and Martin Peters run to hug him.

George Cohen doesn't join in. He prefers to walk back into position ready for the restart and save his energy for later.

Hans Tilkowsli points an accusing finger at centre-back Wolfgang Weber.

Alf Ramsey is impassively chewing gum.

'Good Show! Bit lucky though!' John Cleese is finding it hard to remain calm and collected. He has a fixed grin on his face and his long legs are writhing under the café table as he tries to hide his excitement from the German tourists surrounding him.

At Wembley, Bill Oddie yells in delight – as does his friend 23-year-old Eric Idle, whom Bill met at Cambridge when they were both members of the Cambridge Footlights.

Eric Idle ended his time at university as the Footlights president. One of the first reforms he introduced was to allow women to become members. Eric has just finished a tour of a review called My Girl Herbert *with 26-year -old Germaine Greer, the first woman to join Footlights.*

At the wedding in Richmond there is a suppressed cheer from the men listening on their transistor radio earpieces.

In Tenby, everyone is too busy celebrating to notice that Heinz Kurt-Doerr isn't joining in.

At Wembley, programmes, hats, scarves are being waved in the air.

The English supporters start singing an adaptation of their usual chant:

Oh, when the Reds, go marching in
Oh, when the Reds go marching in,
Oh Lord, I want to be in that number,
When the Reds go marching in!

Already feeling that their presence at Wembley is of little interest to the spectators, bandmaster Michael Hutton and his Royal Marines Band are now standing in the tunnel getting ready to perform at half-time. They can hear the singing, but can't see anything of the game.

Uwe Seeler restarts the game with a back-pass to Beckenbauer.

Kenneth Wolstenholme tells the millions watching at home that England are looking 'ten feet tall!'.

The pace of the game immediately quickens. It's a more open final now. Martin Peters screams at Alan Ball for the ball, but it's too fast and Peters can't control it.

Peters isn't missing Jimmy Greaves, whom he regards as a 'lone wolf'. He feels the team is more balanced with his team-mate Geoff Hurst on the pitch. Bobby Charlton is thinking the same. He later described Jimmy Greaves as 'a luxury. I always felt that he'd score five if you won 8-0 but in matches where a single goal would decide, it was better to have someone like Hurst'.

England's equaliser has its origins in Bobby Moore's early days at West Ham. As a young player, Moore had a mentor in the larger-than-life half-back Malcolm Allison, who once gave the teenager some advice he applied throughout his career:

'Take control of everything around you. Look big, think big. Keep forever asking yourself "if I get the ball now, who will I give it to?"'

Moore said it was 'like suddenly looking into the sunshine' when he was told that. 'It was the single most valuable thing I was ever taught.'

> *Bobby Moore is a quiet captain. He leaves the shouting to others.*
> *'He led minute by minute, second by second, by sheer example,'*
> *Nobby Stiles wrote later.*

'You've had a World Cup Willie!'

3.20pm

With the help of two midwives and a nurse, Anita Dunnington gives birth to a healthy baby boy in a delivery room in Royal Oldham Hospital.

'You've got a little boy! You've had a World Cup Willie!' exclaims one of the midwives.

'What?' Anita asks weakly.

'A World Cup Willie! You've had a little boy on World Cup day!'

Anita has no idea what they're talking about, and is too exhausted to ask more.

It's immediately clear to Clive Bradburn and the rest of the Maidstone fire crew which house on South Park Road needs their help – flames and smoke are pouring out of a chimney. They knock on the front door and a very upset old lady answers and takes them into the lounge – they can hear the roar of the flames in the flue. Clive and a colleague get a stirrup pump and buckets of water from the engine. They could tackle the fire from the roof, but it will be quicker to use a stirrup pump by the fireplace in the lounge.

The leading fireman spots that something vital is missing.

'Where's your telly?' he asks the old lady, desperate not to miss any of the final. She explains that it's in the back room, unused and still in its box.

**People think I was a bit of a fancy-dan because I was a
ball player. I would read the game and pick things off,
but people who know me know I could put my foot in.**

Martin Peters

3.22pm/4.22pm Bridge Time HMS Mohawk

Martin Peters loses the ball to Wolfgang Overath and chases
after him, tugging at his shirt.

Referee Gottfried Dienst blows his whistle and runs up to
Martin Peters. Peters obligingly turns round to show him the
number 16 on his back. Dienst writes something in his notebook and wags his finger at the England striker.

*Some years after the game, Martin Peters asked Gottfried Dienst
why he booked him, but he replied that he never did.*

*'That was your first tackle, Martin. I'd never seen you tackle
anyone before that!' Jack Charlton teased him later.*

From the free kick, Karl-Heinz Schnellinger floats a ball into
the England area and Uwe Seeler, gracefully as ever, jumps
above Bobby Moore and heads it down towards the feet of
Gordon Banks, who dives forward onto his knees and scoops
up the ball.

*Gordon Banks is another player from a poor family. As a child
in Tinsley near Sheffield, he wore clogs to school, with steel caps
fitted by his father to make them last longer. Like many of the
England players, he left school early and got himself a job. At 15,
Banks was a bagger with a local coal merchant in Catcliffe, south
of Rotherham; the hard physical work of an eight-hour day turned
out to be ideal training for the future goalkeeper.*

One day, he went on from work to watch a local amateur team called Millspaugh. At the start of the game, their trainer, who had seen Banks play as a schoolboy, came up to him and said that as their goalkeeper hadn't turned up, did he fancy a game. It was a real Roy of the Rovers moment. He was delighted at the chance and went straight onto the pitch in his work clothes. He always remembered the surprise of his new team-mates when a cloud of coal dust billowed around the goalmouth after he blocked a shot with his legs.

The sun finally comes out at Wembley. The shadow from a floodlight stretches across the pitch. In the royal box, the Queen and the Duke of Edinburgh have sunglasses on.

Franz Beckenbauer is playing increasingly further forward and joining the attack.

Uwe Seeler chips a ball over the heads of the English defence to Helmut Haller – but he's offside.

Free kick.

In South Park Road, Maidstone, the fire crew has put a canvas sheet in front of the fireplace to stop burning soot setting fire to the lounge. One fireman is pushing a rod up the chimney, another is screwing the next rod to its base, and another is operating the stirrup pump with his foot. Water from a bucket is being sucked up by the pump and spraying onto the fire from the top of the rod.

The men are watching the television as they work. The leading fireman got it out of its packaging and set it up in the lounge. It took a little while to warm up, but is now working nicely.

The crew has never worked so quickly – they want to get back to the station as quickly as they can.

Midshipman Dixie Hughes in on the bridge of HMS *Mohawk*, a tribal-class frigate on patrol off Rhodesia. One of his duties is to keep an eye on the Portuguese frigate that has been sailing with them for the past few days.

On the bridge, no one is following the fortunes of England as they have to concentrate on the welfare of the ship, but elsewhere on board, the BBC commentary is being broadcast over the ship's tannoy. Dixie Hughes isn't too bothered as he's a rugby fan.

On Tuesday, during the semi-final between England and Portugal, there was a remarkable sight in the middle of the ocean. The British and Portuguese frigates sailed side by side at about 10 knots. Both crews were up on deck – each listening to radio commentaries of the game in their respective languages over their tannoys. Once the game was over, and with the British crew celebrating a sweet 2-1 victory, the two ships sailed apart and resumed their patrols.

HMS Mohawk *is in the southern Indian Ocean as part of a British economic blockade of Rhodesia, whose government unilaterally declared independence in November 1965. Rhodesia's prime minister, Ian Smith, objected to British preconditions for independence that included an end to racial discrimination. He said the rest of the world was 'too corrupted, too prejudiced to see the advantages white rule gave the people of Rhodesia'.*

Harold Wilson is putting economic pressure on Smith's regime with a series of sanctions that include an oil blockade. The South African and Portuguese governments are happy to assist Rhodesia in defying the sanctions. The Portuguese navy is making sure the Royal Navy doesn't stray into the waters of the Portuguese colony of Mozambique.

> **I think about [Munich] a lot ... This was a great team
> with great players, and suddenly it was no more.
> I kept asking myself, 'Why me? Why should I be left?'**
>
> *Bobby Charlton*

3.24pm

Hurst.
  Stiles.
  Ball.
A deflection to Bobby Charlton just outside Germany's
penalty area – he shoots with his left foot, aiming for the right-
hand German post. Hans Tilkowski dives and stops it.

At his microphone up on the television gantry, Kenneth
Wolstenholme says, 'There's Bobby Charlton. A lot of England's
hopes rest on him this afternoon.'

*Kenneth Wolstenholme first saw Charlton play for England school-
boys at Wembley in 1953. He recalled that it was hard to get into
the dressing room because of all the scouts who wanted to sign
him – at one point there were 18 clubs chasing the teenager. Cissie
Charlton remembered there once being a scout in her living room
and another in the kitchen: 'I'd look round and there'd be another
one standing behind me.'*

The television cameras pick up a serious-looking Bobby
Charlton. Jack believes his brother rarely smiles after the tragic
events of 6th February 1958.

*Manchester United were flying back from Yugoslavia, having played
Red Star Belgrade in the European Cup. The BEA twin-engine
Elizabethan stopped at a snow-covered Munich Airport to refuel.*

146

Half-back Duncan Edwards called out as he went down the steps heading to the airport lounge, 'Get your snow shoes on, lads. Short studs are no use in this stuff!'

As the team waited in the airport, the plane developed engine trouble. Two attempts to take off were aborted. At the start of the third attempt, everyone on the plane was nervous and quiet. Bobby Charlton always hated how long the Elizabethan took to get airborne. He looked at his watch and tightened his safety belt. He said to striker Dennis Viollet, 'I'm not taking my coat off this time.'

The plane thundered down the runway. It wasn't gaining height.

Ray Wood turned to Roger Byrne, the United captain, who was gripping his armrests in terror.

'Roger, what's happening?'

'We're all going to be killed,' he replied.

In the cockpit co-pilot Kenneth Rayment screamed, 'Christ, we're not going to make it!'

The plane hit the perimeter fence, a house and a wooden hut filled with tyres and fuel. The Elizabethan finally came to a halt, cut in half, with its tail section on fire. Bodies were strewn in the snow and slush.

Goalkeeper Harry Gregg ignored the pilot James Thain's order to 'Run, you stupid bastard – it's about to explode!' and went into the wreckage and pulled out a baby and her mother. He then found Bobby Charlton and Dennis Viollet still in their seats – both motionless. Harry Gregg grabbed them by the waistbands of their trousers and pulled them clear of the wreckage.

Charlton and Viollet came to on the tarmac. Charlton released his safety belt and, aching all over, staggered to his feet.

'What's the matter, Bobby, what's gone on?' Viollet said, getting up.

'Dennis, it's dreadful,' was all he could say in reply. Charlton placed his overcoat over Matt Busby, who was lying injured on the runway.

Twenty-three people died in the Munich air crash, including eight of the Busby Babes. Bobby Charlton was taken to hospital suffering from minor head injuries. He didn't find out that so many of his team-mates had died until the following morning, when a German in the bed next to him read aloud a list of names in a newspaper, then paused and said, 'dead'.

'I shut my ears to him but he just went on and on. I thought he would never stop. It was the worst moment of my life.'

For the rest of his life, Bobby Charlton has been plagued by feelings of guilt for surviving, 'which can come to me so suddenly at any moment, night or day'.

Jack Charlton was in the Leeds dressing room after a training session when the club secretary walked in and said, 'The Manchester United plane has crashed and they don't know if there are any survivors.' Jack rushed to his parents' home in Ashington with his new wife Pat. On the way they saw a newspaper seller in Newcastle with a paper over his arm with the headline 'BOBBY CHARLTON AMONG THE SURVIVORS' – but they didn't believe it until Cissie showed them a telegram that said: 'Alive and well, see you later, Bobby.'

A neighbour arrived soon after, saying she'd heard the plane was 'an inferno' and 'no one had survived'. Cissie said, 'If that woman had arrived a few minutes earlier, you could have buried me at home.'

The bodies were flown to Manchester. The Old Trafford gymnasium was turned into a temporary mortuary for the players' coffins.

After a week, when Bobby was well enough, he returned to England by train and boat, too shocked to fly. Jack met him in London and drove him home to Ashington. 'I know you want to know what happened and I will tell you, but I don't want you to ask me again,' Bobby said. He proceeded to tell him the story of the crash and how by a miracle he had survived. 'Now I want to forget all about it.'

Bobby said later, 'Jack didn't say much and there were long silences during the journey. But I felt very close to him then.'

Bobby initially refused to return to Old Trafford – he vowed to give up football and spent days lying on the floor of his bedroom listening to Frank Sinatra LPs. Cissie finally persuaded him to come to the local park and kick a football with her. As the family GP Dr MacPherson removed stitches from Bobby's head, they talked – it was a conversation Bobby always remembered. MacPherson told him how during the war he'd been in the RAF and seen his friends shot down, but that he still had to carry on. He encouraged Bobby to play again and sent him home saying, 'I expect to see you at Wembley.'

3.27pm/4.27pm German Time

Shadowed by Franz Beckenbauer, Bobby Charlton takes the ball about 20 yards into the German half before crossing it towards Roger Hunt, who's sprinting into the penalty area. But Wolfgang Weber gets a foot to it first and it spins off for a corner.

Roger Hunt is still struggling to get into the game. Like Bobby Charlton, he's scored three times in the tournament so far and is keen for a fourth.

Alan Ball takes the corner quickly – but the ball goes straight into the arms of Hans Tilkowski.

Roger Hunt isn't enjoying the team's 4-1-3-2 formation. 'It was completely foreign to the way I played at Liverpool. It was mainly a running chasing role.' Ramsey wants him to stick as close as he can to Wolfgang Weber, but as he doesn't feel in the game he decides to 'roam around and come back a bit to get hold of the ball to get a bit of confidence'.

Five-year-old Jurgen Dudek is riding his bike through the sunny streets of Uhingen – the excitement of Helmut Haller's goal and the smashed lampshade was not enough to keep him in front of the television. It's a great time to be riding his bike as all the streets are deserted.

3.29pm

Despite being stopped for speeding on the M1, George Best and Mike Summerbee made it to Wembley in time. Best's white Jaguar is outside in the car park. They are in among the crowd, sitting on benches close to the pitch on the opposite side to the royal box. Summerbee feels envious of the English team – to play in the World Cup final is every player's dream, but he has a suspicion that he'll never be good enough to play for England.

> In November 1965, Northern Ireland only had to beat Albania in Tirana to qualify. George Best and the rest of the Northern Irish squad were appalled at the basic facilities – when they arrived at the stadium the grass was being cut with shears.
>
> The team complained of being bored and were put on an old bus and given a tour of a mental hospital. The game ended in a 1-1 draw and disappointment for George Best and Northern Ireland.
>
> Mike Summerbee did in fact play eight times for England. George Best never made it to a World Cup tournament.

Bobby Moore has the ball. The West Germans have ten men back in defence – only Lothar Emmerich isn't in his own half. Moore takes a shot with his left foot. It flies high over the goal.

Standing behind Kenneth Wolstenholme, because there is no room next to him, is summariser Walley Barnes, the former Wales and Arsenal full-back.

'That's not a bad idea, for Bobby Moore and the occasional defender to come forward and have a crack with the ground as skiddy as it is. It will come off at a tremendous pace. Tilkowski in goal isn't all that good at anticipation on this slippery surface,' Barnes says.

> **At 16 I was rejected from Bolton – imagine that, my home-town team – for being too small, too weak, frail. That was the reason I was what I was: I was frightened, terrified of failure.**
>
> **Alan Ball**

3.30pm

Alan Ball is furious. Siggi Held grabbed his shirt as they both went for the ball – but referee Dienst has given the free kick to Germany.

> *In the last 12 months, Alan Ball has learned to control his temper. In 1964, when playing for Blackpool against Manchester United, he provoked Denis Law by saying, 'You're finished, you're old, step aside...'*
>
> *Punches were thrown and they were both sent off. In 1965, he was again sent off while playing for England's Under-23 side for throwing the ball at the referee.*

An old friend of Alan Ball's, 21-year-old Gordon Taylor of Second Division Bolton Wanderers, is watching from the stands, just opposite the tunnel, only about 15 seats from the pitch. Taylor has come down to London for the weekend with his fiancé, Catherine. He's meeting her in the West End after the game; they're planning to see the musical *The Owl and the Pussycat* at the Criterion Theatre, starring Anton Rogers. Later they'll go on to the Talk of the Town to see an artist in concert they both love – Johnny Mathis.

Gordon Taylor is hopeful that England can win, but he remembers watching the 1954 World Cup final – the so-called 'Miracle of Bern', when the amateur players of West Germany beat the favourites Hungary 3-2.

Gordon Taylor and Alan Ball used to play together for Lancashire schoolboys and for Bolton's junior teams. They first met moments after Ball had spoken to the Bolton manager Bill Ridding about playing for the first team.

'He said I'm too small to become a footballer! He told me to become a jockey!'

Taylor encouraged Alan to write to other clubs. Blackpool recognised his talent and took him on in September 1961.

Jimmy Armfield, Alan Ball's team-mate at Blackpool, is sitting with the rest of the squad in the stands and keeping an eye on the young player too. Armfield has had a great influence on Ball. 'He simply talked me into areas when we didn't have possession of the ball, and I knew when I was in possession I should drag the ball inside so that he could make the overlap run on the outside. He was brilliant at that,' Alan Ball said later.

Alf Ramsey has given Jimmy Armfield instructions to bring the rest of the squad down from their seats in the stands at the end of the game. 'The FA have arranged with the people at Wembley for you all to come down in the lift to the tunnel near the royal box just before the end. There will be some places for you on the bench behind where I am sitting. Can you make sure everyone is down there?'

3.33pm

About five yards into his own half, George Cohen sends a perfect ball for Geoff Hurst, who jumps higher than his markers and heads it towards goal. Hans Tilkowski dives to his right and stops it – but can't hold onto it.

'Ball is there!' Kenneth Wolstenholme shouts.

The Englishman gets it before the keeper, skips and turns and sends the ball across the area – but there's no one waiting. Wolfgang Overath clears it. The West Germans look very panicky – especially Hans Tilkowski.

Gordon Taylor is happily taking pictures of the game with his camera, unaware that his ticket states 'All photographic equipment prohibited'.

3.34pm

The afternoon sun is now strong and the clouds have cleared – the players are casting dark, sharp shadows.

Full-back George Cohen has been disconcerted by the fact that Siggi Held has spent a great deal of the time looking him straight in the eye. He suddenly realises that the German is trying to work out when he is going to make a run. This thought allows Cohen to relax.

3.35pm

Watching the game from the entrance to the tunnel is Wembley ground technician Joe Power. Although he's an Irishman, he's always loved English football. Joe's job is to look after the dog track and the pitch, helping groundsman Percy Young to paint the white lines and assemble the goalposts. During the game he has a different role – Joe is what's known as a bucketman. He has a white bucket and towels with him should the match officials need them. Last Saturday, his bucket of water turned bloody after an Argentinian hit the fourth official at the end of the game.

Bobby Charlton kicks a long ball in front of the West German goal that an uneasy Tilkowski punches with two fists.

'I'm not a thinker. I was instinctive. Give me a ball and I will see what I can do with it,' Bobby Charlton recalled.

3.36pm

In a side ward in the maternity unit at Royal Oldham Hospital, Anita Dunnington is drifting in and out of sleep. She's waiting for a doctor to give her some stitches. A midwife puts her head around the door.

'The doctor won't be long – he's just watching the football.'

In the nursery up the corridor, Anita's new baby boy has a label attached to his cot. It says: 'World Cup Willie.'

3.38pm

England have been looking confident, but then Alan Ball, just outside his own penalty box, sends a clumsy pass to George Cohen that Siggi Held almost intercepts. Under pressure and with his elbows out as usual, Cohen tries to fight Held off, only to lose the ball. Jack Charlton has seen enough. As Held goes to a cross the ball, he slides in and robs him. Corner to West Germany on the near side.

Only Lothar Emmerich, Wolfgang Weber and Uwe Seeler are in

the penalty area. It's a fast cross from Held. Lothar Emmerich just gets to it. Overath takes three quick steps and the orange ball rockets off his boot – Banks sees it late and instinctively puts his hands up and stops it. There's still danger. The ball falls to the left of Emmerich, who just manages to control it. Martin Peters and George Cohen run at him.

'Emmerich must score!' shouts Hugh Johns on ITV.

Emmerich shoots – but Banks has it covered. He hugs the ball as he gets to his feet. Bobby Charlton gulps with relief.

3.40pm

Graham and Sally Saunders and their friends Alan and Sandra Morris are listening to the final on the Mini's radio. They've spent the past 40 minutes yelling and cheering as they've made their way towards Graham's aunt and uncle's house in Ascot. They should be there just in time to see the second half on television. Then they have to get to Earls Court for 7.30pm and the start of the Royal Tournament.

Bobby Moore's mother Doss, at home in Barking, is too nervous to watch the final on the television or listen on the radio – she's gardening.

Hans Tilkowski's mother can't bear to watch either. His whole family has gathered at his home in Herne, but she's gone for a walk in a nearby park instead. She's explained to her family that she gets *Herzklabastern* – heart palpitations – from the excitement.

'Wembley really wasn't made for the faint-hearted,' her son said later.

3.41pm

In an office in the bowels of Wembley Stadium, former policeman Bob Geggie is watching the final on a small television set. He can hear the muffled roar and groans of the crowd coming through the walls. The office door is locked for security reasons because next to him on a desk is the real Jules Rimet trophy; PC Peter Weston handed it over to him earlier this morning. Because of the responsibility he'd been given, Geggie had expected he'd get a prime seat in the royal box, not have to watch the final in black and white in a dingy office.

Geoff Hurst mistimes a pass back. In the stands you can hear the thwack as the ball hits his right shin pad. The ball is now Lothar 'Emma' Emmerich's. As he gallops forward there is no one between him and Gordon Banks. But Bobby Moore is racing in from the right – his right boot arcs round and scoops it from under the tumbling Emmerich. The England fans roar their relief.

3.42pm

Close to the near-side touchline, well into the West German half, Alan Ball passes to Bobby Charlton; Franz Beckenbauer is inevitably not far behind. Charlton whips a cross into the 16-yard box and Wolfgang Weber dives over the penalty spot and clears it high into the air. Ray Wilson heads it back – this time even higher. Geoff Hurst and Wolfgang Weber both jump for it. Hurst wins and heads it to Roger Hunt, who shoots from about eight yards out – his first chance at goal. But Hans Tilkowski puts his hands up, denying Hunt his fourth goal of the competition. Horst-Dieter Höttges clears the ball.

3.43pm

Bobby Moore settles a midfield battle by sending a long ball to Geoff Hurst.

Peters.

Charlton.

Peters can't get to the ball before Wolfgang Weber. Alan Ball trips and loses the ball to Siggi Held.

Seeler. He runs with it – unchallenged. Seeler is 25 yards out – he looks up and skips around Bobby Moore and thumps the ball with his right foot. It's dipping below the bar. Gordon Banks leaps and tips it over. There are groans from the German crowd and relieved cheers from the English. A single photographer behind Banks claps.

A corner to West Germany.

But it's wasted by Helmut Haller, who sends it high over the England goal.

3.44pm

At home in Leeds, Pat Charlton is watching her husband play on television. There are reporters and photographers in her sitting room hoping that she might give birth during the final.

In Royal Oldham Hospital's maternity ward, Anita Dunnington is still waiting to be seen by a doctor.

Alan Ball jumps with Karl-Heinz Schnellinger and the referee blows his whistle. Ball slaps his legs in disgust as another decision has gone against him.

Siggi Held is poised to take the free kick – he has nine men to choose from. A goal just before half-time could be decisive.

Held passes to full-back Höttges, who sends a slow, low easy shot to a grateful Gordon Banks.

3.45pm

Gottfried Dienst blows his whistle for the end of the first half. All 22 players turn for the tunnel and the dressing rooms. Like his team-mates, Bobby Charlton is walking to save energy.

Royal Marines bandmaster Michael Hutton gets the signal for his men to begin their half-time entertainment. Michael tucks his baton under his left arm and follows his men onto the pitch. Two of his Marines give encouraging winks to Gordon Banks as he walks past.

The chimney fire is out in the house in Maidstone.

'Right, it's half-time,' the leading fireman shouts, 'we've got 15 minutes to get back to the station!' Clive Bradburn and his three colleagues start clearing up at top speed. The old lady is delighted – the fire is extinguished and her television set is out of its box and it works.

At Wembley, hundreds of fans are heading for the stalls selling tea and coffee. Eighteen-year-old Scout John Nutkins picks up his box of Jubblys and starts selling the cartons to the German fans around him. He is soon doing a brisk trade.

Not everyone is drinking soft drinks. In the stands, Derek Hogg produces a half-bottle of whisky, takes a swig and then offers it to his 15-year-old nephew Carlton.

Some fans are making a dash for the toilets. Ten minutes is very little time to get there and back. There is an accepted practice of urinating where you are, with a cry of 'watch out, chum!'

'You can improve. And if you do that you will win the cup.'

3.47pm

Father and son dairy farmers Reg and Philip Hodgskiss have been standing behind the England goal in the first half. They are watching the Royal Marines but can't hear a note because of the noise from the crowd and in particular the Brazilian drummer to their right who has been playing non-stop since before kick-off.

In the England dressing room, the players are slumped on the benches. Alf Ramsey is full of words of encouragement. He doesn't mention Helmut Haller's goal.

'You can improve. And if you do that you will win the cup!'

But he also has a warning.

'Remember, the Germans won't throw in the towel. They will fight until the last kick of the match.'

Ramsey urges them all to be more ruthless in the second half and to hold onto possession more. He tells Geoff Hurst to 'push up as far as possible' but he takes Roger Hunt to one side. 'Alf wanted to know what was going on and why I was not doing what I was told... I didn't actually blow up but I replied that I wasn't in the game – I wasn't getting involved,' he said later. Bobby Moore steps in and says Hunt should play as they'd planned.

Alf Ramsey's half-time team talks were influenced by Arthur Rowe, his manager at Spurs, and especially from one particular game during the 1949/50 season. When Spurs went to Grimsby on 19th November 1949, they were six points clear at the top of the First Division, but by half-time they were stunned to be 2-1 down. Alf and his team-mates expected a dressing-room roasting from Rowe – instead he encouraged them.

'Well done, boys! You can do it!' he beamed at his dejected players.

Eight minutes after they returned to the pitch, Alf Ramsey scored, a rare thing for the full-back. 'The crowd seemed as surprised as I was,' he said later. Spurs went on to win 3-2.

Years later, Alf Ramsey recalled, 'The confidence his words inspired was wonderful... When Arthur said something in that quiet manner of his, you knew he wasn't talking for talking's sake. He had said we would win, and after that I don't think anyone in that dressing room was in doubt about the outcome.'

3.52pm

It starts to pour with rain at Wembley. Fortunately, the Royal Marines bandsmen have their music under protective plastic. They are playing a medley of songs including 'The World Cup March', 'Colonel Bogey', and 'A Life on the Ocean Wave'.

In the German dressing room, Hans Tilkowski is impressed at how much his team have grown during the tournament – 'we radiated self-confidence and fighting spirit'.

In Castle Combe in Wiltshire on the set of the 20th Century Fox film *Doctor Dolittle*, the crew have placed a television set attached to a generator in the middle of a field, so that Rex Harrison can watch the final. Sitting next to him is his co-star Samantha Eggar.

It is one of the rare sunny days this summer in Wiltshire for a production that has been plagued by bad luck. The animals have eaten the sets and urinated on its star; the locals have objected to the disruption and a 22-year-old soldier seconded to the SAS named Ranulph Fiennes has tried to blow up a concrete dam the film company built across the village stream.

Rex Harrison has objected to almost every aspect of the production, from the casting to composer Leslie Bricusse's songs. At one stage he was sacked and replaced by Christopher Plummer, but later reinstated.

The crew have nicknamed him 'Tyrannosaurus Rex'.

3.53pm

The buzzers go in the Wembley dressing rooms. One minute to go.

'Excuse me, what would you do if I called you a bastard?'

3.54pm

The Royal Marines Band march off the pitch towards the tunnel. The players walk past them in the opposite direction, heads down, lost in thought.

It's still pouring with rain as the 22 players get in position. England will kick off the second half, now playing right to left.

Kenneth Wolstenholme has a reminder for the BBC viewers: 'If the scores are level after 90 minutes there is half an hour's extra time. If they're still level – a replay here Tuesday night.'

3.55pm

Bobby Charlton stands on the centre spot; either side of him, hands on hips, are Geoff Hurst and Roger Hunt.

Gottfried Dienst blows his whistle and waves them forward.

Bobby Charlton taps the ball to Hurst.

Alan Ball.

Bobby Moore. The ball is moving fast on the wet grass.

Ray Wilson sends a hopeful shot towards the German penalty area. Karl-Heinz Schnellinger heads it obligingly to the feet of Alan Ball, who passes it to Bobby Charlton, accelerating into the right side of the German penalty area, chased by three defenders. Willi Schulz is closest and sticks out a foot for the ball. Charlton trips and tumbles off the pitch. He gets up and he and Schulz briefly shake hands.

Goal kick.

3.57pm

Wolfgang Overath clears the ball from his penalty area; it bounces on the centre spot and up onto Jack Charlton's right arm.

The referee blows his whistle. Charlton stops and wheels round in disgust, pulling his shirt on the right side of his chest to show the referee where he thinks the ball hit him.

Charlton runs backwards, still facing the referee. Swearing.

When playing for Leeds against Liverpool, Jack Charlton once said to a referee who was irritating him with what he thought were poor decisions, 'Excuse me, what would you do if I called you a bastard?'

'I'd send you off.'

'OK, in that case I'll just think you're a bastard.'

3.58pm

Nobby Stiles has a throw-in on the far side, about 15 yards into the West German half. Geoff Hurst taps it back to him. Stiles moves down the touchline, loses control and Lothar Emmerich pounces, scything down Stiles with his left foot. Stiles doesn't react, but looks at the number of the man who tackled him, as if making a mental note.

Throw-in to England.

> *Jack Charlton and Nobby Stiles won their first England cap at the same time, playing against Scotland in the Home Championships in April 1965. Their tough style of play made them surprising choices. Soon after his selection was announced, Charlton received a letter with a Barnsley postmark that said: 'You are the worst centre-half in the land and how you have been picked to play for England I will never know.' He kept it and took it to his first training session with the England squad. He got chatting with Nobby Stiles and showed him the letter. Stiles pulled out an identical one.*
>
> *'Snap!' he said.*

Nobby Stiles throws the ball to Alan Ball, who passes it back to Stiles, who by now is running towards the German penalty area. With one touch Stiles passes it back to Martin Peters. Karl-Heinz Schnellinger wins the ball in the air, but only heads it as far as Jack Charlton. He calmly heads it to Alan Ball, who starts a run down the far touchline. The crowd roar in appreciation.

> *Geoff Hurst wrote later, 'The goals might have given us the game, but the crowd gave us goals...'*

Alan Ball is brought down by the West German Number 2,

Horst-Dieter Höttges, whose studs tear the back of Ball's right sock. Gottfried Dienst awards a free kick to England. Ball lies on the ground clutching at his leg. An apologetic Höttges pats him on the head. Alan Ball gets up and does some theatrical limping.

At the Hendon Hall Hotel, a group of guests from the wedding reception are gathered around a television set placed outside the banqueting room especially for them to watch the match. The groom is Italian and very disappointed that Italy aren't in the final.

3.59pm

George Cohen sends a high, optimistic free kick to Martin Peters on the edge of the penalty area, but Franz Beckenbauer gets there first and heads it away.

Bobby Moore picks it up.

Hunt.

Jack Charlton gets a head to it on the edge of the penalty area. Karl-Heinz Schnellinger falls backwards as he clears it. The leather ball is getting heavier as it soaks up water on the pitch – it trundles through midfield.

Siggi Held versus Nobby Stiles. Held wins. The West Germans are racing forward.

Seeler.

Haller.

The German fans roar them on.

Stiles, running back, is almost onto Haller as Haller passes to Siggi Held, ten yards from the England goal and in space. England appeal for offside. Gordon Banks rushes out. Held is forced to run wide.

The linesman raises his flag. He is offside.

The Skinner family is on their way home on the A303 after a camping holiday in the West Country. They love pitching their tent for a night, paying their ten bob and then moving on to somewhere new the next day. Parents Dennis and Marjorie have decided to break the journey at Stonehenge and are pulling into the car park.

As they walk towards the monument with their children, Geoffrey, Ann and Richard, they can see people huddled together in small groups, some sitting on the fallen stones. Occasionally they can hear a cheer or a groan. The Skinners realise that they've forgotten about the World Cup final, and latch onto a group with a transistor radio.

4.03pm

It's a corner kick to West Germany at the far side of the pitch. The Germans are in no rush to take it – they're conserving their energy.

Siggi Held takes the corner. The ball floats down towards Franz Beckenbauer about ten yards outside the England penalty area. Bobby Charlton gets a chest to it, but it still lands nicely for Beckenbauer, who with his left foot skips the ball around Martin Peters and then with his right tries a shot – but a deflection off an England player takes the speed from it and it goes wide.

4.05pm/8.05am California Time

In San Bernardino, California, English DJ John Ravenscroft (known as John Ravencroft on radio station KMEN as his boss dislikes the 's', and later known to BBC listeners as John Peel) has persuaded some friends to get up early on a Saturday morning to watch the final. John has supported Liverpool since the 1950 FA Cup final, and is delighted that Roger Hunt is playing today for England. John has been trying to explain to his friends why Liverpool legends such as Billy Liddell, Alan A'Court and Albert Stubbins are so important to him – but he's met with bemusement. He said later, 'I think that this may have been the moment it was time to come home.'

John Ravencroft is Mr Morning Man with the 6am to 9am slot. He is allowed to play anything he likes, including songs he claims are from the UK chart but are actually songs from acts he thinks deserve radio play. John's fame and success as a DJ both in San Bernardino and earlier in Dallas have been boosted by the impression he's given that he's a close friend of fellow Liverpudlians John, Paul, George and Ringo. He has in fact never met the Beatles.

At Wembley about 80,000 people shout 'handball!'

The England supporters reckon that Helmut Haller handled the ball, but referee Dienst signals play to continue.

A sarcastic chant of 'Oh my, what a referee, oh my, what a referee' begins on the terraces.

Lothar Emmerich passes the ball to no one. A German attack disintegrates.

Ray Wilson collects the ball and is about to hit it upfield – there's plenty of time – when Bobby Moore runs up and does the job for him. 'He would often do that, Bob,' said Gordon Banks later, 'just to make sure it got to an England player.'

No goalkeeper ever did more than Gordon Banks to fulfil the greatest demand of his position, which is to generate certainty among his colleagues.

Nobby Stiles

4.07pm

The England captain brings down his West German counter-part. Uwe Seeler has a free kick halfway inside the England half. Seeler tells Helmut Haller to leave it for Franz Beckenbauer. Roger Hunt runs back. Bobby Moore waves to Martin Peters to plug a gap in defence.

Beckenbauer looks around, gives himself a long run-up and hits the ball straight onto Bobby Charlton's legs.

Wolfgang Overath collects the ball and has time to send a considered pass over the heads of the English defence to an unmarked Uwe Seeler hovering in the right-hand side of the penalty area.

England appeal for offside.

'Play on!' says Gottfried Dienst.

Jack Charlton, rather late, runs to challenge Seeler, who coolly chips the ball towards Lothar Emmerich – but Gordon Banks jumps high above the Number 11's head and the danger is over.

Applause echoes round the stadium.

Neither side is threatening to score.

4.10pm

Once again, the Royal Marines are standing in the Wembley tunnel, unable to see any of the game, having been ordered by the drum major to leave their seats to get ready for their last performance once the final whistle blows.

Ray Wilson has a throw-in at the near-side touchline in the German half.

Bobby Moore crosses the ball. Geoff Hurst chests it down to

Martin Peters but it bounces awkwardly and high and drops about five feet over the bar.

The applause from the English fans dies quickly away.

Wembley is the quietest it's been all afternoon.

About 4.12pm

The doorbell goes at 73 Longfield Avenue in West End, Hampshire. George Hallett is watching the football with his 13-year-old son Mark. As George goes to the door, Mark looks out the window. A green double-decker bus belonging to the Provincial Bus Company has pulled up outside. They've been too engrossed in the football to notice.

At the door are the driver and conductor in full uniform.

'Sorry to bother you, sir, we haven't any passengers and we could see through your window that you're watching the final – could we join you?' the driver says.

George is surprised but very happy for them to come in. They introduce themselves and take a seat in the lounge.

4.15pm/8.45 Glengyle *Bridge Time*

Franz Beckenbauer robs Bobby Charlton of the ball and it flies in the air towards Alan Ball.

Overath wins it.

Beckenbauer.

Haller by the near-side touchline crosses it.

Gordon Banks watches. He waits. Then leaps above Seeler and punches it with his left fist about 15 yards away.

Emmerich chests it down, and chivvied by Alan Ball, sends a poor, slow, low cross that's easily cleared by Jack Charlton.

Peters and Beckenbauer tussle for it.

It's Haller's. He shrugs in frustration – he can see no one to cross it to.

Beckenbauer.

Schnellinger.

Held. The West Germans are trying to break through England's defence on the far side. Held skips around Ball and his shot hits George Cohen hard in the chest.

Held again.

Jack Charlton and Cohen aren't going anywhere and block the cross.

Corner to West Germany on the far side.

Siggi Held takes it. Franz Beckenbauer catches it on the volley. Bobby Charlton jumps in front of him, but it hits Bobby Moore on the legs and cannons off to the near side. Ray Wilson wins it and passes it upfield to Charlton, who sends Beckenbauer one way and then the other as he advances. But the ball runs away from him and it's Willi Schulz's.

But Charlton isn't finished – he runs at the hesitating Schulz and forces him to make a bad pass to Wolfgang Overath. Roger Hunt closes in and Overath fouls him. The referee blows his whistle – free kick to England just outside the West German penalty area. Overath smiles ruefully at the referee.

Jim Tucker is loving this. He's watching the final on television at his friend Colin Eldon's house in Reigate, having sold his ticket to a tout this morning. Someone else has his seat at Wembley – six rows back from a corner flag. He wonders how much the tout got for it. 'When I was watching the final, I never thought "I wish I was there."'

Tomorrow the tournament will be over and Jim will give up the grocery delivery job with its football-friendly shifts and start a new, more profitable job as a taxi driver.

Divots litter the penalty area. The pitch is suffering after its soaking from the hail storm in the morning and the rain at half-time.

The turf in front of both goals has already been replaced earlier in the tournament. Just outside Wembley Stadium is an area the size of a small field where the replacement turf is grown.

Outside the German penalty area, Bobby Moore quickly takes the free kick. Geoff Hurst is blocked but Jack Charlton is free to jump and he heads the ball down towards the goal. For a second he thinks it's going in – but it's wide.

Now the crowd have something to cheer about.

'When the Reds go marching in' is once more the Wembley refrain.

England just have the edge.

In the Indian Ocean on the merchant ship *Glengyle*, one of the ship's engineers is following the game with particular interest. His name is Gordon Charlton and two of his brothers are in the final. Gordon is listening to the game via a crackly radio. The signal comes and goes, but he can follow most of it.

Like Jack, Gordon was taken on as ground staff at Elland Road after he finished school. But he didn't like the work: cleaning boots, painting and oiling the turnstiles and sweeping the terraces; other members of the staff kept complaining to Jack that his little brother was failing to turn up for work on time and when he did, not doing it properly. Leeds let him go after a year.

Gordon, like his brothers Bobby and Tommy, is going bald. Their mother Cissie is very protective of her sons. She once thumped a Scottish spectator during an international who called Bobby a 'baldy git'.

'You're no lady!' the man's wife shouted at Cissie.

'If he's yours then you can't be a lady either!' Cissie shouted back.

'[While] I know it is irrational I have always been sensitive about my four sons' lack of hair... I have never been able to shake off the feeling that somehow the failure was mine; that I was responsible,' Cissie once said.

Jack Charlton is also protective of 'our kid'. He once saw a comedian make a joke about Bobby's comb-over haircut.

'When he was finished I went to his dressing room and I said, "You're out of order. It was a stupid joke." It upset me greatly, actually. I said, "He's done more for his country than you will ever dream of doing, and people like you tend to piss on him over something like that, and it's very hurtful to him, and it hurts me as well."'

4.18pm

Jack Charlton robs Uwe Seeler of the ball and passes it back to Gordon Banks – the first English pass back to the goalkeeper of the match.

Banks bounces the ball once and throws it over-arm to Nobby Stiles deep in the midfield. Stiles sends the ball to Ray Wilson, running up the touchline ahead of him. Wilson looks up – Roger Hunt and Geoff Hurst are in the penalty area with only three German defenders around them. Hunt starts to jump for Wilson's cross but he's nudged by Willi Schulz. The English fans roar in outrage.

The referee is unmoved.

A German counter-attack is stopped by Jack Charlton, who then outruns the short Siggi Held with his trademark long strides and pounds into the German half. The ball ricochets off Helmut Haller and into Charlton's face. Haller runs for the ball.

But heading for Haller as fast as he can is Nobby Stiles. Stiles slides in, Haller jumps over his boot and tumbles onto the turf.

Gottfried Dienst blows his whistle and runs towards Stiles. Stiles is outraged – he reckons Haller took a dive. Alan Ball pats the referee on the shoulder and then persuades his friend to shake hands with the German forward.

> **You enjoyed playing against West Ham because they let you play. But they didn't let you win.**
>
> **Gordon Taylor, Bolton Wanderers**

4.23pm

Up in the stands, nine-year-old Ray Winstone is gripped. He's there with his dad Ray Senior. They are both avid West Ham fans and young Ray is clutching both a World Cup Willie pennant and a West Ham pennant. The Winstones have been to every England game; Ray Senior is a popular figure in the east London fruit-and-vegetable trade and has used his many contacts to secure tickets.

Bobby Moore crosses the ball swiftly, almost the full width of the West German penalty area, to Geoff Hurst, who heads it towards goal, in the direction of Bobby Charlton. Franz Beckenbauer runs back and blocks Charlton, but trips and slams into Hans Tilkowski's face. Beckenbauer holds his head. Tilkowski gets slowly to his feet, his black strip now smudged with white paint. Bobby Charlton is on his knees on the goal line, sweat staining the full length of his red shirt.

'The concentration was intense and it was exhausting – we both ran a lot without the ball. But we had to...' Charlton said later.

4.24pm

It's a corner from the far side of the pitch.

The German midfield players walk slowly into the England penalty area to the sound of 'Eng-land! Eng-land! Eng-land! Eng-land!'

Uwe Seeler and Martin Peters jump for Siggi Held's cross. Peters jumps higher. The ball bounces once in front of Franz Beckenbauer, who thumps it high over Jack Charlton and the England goal.

Walley Barnes, in the commentary box with Kenneth Wolstenholme, says, 'It's significant that the West German side do use the quick, long ball when they can get away with it and they've caught the English defence napping once or twice in the last ten minutes.'

Banks.

Wilson.

The ball's blocked by Höttges, who slips.

Bobby Charlton.

In a classic West Ham move, Hurst sends a zipping cross that bounces just in front of Roger Hunt near the German penalty spot. Hunt and Wolfgang Weber collide and the ball goes spinning towards the left of the goal. Alan Ball, Wolfgang Weber and Hans Tilkowski all run for it. Ball dives between them and he and Tilkowski fall – the goalkeeper flies over the line almost hitting his head on a stills camera, and Ball lands flat on his face.

Geoff Hurst, a photographer behind Tilkowski and 80,000 England supporters shout for a corner. Ball lies with his ear to the ground as if listening for something.

4.25pm

Bobby Charlton takes the corner quickly. Hunt and Hurst jump but Hans Tilkowski confidently punches the ball clear with his right hand.

In Barking, Bobby Moore's mother Doss is still gardening, unable to cope with the stress of watching her son on television.

For journalist Hans Gebhardt and his family, the World Cup has been a revelation. They don't know a great deal about football but as they have three weeks' holiday in London, they thought it would be fun to go to Wembley. They bought tickets for the stands, Gate J, Block 51. Hans' eldest son spent the evening of his 18th birthday watching England beat Argentina.

They've been intrigued by the chants of 'Rule, Britannia' and 'When the Reds go marching in'; the long, patient queues for the Tube initially ignored by Europeans, and the friendly policemen pointing them in the right direction with a polite, 'This is the end of the queue, thanks'; and the flat and bitter taste of the beer in the pubs. The whole trip has set Hans back about 1000 marks, but it's been worth it.

4.26pm

Franz Beckenbauer, Siggi Held and Lothar Emmerich are

trying to find a way through the English defence. The tireless Alan Ball has had enough of watching them pass it back and forth and runs from midfield; he robs the hesitant Emmerich. The crowd roar their appreciation.

Stiles.

Peters.

Bobby Charlton then takes the ball to the Germans, sprinting past his marker Franz Beckenbauer; he passes to Martin Peters before Wolfgang Overath can get to him. Wolfgang Weber slips inside the 'D', giving Martin Peters a valuable second to turn and find some space, and for Alan Ball to get into the area. Three yards from the touchline Ball shoots low. Hans Tilkowski dives and the ball spins out.

England corner on the far side.

'Undoubtedly when England dart in behind this defensive wall of Germany they're getting them in trouble.' says Hugh Johns on ITV. Wembley is loving this.

Standing quietly behind Hugh Johns in the commentary box is another new ITV signing called Barry Davies. Davies looked after the games at Roker Park and Ayresome Park for the network and hoped that he might be in with a chance to commentate during the final.

After the quarter-finals, all four of ITV's commentators had to phone John Bromley, the executive editor, to find out his decision. Barry Davies wasn't too surprised when Hugh Johns got the job.

Barry Davies' first broadcast commentary was in February, when Chelsea played AC Milan in the Fairs Cup. Jimmy Greaves signed Barry's match programme and wrote: 'Here's to the first of many...'

At Loughton Methodist Church in Essex, Geoffrey Cochrane and his new bride Pat are in the vestry signing the register, watched over by the minister. There are some noticeable gaps in the congregation. None of Geoffrey's five best friends have turned up – even though they promised they would, the lure of the football was too strong.

Two of Pat's cousins have transistors with earpieces to keep in touch with the game.

> **It was as though the players on the field actually connected with the energy in the stands.**
>
> *Terence Stamp*

'I feel like I've got electricity running through me!'

4.27pm/5.27pm Spanish Time

Alan Ball pauses by the corner flag. The ball is wet and heavy, so he really has to dig it out of the turf as he kicks. With head down, he strikes. Two German defenders jump for the ball; Jack Charlton doesn't even try.

It falls to Geoff Hurst, who sends the ball one way and then the other to fool Uwe Seeler. Martin Peters and Roger Hunt move away from the goal to keep onside.

Hurst shoots with his right foot. Horst-Dieter Höttges slips as he clears the ball.

It spins into the air behind him and in front of Martin Peters, six yards from the goal line.

Peters watches it for a second.

He thinks, 'Hell, it's coming to me!'

He flashes a look to check he's onside.

Then he volleys the ball into the back of the net with his right foot.

England 2 West Germany 1

Peters turns and runs with his arms in the air, pursued by Roger Hunt and Geoff Hurst. Gordon Banks runs the length of the pitch to join the celebrations.

Nobby Stiles kisses the turf.

An overjoyed Jack Charlton, who was just behind Peters, thinks, 'I'm glad it wasn't down to me. I would have kicked the bugger over the bar!'

The two men in white coats above Gordon Banks' goal are leaping up and down, arms in the air.

'There's Martin Peters – the man who scored the goal that could well have won the World Cup for England!' Kenneth Wolstenholme exclaims.
    The sound of Walley Barnes clapping is picked up on his microphone.

As Bobby Moore passes him, Martin Peters splays out his fingers, palms down. His fingers are tingling with excitement.
    'I feel like I've got electricity running through me!' he says with a grin.

Bobby Charlton turns to Nobby Stiles. 'Nobby, Nobby, we've won! We've won! They can't beat us now. We've made it!'

Willi Schulz slaps the ground in anger.

'Eng-land! Eng-land! Eng-land! Eng-land!' chant the Wembley crowd.

In the vestry of Loughton Methodist Church in Essex, Geoffrey and Pat Cochrane hear Pat's cousins give a muffled cheer.

'Shall we send out to find out the score?' the minister says with a smile.

'Come on, Germany! Give us a game!'

In the bar in Ibiza, John Cleese is overjoyed and clapping wildly, but he's not sure if that was the best thing to shout.

In the sitting room of Number 20 Clarence Grove in Liverpool, Carl Gillwood leaps up and down in front of his family's Radio Rentals television set in total ecstasy. He looks at the cardboard Jules Rimet trophy that he and his friends play for out in the street. It looks like the real thing will soon be England's.

> *Ken Jones of the* Daily Mirror *is viewing the goal with particular satisfaction. In this morning's edition, he not only predicted that Jimmy Greaves wouldn't be playing, but he also predicted England's tactics and in particular Martin Peters' role. 'See how Geoff Hurst and Roger Hunt set off when England have possession, seeking to pull defenders wide and opening up gaps for others... see how Martin Peters performs a double role of defender and attacker, coming late into the German penalty area and trying to finish with a header or a shot.'*

4.29pm

As the Germans restart the game, Martin Peters wonders if England have won the World Cup – all thanks to his goal.

Then he remembers Alf Ramsey's warning about the German's determination to the last.

4.30pm

On a golf course in Manchester, Denis Law of Scotland and Manchester United is having trouble concentrating on his game. Law had decided that he couldn't bear to watch England in the final, but he keeps wondering how his Manchester United team-mates Bobby Charlton and Nobby Stiles are getting on.

It is raining and once again, Law is being beaten by his friend. He looks set to lose their £25 bet.

For Denis Law the rivalry with England went deep. Before a Scotland–England international at Wembley in April 1965, Nobby Stiles went up to him and wished him luck, putting out his hand.
   'Get lost, you little English bastard,' Law said and walked off.

At Wembley there's another England attack, this time down the near-side touchline. The Germans are tired and their marking is looser.

Ball.

Peters.

Alan Ball again. Karl-Heinz Schnellinger slips as Ball steps left around him. In desperation, Willi Schulz slides in aggressively with his right boot and brings Ball down. The Englishman rolls dramatically a few times and comes to rest with his face in the grass.

Martin Peters jogs over to take the free kick, but Ball is in no mood to surrender anything unless he has to. He gets up, keen to take it quickly. Again his head is down as he kicks. It's too high for George Cohen and Jack Charlton can't get there in time. The ball is cleared by Horst-Dieter Höttges.

Nobby Stiles neatly stops the German break by robbing Siggi Held of the ball – to loud cheers from the crowd – and he then chips it towards Roger Hunt and Alan Ball.

The referee blows his whistle for offside. But Alan Ball cheekily plays with the ball and kicks it over Hans Tilkowski's head and into the goal. The crowd cheer again. Gottfried Dienst is not amused and walks towards Ball, hands on hips. Alan Ball is lucky – he gets no more than a talking-to for a bookable offence.

Twenty-four-year-old Frank Horrocks has a great seat just four rows from the front, almost level with the West German six-yard box. He is amazed to see some England fans in the stand behind the goal to his right starting to head for the exits.

Martin Peters runs over the centre circle with Bobby Charlton ahead of him. He passes and Charlton strikes it with his left foot – it doesn't trouble Hans Tilkowski. Bobby Charlton is yet to have a shot on target.

'Now let's get this done, Bobby, because another goal will finish them off,' he thinks to himself.

4.32pm/4.32pm Tunisian Time

Eight minutes to the final whistle.

In the middle of the Tunisian desert, a large, battered Mercedes taxi pulls up alongside a coach outside a roadside café. Two hot and tired English families – Ron and Barbara Thomas and their 12-year-old daughter Ann, followed by Gordon and Sheila Smith and their ten-year-old daughter Mary – get out and head for the cool of the café in search of a drink.

The two families met at the Hotel Marhaba in Sousse on

the coast, where they are both staying as part of a two-week Wings package holiday – it's one of the first foreign trips the Thomas family have made. They've hired the taxi for the day to take them to see the holy city of Kairouan.

The café is full of tourists and about half a dozen Tunisians, all seated at tables; everyone's attention is on a black and white television showing the World Cup final.

'Oh, that's good!' Barbara Thomas says when she sees the television – she didn't think they'd get a chance to see the final.

The Thomas family is from Leeds and they are keen to see how Jack Charlton is getting on. They all order Cokes and as the two families find seats, they take in the voices of their fellow tourists and realise that they are all German.

German centre-back Willi Schulz passes from the centre circle to fellow defender Horst-Dieter Höttges on the near-side touch-line. Höttges sends a long ball to Karl-Heinz Schnellinger, who shoots from the edge of the box – straight at Gordon Banks. The man who was rated the world's best full-back before the World Cup is not having his greatest game.

Bobby Moore tells Banks to slow down to waste some time, but Banks ignores him and throws the ball over-arm to Alan Ball on the far touchline. Ball looks the least tired player on the pitch and makes Karl-Heinz Schnellinger look foolish as he darts around him, leaving the German on the floor.

> '*Schnellinger realised that he was involved in not so much a football match as the ordeal of his life,*' was Nobby Stiles' verdict.

Geoff Hurst has some space 20 yards out – he gets the ball onto his left foot and sends it high and wide. It ends up on the greyhound track far behind the German goal.

The English fans are once more singing 'When the Reds go marching in'.

Although there are no opposition players in his half, Jack Charlton is only too happy to waste some time by passing the ball back to Gordon Banks. Some in the crowd whistle and boo.

Bobby Moore once said of Jack, 'Some days... I'd look at him and I'd wonder how this big giraffe played football. We used to argue black and blue because I wanted to get the ball down and play the game and he wanted to hoof it away to safety.'

Alf Ramsey told Charlton one of the reasons he picked him was because he knew he didn't trust Bobby Moore. Charlton asked him what he meant.

'If Gordon Banks gives the ball to you as a central defender, you'll give it back to Gordon and say "Kick it!" but if you give the ball to Bobby Moore, Bobby will join in the build-up midfield, through to the forwards, and if he makes a mistake at any stage, I know, because I watched you play, you will always go across and play behind him and allow him to make the mistake.'

Charlton has always been a bit bemused by Bobby Moore – the way he doesn't shout or encourage his players on the pitch ('I believe all centre-backs should be shouters,') and the way he reacts to victory. 'When we won, most of us would be boisterous. Bobby would take off his shirt and smile. He wasn't like us. He was one of us, but he wasn't like us.'

4.33pm

Seven minutes to the final whistle.

The singing has stopped and the English fans chant has changed to 'We want three! We want three!'

England's players look happy to oblige. Alan Ball on the far side passes across to Geoff Hurst. Bobby Charlton claps his hands then opens his arms – he wants the ball. But Hurst has seen Martin Peters running to his left. Peters' shot goes three feet over the bar.

Jimmy Armfield signals to the nine reserves – the time has come for them to make their way from their seats in the stands to the England bench for the final whistle. Jimmy Greaves is already there.

4.34pm

Six minutes to the final whistle. The crowd are now singing 'Rule, Britannia'. The sun is shining once more on Wembley.

The West German defenders are pushing forward as far as they dare.

Jack Charlton is getting irritated by referee Gottfried Dienst as he keeps taking his watch out of his pocket and putting it back again. It's putting him off.

It's a throw-in to Germany. The Germans have an urgency to their play now. Siggi Held passes to Lothar Emmerich – but George Cohen is instantly on him.

Cohen always credited his swiftness on the pitch to his humble origins in working-class Fulham. 'The biggest assets I had were speed and strength. I was chunky, never fat. We didn't have the food to be fat.' The majority of the England team came from communities dominated by the foundry, docks or pit. None could be described as middle-class.

Nobby Stiles and Siggi Held tussle for the ball; Stiles slips as he tackles. Gottfried Dienst, just a few feet away, blows his whistle for a free kick to West Germany just outside the England penalty area. Stiles swings his arms theatrically in disgust.

Gordon Banks is on his goal line. The six-man England wall is diagonally across the far corner of their penalty area. Lothar Emmerich floats the ball in and Wolfgang Weber gets his head to it, but Jack Charlton and Gordon Banks watch it go wide. Banks is furious that Weber is so loosely marked. They cannot afford to make mistakes like that so close to full time.

4.35pm

Five minutes to the final whistle.

In Royal Oldham Hospital's maternity ward, a doctor finally arrives to give Anita Dunnington her stitches. She's been wondering where everybody is.

'Have you been having your tea?' Anita asks.

'No, we've been watching the match...' the doctor replies.

It's a West German corner on the near side – but it's a tired, poor ball from Franz Beckenbauer that Bobby Moore easily intercepts. Martin Peters chips it to Alan Ball. The crowd are cheering every move by the England team now.

Roger Hunt sprints towards the German goal with Willi Schulz close behind. Hunt passes to Bobby Charlton, who is running up the middle – with his first touch he thwacks it four yards to the right of the West German goal. Again he's missed and again he's face down in the mud. Wolfgang Overath helps him up.

'I'll tell you what,' Jack said later, 'if he had hit that properly it would have probably killed the goalkeeper...'

4.37pm

Jack Charlton calmly intercepts a long ball intended for Siggi Held, then makes a poor pass himself.

Weber.

Schnellinger.

Lothar Emmerich miskicks his shot on goal and Gordon Banks scoops the ball up with no trouble. He throws it accurately to Alan Ball at the halfway line.

Ball passes to Geoff Hurst. Roger Hunt is to Hurst's left and Ball is now moving up on his right. Twenty yards out Hurst tries a shot – it goes wide, just like Bobby Charlton's moments before.

Hunt shouts at Hurst in frustration. Hurst looks tired and his right eye is slightly closed after his collision with Hans Tilkowski in the first half.

'Alf's idea was the less number of passes you take, the less chance there is of you making a bad pass,' said Jimmy Leadbetter, who was an inside forward at Ipswich Town under Ramsey. 'If I had to say an ideal number of passes, I would say three,' the England manager once said.

In the Wembley office where he's been watching the final on television, former policeman Bob Geggie picks up the Jules Rimet trophy and puts it into his deep coat pocket. It looks as if the Queen will need it to give to Bobby Moore in a few moments. Geggie makes his way through a maze of corridors until he reaches an anteroom. He's right under the royal box.

4.38pm

Only two minutes to the final whistle.

On the edge of his penalty area, Franz Beckenbauer is not giving Bobby Charlton a moment to shoot. Karl-Heinz Schnellinger robs Charlton of the ball.

Seeler.

Wolfgang Overath skips around Martin Peters, and tries a shot – but it's two yards to the right of the England goal.

There's a groan of relief from the England fans.

Kenneth Wolstenholme starts to wind up his commentary: 'Thirteen years ago the Hungarians showed that England were no longer masters of football. And in those 13 years, England has fashioned a team which is on the threshold of being the world champions!'

On 25th November 1953, Hungary played England at Wembley in a game that was billed as 'The Match of the Century'. It was a one-sided contest – England were thrashed 6-3. It marked the end of the international career of one England full-back – Alf Ramsey.

The crowd are whistling for the end.

Bobbies in helmets and capes are taking up positions closer to the pitch to stop any invasion by enthusiastic supporters at the final whistle.

Gordon Banks' goal kick is headed back into the England half by Horst-Dieter Höttges. Martin Peters then heads it.

In the centre circle, Franz Beckenbauer jumps higher for the ball than a tired Bobby Charlton and heads it towards Siggi

Held. Held hesitates and Jack Charlton – coming up from behind – leaps above him to head it.

Gottfreid Dienst blows his whistle, believing Charlton has pushed Held.

A free kick to Germany ten yards outside the box.

It's the last thing England want.

Lothar Emmerich claps his approval.

Nobby Stiles protests to the referee. Jack Charlton joins in, telling Dienst angrily, 'I never saw the guy. I just jumped to head the ball!'

'I did not go down on purpose. He jumped into my back, he was heavier than me and then I fell [forward],' Held said later.

Hugh Johns tells the ITV audience: 'Referee Dienst is certainly not making a lot of friends among the England spectators here at Wembley.'

The England players look over to their bench and get the sign that there are only a few seconds to go.

'Bloody Germans'

4.39pm/4.39pm Tunisian Time/5.39pm Spanish Time

There is panic in the England defence.

Almost everyone is shouting and swearing at somebody.

Referee Dienst gestures to Nobby Stiles to calm down.

Martin Peters is trying to get the referee to move the ball back. Nobby Stiles is pulling the wall of five men into some sort of shape and checking with Gordon Banks that he can see the ball and the kicker. Alf Ramsey had been concerned about the danger of free kicks in this position and Lothar Emmerich's skill at taking them, and he'd given Stiles the responsibility of setting the wall. They have rehearsed for just this eventuality many times.

The England players are still cursing.

Referee Dienst moves the England players back. All the Germans except Franz Beckenbauer and Lothar Emmerich, who is going to take the free kick, are in the England penalty area.

Emmerich sprints in and hits the ball with all the energy he has left – it flashes past the England wall and strikes George Cohen on the right knee, knocking him over. The ball falls to the feet of Siggi Held, who shoots across the goalmouth – it's going wide but then hits Schnellinger on the back.

All the pace goes from the ball.

Gordon Banks and Ray Wilson are wrong-footed.

The England players shout 'handball!' Linesman Tofik Bakhramov raises his flag – then drops it.

Wolfgang Weber runs for the ball.

Ray Wilson stretches out a leg.

Gordon Banks dives to his left – but Weber, with the tip of his boot, sends the ball flying into the net above the goal-keeper's hands.

England 2 West Germany 2

'How the hell did you let that happen?' Bobby Moore yells.

In the cottage on the hill in Tenby, Heinz Kurt-Doerr can

contain himself no longer. *'Tor! Tor!'* (Goal! Goal!) he yells. The roomful of English and Welsh turn and stare at him.

In the stands behind the royal box, Alan Ball's girlfriend Lesley faints. 'It was as though the whole atmosphere had been sucked out of the stadium,' she said later.

In the anteroom several feet below her, Bob Geggie, poised to pass the Jules Rimet trophy to an FA official who will in turn give it to the Queen, hears the crowd howl and wonders what's happened.

On the England bench, Harold Shepherdson looks at his stop-watch. Four seconds to go.

As the Germans in the café around him celebrate, John Cleese, crying inside, applauds the equaliser.

Jack Charlton looks at his brother, who is standing on the goal line staring at the ball in the back of the net. Tears are running down Bobby's face. 'This is it, we've had it now,' he's thinking.

Alan Ball runs to get the ball and then sprints with it to the centre circle – he thinks there may be a chance to make it 3-2.

The television room in the Scott Arms pub near Corfe Castle in Dorset falls silent. A dozen boys are glued to the set. They're from the Royal Manor School in Portland and are at a school camp nearby. One of the customers watching with them is a short, squat man in his late fifties wearing a sports jacket and Fred Perry shirt. The boys have realised that he's German and have nicknamed him 'Helmut'.

He can see the boys' bitter disappointment at Weber's goal.

189

'Bloody Germans,' he says.

All the boys burst out laughing.

In the Tunisian café, the Thomas and Smith families remain seated as the West German tourists and the half-dozen Tunisians dance and punch the air.

In 1966, West Germans are popular in Tunisia and are considered better tippers than the British, who are allowed to take only £50 out of the country by Harold Wilson's government.

As the German players surround Weber, the English are protesting to referee Dienst about what they saw as Schnellinger's handball.

The English fans are booing.

Jimmy Armfield saw Weber's goal but the rest of the England squad were behind him as they walked up the tunnel and missed it. Jimmy sits down on the bench behind an impassive Alf Ramsey.

Six years later, Nobby Stiles was back at the FA training camp at Lilleshall, this time to learn how to be a football coach. They were shown a film of the West German equaliser and Nobby was furious when Charles Hughes, the director of coaching, asked, 'What went wrong here?' When greeted by silence Hughes declared that there were too many people in the wall. Nobby was livid and put his hand up to say something – what did this man know of their well-rehearsed plans? He was just about to vocalise his anger when a colleague next to him told him urgently to put his hand down – 'if you want to get your coaching badge'. You could fail the course for arguing with Charles Hughes.

Dave Corbett's phone rings (he's recently had one installed, so no more trips to the phone box for Pickles) – it's his agent George Skinner.

'Dave, there's going to be a celebration at the Royal Garden Hotel in Kensington High Street after the final ends – all the players are going to be there, and I've got us an invitation to get in! Bring the dog! Get up here! I'll meet you at the front.'

'You won it once. Now go and win it again.'

4.40pm/9.10pm Glengyle *Bridge Time*

The game restarts. Bobby Charlton passes to Geoff Hurst.

Almost immediately Gottfried Dienst blows his whistle. Jack Charlton waves his hand contemptuously at him. His brother can't believe it – he thought there was another ten minutes to play. Uwe Seeler walks up to him and says, 'Bobby, that's football.'

German manager Helmut Schön walks briskly onto the pitch. He starts encouraging his tired team. Siggi Held is oblivious to his words.

'Everyone was just focused on themselves.'

An exhausted Gottfried Dienst sits down on the pitch and looks at his watch.

Alf Ramsey strides onto the pitch with Harold Shepherdson and Les Cocker following behind with drinks and oranges. Ramsey is furious at how many scoring chances they missed and is trying to contain his anger.

But he is also thinking about what he should say to his

exhausted players. He knows he doesn't always express himself well.

Alf Ramsey hid his lack of education by affecting phrases that he thought made him sound more intelligent. Sometimes he was caught out. Once, when the England squad were in a lecture room discussing club chairmen, Alf said to Jimmy Armfield, 'Haven't you anything to say on the subject, Jimmy?'

'Not really. There's little choice in rotten apples.'

'Come, Jimmy. I would have thought you, of all people, would have had something more poignant and articulate on this subject. "Little choice in rotten apples"? We are English, Jimmy. We speak English, the language of Shakespeare.'

'That is Shakespeare, Alf,' Jimmy replied.

Ramsey wrote in 1952 that he read a great deal to 'develop a command of words so essential when you suddenly find yourself called upon to make a speech... I always try to put up some sort of show when asked to say a few words.'

The manager looks at the team. George Cohen is exhausted – not only has he played 38 games for Fulham this season but he's also been in all of England's games at Wembley, which has really drained him. 'Fans always assumed you should do well at home and they'd soon get on your back if you didn't,' Cohen said later.

Nobby Stiles is ranting, furious with Alan Ball about something. Alf Ramsey takes his arm to calm him down. Bobby Moore and Jack Charlton are sitting down.

'I knew that I must not indicate, either by word or expression, the least degree of sympathy for the team because they had to go on playing,' Ramsey said in an interview.

Ramsey finds the right words: 'Look at the Germans. They're finished. They're flat on their backs. Stand up! Stand up! Don't let the Germans think you're tired. You're the better team – you're the fitter team. You won the World Cup once. Now go and win it again!'

'Make no mistake, if the wrong thing had been said in those tense seconds, we could have lost the Cup,' Geoff Hurst said later.

In the south-east London suburb of St Paul's Cray, the Harris family are squeezed into their front room, watching the match on television. They are all in their best clothes. Today at five o'clock at the church of St Peter and St Paul, little Billy Harris is going to be christened. His parents Bill and Sheila are there along with Bill's parents, his brothers and their wives. They are all poised to head out of the door. Wolfgang Weber has thwarted their plans.

They hadn't thought about the possibility of extra time. Father Roskilly will be waiting for them.

There's a moment's panic, then Bill's brother David has an idea. 'Why don't I ring Father Roskilly and see if we can delay it?'

They all agree it's worth a try and someone searches for the priest's number.

Gordon Taylor looks at his watch. He has also failed to take the possibility of extra time into account. He can't see how he's going to get from Wembley to the West End in time to meet his fiancée for *The Owl and the Pussycat*. As he looks at the two teams on the pitch, it's clear to him that the Germans are keen to get extra time started; the momentum is with them, but Alf Ramsey is sensibly taking his time.

Reg and Philip Hodgskiss are also looking at their watches. Although they've been on their feet for over two hours, they're not tired – farmers are used to standing. Their main worry is that they have to be back at their Staffordshire farm in two hours to milk their 60 cows.

On the merchant ship *Glengyle* in the Indian Ocean, Gordon Charlton is reluctantly making his way down to the engine room for the start of his shift. There's no radio signal in the bowels of the ship.

Wembley is buzzing with excitement. The flags are still being waved and the hunting horns still being blown. A well-dressed middle-aged man drops to his knees on the terraces, bows his head and puts his hands together in prayer.

'God, please – you cannot let us lose to the bloody Germans...' he says.

When the man gets up, he looks ready to face extra time.

Up in the press box, Barry Davies leans over to the German commentator next door and tells him that his country deserves to be on level terms.

Alf Ramsey is walking round the players, having a quiet word with each of them.

'Attack, attack, every time you attack!' he urges Alan Ball.

Some of them are sucking oranges.

Ball throws his orange peel off the pitch.

4.42pm

In St Paul's Cray, the Harris family hold their breath as David Harris phones the parish priest. They are due at the church in ten minutes; he might already be there. Someone answers.

'Father Roskilly. It's David Harris here, William Harris's brother. Is it possible you could delay Billy's christening until after the football's finished?'

'Of course!' There is relief in Father Roskilly's voice. 'I'm watching it too! I'll see you when the game's over.'

'Thanks, Father!'

The Harrises give a cheer.

4.43pm/8.13pm Iranian Time

It's a warm, balmy evening in Tehran. On a veranda at the back of a house on the northern side of the Iranian capital, Brian Moore's Wembley commentary is coming out of a short-wave radio tuned to the BBC World Service sports programme *Saturday Special*. Bill Denley and his young sons, Gareth and Ian, are hanging on every word. The signal keeps coming and going, so they've attached two wires to the radio's aerial and rigged them so they run up the outside wall of the house.

Both teams take up their positions once again. They look tired. Nobby Stiles and Alan Ball haven't bothered to roll their socks up. But as Jack Charlton said later, 'every man-jack of the England team seemed suddenly to have a streak of tempered steel in his make-up. Our motto had become "They shall not pass".'

> *I was up against [Schnellinger] all afternoon and I just kept grinning at him and then going past him... I had him on toast.*
>
> *Alan Ball*

> **The English got cracking as if they had inserted new batteries into them.**
>
> *Hans Tilkowski*

4.45pm

England are now playing left to right.

Siggi Held kicks off for West Germany, passing left to Lothar Emmerich, who skips around George Cohen. Nobby Stiles blocks him and the ball goes out for a throw-in on the near side.

Kenneth Wolstenholme is talking about the need for players to 'pace themselves', just as England's Number 7 is proving him wrong. Alan Ball has taken the manager's instruction to attack to heart. At the centre circle he picks up a long clearance from Jack Charlton. Ball manages to nip around Wolfgang Weber to the edge of the German penalty area and strike the ball sweetly and with power – sending it straight towards the top of the net. Hans Tilkowski just manages to tip the ball over with his left hand and deny England the lead. 'It gave me a big lift and I felt I was well and truly on my way to something special,' Ball wrote later.

On the regular late-afternoon Red Funnel ferry between the Isle of Wight and Portsmouth, a large crowd has gathered on the port side of the ship. They are huddled around a transistor radio, listening to Brian Moore and Alan Clarke's World Cup commentary.

The ship's tannoy crackles into life.

'Would the passengers congregating on the port side of the ship please move into the centre of the vessel.'

The number of people listening to the radio is causing a significant list to port, and the captain needs it correcting as soon as possible.

The West German Number 3, Karl-Heinz Schnellinger, has stopped running and is bent over – he's got cramp in his left leg. Alan Ball casually walks past to check the damage. He feels he's partly responsible for Schnellinger's cramp, as the German has been trying to follow him all afternoon as he's scampered around the pitch. 'I could have gone on until nightfall,' Ball said.

Just outside the penalty area, Lothar Emmerich thumps the ball into George Cohen's left knee. The Germans just can't find a way through the England defence.

4.46pm

Bobby Moore is a constant, reassuring presence to the England players. In the words of David Miller of the *Sunday Telegraph*, he moved 'like a bank manager among junior clerks, correcting, re-directing and discreetly scolding'.

Bobby Charlton runs up the left wing, the front of his shirt discoloured with vertical stripes of sweat and mud. He pauses. Beckenbauer is too tired to challenge him. Bobby passes to his brother, who's made a run to his left along the touchline. Jack kicks a high ball into the six-yard box with his first touch. Hans Tilkowski jumps higher than Hurst and pats the ball out of play. The German goalkeeper limps back to his line.

Alan Ball takes the corner – a short ball to Roger Hunt who passes it back. Ball crosses towards Martin Peters, who, at full stretch, heads the ball behind him. Franz Beckenbauer, competing against the taller Jack Charlton, heads it poorly and the ball finds Peters once more.

Peters to Bobby Charlton.

He hasn't much time – he thumps a fast ball that hits the base of the right-hand post and cannons back into Tilkowski's face.

'Perhaps it's not going to be our day...' thinks Peters.

With a smile, an exhausted Horst-Dieter Höttges signals to Geoff Hurst to slow down a bit.

The German trainer trots round behind the West German goal to see how Tilkowski is.

England have had two shots on target in the last four minutes.

4.47pm

Roger Hunt, moving swiftly on the left wing, tries to make it three. The ball is an orange blur passing through the West German defence but it just skims the wrong side of the post.

Nineteen-year-old Reiner Hammeran is studying at a summer school in London with two friends from his home town of Rietberg. They have a good position at Wembley, level with the West German goal line. They were here on Thursday night to see the third-place play-off between the Soviet Union and Portugal. It had been a spontaneous decision and they were doubtful they'd get a ticket. But as they approached Wembley, they were taken aback by the number of ticket touts. 'It was like a bazaar! There were many people who held tickets and offered them to us,' Reiner recalled; they didn't hesitate and bought tickets that were originally 15 shillings for 20 shillings. Reiner felt the price was fair; 'after all, I got to see Eusébio play.'

Because it worked so well, Reiner and his friends tried again this morning – and succeeded. Although the teenagers are in a block with English supporters, everyone has been very friendly. He came to England to improve his English – the World Cup has been a bonus. And this time the tickets were even cheaper than for the third-place play-off – only 15 shillings.

4.48pm

England's corner.

Alan Ball runs up to take it. The crowd chant 'Eng-land! Eng-land! Eng-land!' The sun is the brightest it's been all afternoon. Hans Tilkowski has put on a cap to shield his eyes. The air is humid; the flags on the stadium roof hang limp.

Martin Peters jumps too early and Wolfgang Weber clears it.

Ball.

Bobby Charlton passes it wide to Ray Wilson on the run, who chips the ball into the West German penalty area. Willi Schulz heads it away with ease.

Ball loses it and West Germany have the chance to attack – captain Uwe Seeler surges into the England half. He crosses left to Lothar Emmerich. The England defence has a moment to regroup, so when Emmerich passes to Siggi Held in the box, Nobby Stiles is quickly onto him.

Held fouls Stiles.

Free kick.

Stiles applauds the referee.

4.49pm

The Royal Marines bandsmen have now been standing in the Wembley tunnel for 40 minutes, unable to see the game. Occasionally the drum major walks from his position in sight of the pitch and down the line of Marines to tell them what's going on.

'It was very frustrating. The cheers could have been anything – someone taking their knickers off in the centre circle for all we knew,' said Michael Hutton.

As Gordon Banks takes the free kick, few of the England players look keen to receive it. For the first time they look tired. Hands are on hips, shoulders are forward.

Bobby Moore, however, looks as if he's just started the game.

4.52pm

Siggi Held is making a good run – he goes past Alan Ball into the England penalty area, darts past a lunging Jack Charlton and just before the touchline, hits a cross in front of the goal.

But there's no one there to receive it.

On a council estate in Northolt, Len Russell is in his front room watching the final on television with his wife Gwen and three of their children, Colin, 11, Tina, nine, and Kevin, aged one. There is a knock on the door.

'Who the bloody hell is that?' exclaims Len.

Colin goes to the door. Standing on the doorstep is a man in a suit.

'Prudential!' the man says. He's come to collect the family's monthly insurance payment.

'But it's World Cup final day!' Colin says, incredulous.

'I know! Everyone will be in this afternoon!' the insurance man says cheerfully.

'For bloody hell's sake, who comes round on the day of the World Cup final...?' Len mutters as he searches for his cheque book. The man from the Prudential smiles as he takes Len's cheque, makes an entry in his book and says farewell. Still muttering, Len goes back to his seat in front of the television.

> *Millions of people on all continents were eyewitnesses that this was no goal. Victory wasn't stolen from our team, but it was cheated of a chance of victory. Nobody can know how this game might have ended without that decision. I don't think the English will ever be truly happy with that 'victory'.*
>
> *German football magazine* **Kicker**, *31st July 1966*

> *The referee goes to the linesman, well, I don't know in which language they conferred or if they spoke at all. Suddenly, England got a goal as a result of this short conversation. That was very strange.*
>
> *Siggi Held*

4.55pm

Two yards inside his own half, Nobby Stiles hits a fine pass over Karl-Heinz Schnellinger's head, aiming at Alan Ball. 'I knew Bally had the beating of Schnellinger – by now it was written in the sky at Wembley,' Stiles said.

But Ball doesn't think he's going to reach it in time. He's exhausted, having probably run further than anyone else on the pitch. 'I was finished...'

Geoff Hurst is making a run into the West German penalty area. But Ball does reach the ball and hits it, first time, towards the near post. 'I didn't even know who was in there...'

Hurst realises that he's made his run too soon – the ball is falling behind him. He turns his back to the goal. 'I needed to adjust my body and take a couple of touches to get the ball into a shooting position.' He hooks the orange ball with all his strength and topples over.

The ball flies over Hans Tilkowski's outstretched arms – he touches it with his finger tips.

It hits the underside of the bar.

The net shakes.

Spinning, the ball then smacks the ground and bounces up.

Wolfgang Weber runs in and heads the ball away over the bar for a corner.

Lying on the ground, Geoff Hurst sees Roger Hunt stop running towards goal, turn and put his hand in the air.

Tilkowski, Höttges and Hurst look to the linesman on the near side and then back to referee Dienst.

Bobby Charlton runs over celebrating, waving his hands in the air. Wolfgang Weber tries to stop him.

German television commentator Rudi Michel shouts, '*Achtung! Achtung! Nicht im tor! Kein tor! Oder doch...?*'

On BBC Radio, Alan Clarke is saying: 'It must be a goal. I would have thought that went in...'

Hugh Johns on ITV isn't so sure: 'No, they haven't given it! The linesman says "no goal". The linesman says "no goal".'

Directly behind the linesman, and only about 15 seats from the pitch, Bolton Wanderers player Gordon Taylor is convinced it's a goal. 'He's got to give it! He's got to give it!' he shouts.

'*Nein! Nein! Nein! Nein!*' the German players are shouting as they surround referee Gottfried Dienst. Alan Ball pulls Dienst towards Bakhramov, even though Ball couldn't see whether it was in or not.

Dienst and Bakhramov have a brief conversation.

Engineer Ken Ashman is sitting at Wembley with four German work colleagues. One points to the linesman.

'He will give a goal. He is a communist.'

Twenty-six-year-old barrister Kenneth Clarke (who failed to win the safe Labour seat of Mansfield for the Conservatives in the General Election in March), is sitting right behind the linesman. Clarke has a smattering of Russian and tries it out by shouting at him as loudly as he can. Everyone around him is shouting too. 'I can't quite remember what I said, but it seemed to work...'

'Is the ball behind the line?' Dienst says.

'Yes, behind the line. *Tor!*' Bakhramov replies, nodding vigorously and pointing to the centre spot.

Dienst turns away, blows his whistle and waves at the centre spot.

'It's in! It's in!' Judith Hurst shouts from her seat above the royal box.

'No, it isn't!' some German fans behind her shout back.

'*Tor...*' says German TV commentator Rudi Michel. He's then silent for a long time.

Uwe Seeler is pulling his players away from Dienst.
  '*Es ist immer noch Zeit!*' ('There is still time!') he says.

Now the England players can celebrate. Martin Peters lifts up and hugs Geoff Hurst, who shouts with joy. Then Alan Ball, Roger Hunt and Bobby Charlton hug each other.

In a stand level with the West German goal line, student Reiner Hammeran is convinced that it's a goal. Why else would Roger Hunt turn away and celebrate?

'Was it a good 'un?' Jack Charlton calls to Roger Hunt.
  Hunt holds his hands two feet apart.

England 3 West Germany 2

4.56pm/8.26pm Iranian Time

Hans Tilkowski is furious. 'It was the third time in a few weeks I had been unlucky, each time on British soil. First we lost 1-0 to England and had a goal disallowed. Then, in May, I was in the Cup Winners' Cup final with Borussia Dortmund, and Liverpool's equaliser should have been chalked off, as the ball had gone out of play.'

Siggi Held can't understand why the linesman had been standing still, looking as if he didn't know what to do. Held knows that the linesman normally runs back to the halfway line when a goal is scored. 'Suddenly, he was of the same opinion that the ball had crossed the line. If he'd given the goal, then he should have moved towards the halfway line right away. But he did not. It was a very strange reaction.'

Barry Davies agreed: 'He became a hero by doing something that linesmen aren't supposed to do; if he thought it was a goal he should have run back to the halfway line – that's what it says in the rule book.'

Harold Wilson turns to Lord Harewood in the royal box and says, 'I was criticised for my visit to Russia the other day – well, it paid off, didn't it? The linesman was a Russian!'

'This goal will remain the most discussed in football history,' the Italian newspaper Corriere della Sera *accurately predicted the following day.*

In Germany, it is what the final is most remembered for. Welt am Sonntag's match report headline was: 'RUSSIAN LINESMAN DECIDES WORLD CHAMPIONSHIP'.

Some German fans believe that it was the start of the Wembley curse – a succession of games in which the English were unable to defeat their German rivals. In Germany the phrase 'Das Wembley Tor' has come to mean any unfair decision.

Kenneth Wolstenholme once asked Roger Hunt why he hadn't kicked the ball into the back of the net. 'Because I'd already seen the ball swerve well over the line. Anyone who says the ball didn't cross the line after it hit the crossbar was not standing where I was.'

Bobby Charlton says, 'Whenever the Germans ask me about it, I always say "Are you suggesting that if that goal hadn't happened you would have beaten us?" Not one of them says "yes"...'

Years later, Gottfried Dienst said, 'Hurst shot on goal on the turn, the ball bounced on the underside of the bar. I was – there is no reason not to admit it – unsure and looked to my Russian colleague Bakhramov, who kept his flag at eye level. I didn't know exactly what he wanted to indicate by that.'

But Bobby Moore admitted, 'We won the World Cup on the best appeal of all time. I believe that old Bakhramov was convinced by [Roger's] reaction.'

In the days that followed, a rumour started that Tofik Bakhramov said the word 'Stalingrad' after the final whistle when the West German players confronted him and asked why he gave the goal. There is no evidence for this claim.

He said later, 'I didn't see the ball in the goal. But I saw how the Englishman Hunt raised his arms in the air after the shot by Hurst. I also saw that the German goalkeeper gave the impression of being inconsolable. Therefore, it must have been a goal.'

According to the West German newspaper Frankfurter Allgemeine Zeitung, *'The greatest achievement of the German team was the excellent attitude with which they accepted the goal and thus the victory of the English. They have done with this prudence more for German sports and German reputation than winning the title could ever have achieved.'*

The West Germans restart the game.

It's estimated that 70% of British adults are now watching the World Cup final.

In a BBC studio in Bush House, Paddy Feeny, the presenter of the World Service programme *Saturday Special*, is absolutely furious – he's been told the World Service schedule cannot be altered – not even for the World Cup final. He interrupts Brian

Moore's commentary to tell his millions of listeners across the globe that he's sorry but they are leaving the dramatic events at Wembley for a half-hour news programme.

On their terrace in Tehran, Bill Denley and his two sons can't believe their ears as the Wembley roars are replaced by the World Service theme 'Lili Bolero' and the latest world news. They are going to have to wait patiently for the result.

4.57pm

Bob Geggie is not happy. When he was in the Wembley office guarding the Jules Rimet trophy at least he had a television to watch the game; he's now in an anteroom under the royal box and the sound of the crowd is the only way he can make a guess at what's going on.

On the far side, Franz Beckenbauer sends a hopeful cross that Jack Charlton has plenty of time to head away. It hits Bobby Moore in the chest and thankfully for England, rolls back to Gordon Banks.

The warden at the training camp at Lilleshall is taking his dog for a walk – he can't bear to watch the television any more, as the tension is too great.

Karl-Heinz Schnellinger attempts a cross, but Ray Wilson blocks him and gets the ball full in the face. For a second he's stunned, then runs back to defend.
Beckenbauer has the ball.
Overath.
Haller.
Held is in possession on the near side, just outside the England

penalty area. Martin Peters robs him of the ball but hesitates. Held recovers and the two men spin round as they fight for the ball.

Held wins and starts a run towards goal – there is no one between him and Gordon Banks.

The referee blows his whistle for a foul against Peters.

Nobby Stiles shouts at Peters that he should have cleared the ball as soon as he got it. Peters shouts back that he should have covered him. Stiles comes up and reinforces his point by gesturing upfield. Peters is too tired to carry on arguing.

4.58pm

'Attack! Attack! Attack! Attack!' the England fans chant.

George Cohen miskicks and the ball runs to Lothar Emmerich on the near-side touchline. Emmerich pushes forward and passes the ball through Jack Charlton's legs, but before Siggi Held can get it, Cohen, who has raced back into defence, slides in and intercepts the ball. Gordon Banks sprints out of goal and stops it going out for a corner.

Banks is enjoying himself – he relishes the drama. 'Thrive on pressure, Gordon. You get no juice out of an orange unless you squeeze it,' Alf Ramsey once said to him.

Karl-Heinz Schnellinger stops a pass from Alan Ball with his hand.

Dienst blows for a free kick.

'Ninety-seven thousand referees gave that decision!' declares Kenneth Wolstenholme.

5.00pm

Gottfried Dienst blows his whistle. It's the end of the first half of extra time. The teams have a couple of minutes before they must change ends. Four of the West German staff sprint on with water.

The England players walk slowly towards their bench. Les Cocker brings a bucket of water to the edge of the pitch.

As Alf Ramsey talks to Bobby Moore, Jack Charlton kneels in front of the bucket and scoops water up into his face. Behind the bucket, Ray Wilson is being supported by Les Cocker and Harold Shepherdson, who both look concerned. They pick up the bucket and Wilson splashes his face with water. In an era of no substitutions, it's vital to get Wilson fit and ready for the last 15 minutes.

Alan Ball is lying on the ground having his legs massaged by team doctor Alan Bass. Alf Ramsey bends down and gives Ball an encouraging pat on the back.

Gordon Banks puts a wet sponge on the back of George Cohen's neck. The weather is still hot and humid.

Alf Ramsey brings George Cohen over to Wilson and asks him to keep an eye on him.

The England fans are chanting the manager's name.

Revived, Alan Ball shouts 'Come on!' to his team mates.

Wilson gives a thumbs-up to the referee.

Nineteen-year-old PC Don Childs has been a policeman for only two months and this is his very first football match. He's finding the atmosphere, the tension and the noise of the crowd overwhelming. He is part of a squad of men stationed around the edge of the greyhound track to prevent a pitch invasion.

At his palace in the cathedral close, the Right Reverend Robert

Mortimer, the bishop of Exeter, is sitting in front of his television, engrossed in the final. In the cathedral there is a congregation waiting for him to lead a confirmation service. Bishop Robert has forgotten all about it.

5.02pm

England will kick off the final period of extra time, playing right to left.

Bobby Moore taps the ball to Roger Hunt, who attempts a one-man assault on the German midfield, before he is tackled by Franz Beckenbauer.

Overath.

Held.

Jack Charlton kicks it out of touch.

Held throws it back to Emmerich, who sends a weak pass back.

George Cohen pounces and kicks the ball upfield.

Schnellinger.

Overath.

Emmerich – in the England penalty area.

Again, Cohen is there. Elbows out.

Hurst.

Ball.

Hunt on the halfway line.

Ball again running in front of Bobby Charlton. A cheeky back-heel to Wilson. He's enjoying himself.

Wilson's cross is intercepted by Wolfgang Weber and cleared by Beckenbauer.

5.04pm

At Cathy and Joe Matos' wedding reception at her parents' small house in Barnet, no one is listening to the speeches or interested in the catering – everyone is watching the football. Cathy's mother Ethel is mortified. She doesn't even like or trust her new son-in-law. Cathy shares her mother's misgivings about Joe.

Once the game is over they are jumping into his Alfa Romeo and driving south to an old-fashioned pub in Crawley that Cathy has booked for their wedding night.

Franz Beckenbauer is walking back from midfield – earlier he would have sprinted. West German shots on goal are accurate, but lack pace, and their passing is becoming erratic.

The English have the greater stamina. Those punishing hours in Stalag Lilleshall are paying off.

5.05pm

Throw-in to England on the far side, about halfway into the West German half. Overath can't wait for the ball boy to collect it – he picks it up and chucks it towards George Cohen.

Stiles' speedy dribble forward is stopped by the defence. The ball falls to Geoff Hurst who hits a weak shot that doesn't trouble Tilkowski for a moment.

As Tilkowski throws it towards midfield, Hurst limps a little and bends over to catch his breath. Roger Hunt is also limping and his socks are now around his ankles.

Tofik Bakhramov flags that Siggi Held is offside. Held is indignant – his anger fuelled by the linesman's earlier goal decision.

> **Without doubt it was my most difficult and important task of the whole ten months we spent in the Far East. I fear that I would have been lynched had I lost the commentary.**
>
> *Philip Hall*

5.05pm/00.05am Borneo Time

In a jungle clearing in north-east Borneo, 21-year-old Corporal Philip Hall is in his radio shack waiting for the BBC's World Cup coverage to resume. He is not alone. Behind him are about 40 other men from B Company of 1st Battalion the Royal Hampshire Regiment, many of whom are chain-smoking, and all of whom are sweating in the jungle heat.

Corporal Hall is responsible for communications for the regiment and he is trying to keep the HF radio tuned to the BBC World Service. The radio has no speakers, only headphones with the volume turned up as high as possible. It's hard for the men at the rear of the shack to hear what's going on.

The radio shack has relayed all the games broadcast by the BBC, and Corporal Hall has also kept jungle patrols updated with scores throughout the tournament, using codewords such as 'Team A-1 Team B-2'. He's well aware that military radios should not be used for football updates.

The British army is in Borneo, together with Australian and New Zealand troops, to defend the newly formed Federation of Malaysia from attacks by the army of President Sukarno of Indonesia.

In Exeter, the bishop's viewing is interrupted by the dean, the Very Reverend Marcus Knight, who informs him that there is a confirmation service that he needs to attend. The dean promises to keep him informed of the score.

After an inaccurate cross from Overath to Haller on the right, their captain impatiently claps his hands. Ray Wilson passes the ball back to Gordon Banks and the England fans whistle their disapproval. They want a fourth goal.

'Move, you little bastard, keep moving!'

5.07pm

Bobby Charlton has the ball just outside his penalty area. He stops and looks to his right. His Manchester United team-mate is unmarked.

Stiles.

Ball.

Stiles glances up and sees the West German goal.

'Yes, near post, I'll go for that,' he thinks.

Suddenly all his strength leaves him. 'The sensation was of whoosh...' He slices the ball and it rolls off closer to the corner flag than the goal.

The English fans groan.

For a second, Stiles is terrified his bowels have emptied – and he's not wearing a jock strap or underwear. He's OK, but still has no strength.

'Move, you little bastard, keep moving!' Alan Ball yells at him as he sprints past. Stiles can only just manage a jog.

5.08pm

Geoff Hurst has a throw-in in the same spot as George Cohen five minutes ago.

Bobby Charlton passes to Alan Ball and points towards

Roger Hunt in midfield as he does so. Tackled by Haller, Ball still has the energy for an impressive dive. Haller is quick to apologise and help the Englishman up.

Every second is precious.

Bobby Charlton takes the free kick and taps it to Alan Ball, who, for the first time in the game, meekly passes it back. Charlton's cross is too high for Martin Peters.

Beckenbauer nabs it and advances.

Emmerich.

Held keeps the flow forward. He moves briefly to the left, then decides to shoot. Gordon Banks doesn't even move as the ball sails high over his goal and bounces across the dog track.

As a ball boy runs to retrieve it, all 22 players have a few welcome seconds to get their breath back.

Although the crowd are still singing 'When the Reds go marching in', there are very few banners and flags being waved around Wembley now. Some fans have been standing in the humid stadium for over four hours.

5.09pm

Jimmy Greaves, watching by the England bench, feels totally exhausted as if he's been playing himself.

Beckenbauer in midfield passes to the other German involved in almost every attack – Siggi Held. Held is 30 yards out. He sees off Alan Ball and Bobby Charlton and tries a shot that bounces off Big Jack. Held controls it – but with his hand. 'Handball!' The English defence freeze and put their arms up. But Held keeps going and tries a second shot that forces Gordon Banks to dive. However, Gottfried Dienst has blown his whistle.

'A close shave' in the words of Hugh Johns.

5.11pm

In the royal box, the Queen keeps asking Sir Stanley Rous, 'How much longer to go?'

Tilkowski has the ball. His penalty area is full of divots and his six-yard box is more mud than grass. The England half looks as if it's from a different pitch.

Beckenbauer.

Schulz.

Jack Charlton slides to intercept the German's pass.

Emmerich.

Charlton is still on the grass.

Tireless Siggi Held is now by the far corner flag. Dienst ignores English appeals for offside.

Held hits an effortless cross.

His captain runs into the penalty area and jumps – but Ray Wilson just gets there first. Seeler and Wilson clash heads.

Without Wilson's quick thinking that could have been the equaliser. Wilson looks groggy, but he slowly gets to his feet. His mistake that resulted in the first goal is long forgotten.

'That pass was the perfect way to remember Bob.'

5.13pm

At Exeter Cathedral, the confirmation service is finally underway.

Bobby Moore trots forward from midfield with the ball.

Roger Hunt is to his left. Despite his half-time telling-off from Alf Ramsey, Hunt is enjoying himself more than any other game in the tournament; he's finding more space because the Germans are tiring.

Moore passes to him. Höttges, in two minds, is slow to come out and challenge him. Twenty yards out, Hunt fires off his most powerful shot of the day. It swerves around the far post.

A loud groan from the England fans eases the tension.

Right now, ITV should be starting a repeat of the series *The Adventures of Robin Hood*.

5.15pm

Eighteen-year-old Mike Williamson has a fantastic view of the game; his seat is close to the pitch and the England goal. He's a drummer in a pop band called Gulliver's People and he bought his ticket for the final for a fiver from their keyboard player who didn't want to go. Half an hour ago, Mike was in tears when the West Germans equalised – but now he's more optimistic of victory.

Mike can see about five people clearly getting ready to run onto the pitch when the final whistle goes.

'The Germans throwing every man into the England box now, trying to find just this one more goal that will force a replay...' says Hugh Johns.

The crowd starts whistling for full time.

5.16pm

Centre-back Willi Schulz picks up a ball from Lothar Emmerich and sends a cross to England's far post. Helmut Haller neatly avoids Jack Charlton and heads it towards Seeler, who's running along the six-yard line. The ball is too fast. Seeler can't shoot, but he can play it back to Schulz, whose second cross is headed away by George Cohen.

The whistles are even louder than before. Could the Germans equalise in the final minute once more?

Siggi Held wastes no time with the corner from the far side. He bangs in a cross. Gordon Banks punches it away, almost angrily.

Referee Dienst looks at his watch. One minute to go.

5.17pm

Horst-Dieter Höttges has the ball just inside the England half. He sends it to Wolfgang Weber, who crosses, then slips.
　　Bobby Moore, in the penalty box, coolly chests it down.
　　He passes the ball to Roger Hunt and then calls for it back. Hunt obliges.
　　'Kick the f*****g thing out of the ground!' Jack Charlton shouts at Moore. 'No footballer had ever been less susceptible to such a classic request from the old, hard school of defence,' his brother Bobby said later.

Martin Peters glances across at the referee, who is looking at his watch. He puts his whistle in his mouth.

In the stands, Mike Williamson is also watching Dienst with the whistle. He's heading for the pitch. With about five other fans, he begins climbing over the low concrete wall that surrounds the dog track. At the other end, three young men have the same idea.

Gottfried Dienst waves 'play on'.

Thousands in the crowd are whistling.

Bobby Moore's legs are weary. But he has the ball.

'Get rid of it!' Gordon Banks shouts.

Moore pauses. He looks up. Most of the Germans are in the England half. He kicks a spectacular, long, left-footed shot downfield to Geoff Hurst who's ten yards inside the West German half.

Jimmy Armfield will never forgot that moment. 'That pass was the perfect way to remember Bob.'

'I will never be able to play this bloody game, because Bob has just done something that is unheard of,' thinks Jack Charlton.

The exhausted Hurst can sense that Wolfgang Overath is chasing him.

Judith Hurst grips Tina Moore's arm.

Mike Williamson and the others have made it onto the grass. Six policemen are chasing them. At the West German end, three young men in suits run across the greyhound track.

'And here comes Geoff Hurst, he's got...' starts Kenneth Wolstenholme.

As he runs, Hurst can hear Alan Ball shouting to him to his right. 'Here! Square! Give it!'

'Some people are on the pitch – they think it's all over...' Kenneth Wolstenholme is almost shouting.

Wolfgang Overath veers slightly towards Alan Ball.

The ball bounces on a divot.

Geoff Hurst hits the ball as hard as he can.

'The feel, the sound of leather on leather were exactly right...'

The ball rockets into the top corner of the net.

'...it is now!'

'It's four!'

Wembley erupts.

> **England 4 West Germany 2**

> **I do wish he would let his hair down occasionally and throw his cap in the air. It would do him a power of good.**
>
> **Victoria Ramsey**

> **It looked like copulation. I don't know what Nobby was doing, but I didn't enjoy it very much, after all we were only 50 yards from the Queen...**
>
> *George Cohen*

On the edge of the dog track, PC Don Childs throws his helmet into the air with delight. Unfortunately, the helmet flies backwards and into the crowd – he looks desperately to see where it landed.

On the grass, Mike Williamson is grabbed by a number of policemen.

'Now we don't want anyone being naughty and running on the pitch,' one of them says as they hold him by his arms and legs. And they gently lower him back into the crowd.

Bill Oddie, five foot three inches in height, can't see what's going on as everyone in front of him is standing up. Eric Idle explains that Geoff Hurst has scored.

Referee Gottfried Dienst blows his whistle for full time, but as Karl-Heinz Schnellinger is still running with the ball, both Alf Ramsey and Jimmy Greaves think the game is still in progress.

'Sit down, Harold!' Alf snaps at trainer Harold Shepherdson.

Behind Alf, Jimmy Armfield, in his lucky red jumper, is sure it's over and puts his arms on Alf's shoulders and shouts: 'We've done it!'

The German players follow Gottfried Dienst into the centre circle; Franz Beckenbauer is remonstrating with him. Helmut

Schön walks on to calm them down and grabs the hands of Beckenbauer and Wolfgang Weber.

Ignoring the players, Dienst and Bakhramov shake hands. A few feet away, Siggi Held claps them sarcastically.

Uwe Seeler and Dienst shake hands, and Dienst touches the German captain's cheek in commiseration. Seeler then shakes hands with Bakhramov.

Beside the royal box, Bob Geggie hands the Jules Rimet trophy to an FA official.

Jack Charlton sinks to his knees, looks up to the blue sky, bows his head and covers his face with his hands. He says a prayer of thanks.

Nobby Stiles jumps on top of George Cohen and they fall on the ground. 'George, we won the World Cup!'

'What the bloody hell do you think you're doing? It's like being kissed by a piece of liver!'

The German players are near to collapse. 'I never remember being so exhausted as I was at the finish that afternoon,' said Franz Beckenbauer.

Alan Ball still has the energy to do cartwheels across the Wembley turf.

A line of caped Bobbies now ring the pitch.

Ken Ashman has been watching the game from the stands with four German work colleagues.

A Cockney leans over and very slowly says to him, 'We... think... you... played... very... well.'

Ken doesn't want to embarrass the man and so replies politely, '*Danke schön.*'

In the Tunisian café, a local man turns the television off in disgust. There is silence. The Thomas and Smith families are overjoyed but dare not speak. The West German tourists are distraught and start walking out of the café and onto their coach.

As the coach disappears in a cloud of dust, the bar owner turns on the television – not to see the celebrations, but the presentation of the trophy.

'We want to see your queen, we respect. We respect,' he explains.

In Ibiza, John Cleese's performance as an ultra-sporting English upper-class twit is drawing to an end. Smiling apologetically and with much shrugging of shoulders, he leaves the miserable German tourists behind and heads for his villa to meet up with the sunbathing Graham Chapman.

Alf Ramsey is slowly getting up from the bench.

'It was because I did not want to forget that I stayed as I did. My pleasure was to see what was happening.' As Bobby Charlton said later, 'He had done what he was good at, all the planning and preparation, but he wasn't ready for the winning bit.'

Alan Ball looks across at Jack Charlton on his knees, Bobby Charlton crying and Ray Wilson almost in tears and thinks, 'What's going on here?' He can't comprehend why they are so emotional. 'I just thought we could do this every four years,' he said later.

Jack Charlton looks up and Bobby is standing next to him. Jack gives him a hug and lifts him into the air.

'Well, what about that, kiddo?' Jack says.

'What's there to win now?' Bobby replies.

'We'll have to win it again!' laughs Jack.

It's the first time Bobby's cried over a football match. 'The sound of the public just got to me. It was a very emotional thing. Afterwards I thought I was a wee bit unprofessional crying – but now I don't see any other way I could have handled myself. It was a lovely, fantastic moment.'

In San Bernardino, California, DJ John Ravenscroft is also crying. His American friends' bafflement grows. 'Grown men did not cry at all, let alone at the result of a football match,' he said later.

George Cohen is standing by himself on the Wembley pitch, taking it all in. 'Thank God for that: it's the end of all football at least for a couple of weeks.'

Gordon Banks shakes Hans Tilkowski's hand. The German is in tears.

Jimmy Greaves walks onto the Wembley turf looking impassive, but then finds Nobby Stiles and hugs him. Stiles ruffles his hair. 'Even in this moment of triumph and great happiness, deep down I felt my sadness. I had missed out on the match of a lifetime and it hurt,' Greaves admitted.

Jack Charlton puts his arm around Jimmy Greaves. 'He'd been a part, and now he wasn't.'

Bobby Charlton watches Jimmy Armfield, Ron Flowers and the other members of the squad come onto the pitch to congratulate the team and feels deeply sorry for them all.

In the middle of the Indian Ocean, down in the engine room of the *Glengyle*, Jack and Bobby's younger brother Gordon is wondering if England have been victorious. The captain comes running down the companionway and above the noise of the engine shouts, 'We've won! We've won!'

> *Cissie Charlton claimed that 'a new sound filled the warm air of the Oriental ocean that night... one by one British ships began to sound their sirens until all were chorusing their congratulations'.*

No one is swapping shirts. According to Jack Charlton, 'It wasn't the sort of shirt you would want to swap.'

As the Germans leave the pitch, Helmut Haller, who scored the first goal, jostles referee Gottfried Dienst for the match ball. Dienst lets him have it. Haller wants it as a souvenir and as a present for his son Jurgen's fifth birthday. Although there is a tradition in English football that the scorer of a hat-trick keeps the ball, Geoff Hurst is too caught up in the excitement of winning the World Cup to be bothered.

5.20pm

The England players start to assemble at the bottom of the 39 steps that lead up to the royal box. These are steps that Bobby Moore knows well. He walked up them to collect the FA Cup in 1964 when West Ham beat Preston North End, and then a year later when they won the European Cup Winners' Cup, defeating 1860 Munich.

'Thank you. Thank you. Thank you.'

At the foot of the steps, Alf Ramsey shakes the hands of all his players as they file by. He hugs Bobby Moore.

'Well done,' he says to Alan Ball. 'You'll never play better in your life.'

As he leads his team up the steps, Moore feels 'misty and unreal'.

Spectators lean over to pat the players on the back.

The steps are made of brick and not the usual wood, which makes them difficult to walk on in studs.

When he reaches the top, Bobby Moore, always concerned that everything should be neat and clean, suddenly realises his hands are dirty with mud and sticky with orange juice and that he's about to shake the Queen's white-gloved hand. Moore wipes his palms on his back of his shorts, then the front of his shirt and then on the purple velvet drape covering the wall in front of the royal box. He bows and shakes the Queen's hand.

The Queen remembers that before the opening game against Uruguay she had pointed to a red, white and blue floral display and said to Bobby Moore, 'The right colours, I hope they bring you luck.'

'They were the right colours, after all,' she says and smiles as she gives the England captain the Jules Rimet trophy and his gold winner's medal.

Bobby Moore then shakes hands with Lord Harewood and Harold Wilson. Finally, he lifts the Jules Rimet trophy high in the air for the Wembley crowd to see.

They roar their appreciation.

'It's 12 inches high, it's solid gold, and it means England are the world champions!' exclaims Kenneth Wolstenholme.

As she watches her husband proudly holding the trophy, Tina Moore thinks about their secret battle with cancer.

Doss Moore has come in from the garden and is watching her son with the trophy. She is determined not to cry.

Geoff Hurst is next to collect his medal... then Bobby Charlton... Roger Hunt... Martin Peters... Jack Charlton (who thinks, 'Hell's bells – it's in a cardboard box!' then slips on the first step down)... Ray Wilson... Alan Ball... George Cohen... Nobby Stiles...

Kay Stiles, watching with the wives, wishes that she could grab a moment with her husband to tell him to put his teeth in. Reserve player Ian Callaghan still has them in his pocket.

...and last to shake the Queen's hand is Gordon Banks.

The Duke of Edinburgh smiles at them all as they walk past.

> *Jack Charlton has met the duke once before when on National Service with the Royal Horse Guards. One of his tasks was to replace the divots on the Windsor Great Park polo pitch after a match. Bunking off for a smoke in the bushes, Jack and a friend approached a man for a light. It was Prince Philip. The two embarrassed soldiers ran off as quickly as they could.*

As he looks at his medal, all Alan Ball can think about is the fact that three and a half years after being rejected by Wolves and Bolton, he has proved himself to his dad.

Down on the pitch, Alf Ramsey watches his players and applauds.

As Bobby Moore walks down the steps from the royal box a fan reaches out to try and touch the trophy. Bob Geggie flinches. He decides to follow the players out onto the pitch and make sure no one tries to grab it.

Fans are patting the victors' backs. Geoff Hurst loves the fact that the spectators are so close. 'I knew fans who had waited 40 years to get such a chance. Wembley gave it to you straight after the match. All that was part of the Wembley magic.'

The West Germans head for the steps to the royal box. A photographer captures Uwe Seeler leaving the pitch, head down, flanked by an FA official and a Wembley security guard. To Seeler's left, Helmut Schön is marching off the pitch, rolling up the sleeves of his tracksuit. Behind them all, Michael Hutton's Royal Marines look on impassively.

> *Uwe Seeler keeps a copy of the photograph in his basement. 'I would have thrown it away long ago, but an inner voice says "no". The image is a record of how brutal sport can be...'*

As Seeler climbs the steps his mind feels empty and he aches all over. Every step feels unusually high. Finally he reaches the top.

Seeler bows to the Queen and says 'Thank you' as he receives his silver runners-up medal. The Queen and Seeler have met before at an official function and he was impressed that she knew about his career at Hamburg.

Helmut Haller has the orange match ball under his arm as he collects his medal.

BBC1 should be showing a 20-minute Laurel and Hardy film from 1932 called *County Hospital*.

'If you strut around and look as if you think you belong, nobody's going to query.'

In a house in Finchley, north London, about five miles from Hendon Hall, 26-year-old Ian Lyons and his two friends Harry Klahr and Tony Hurst are leaping up and down and hugging each other.

'Why don't we go and welcome the team?' Harry Klahr says.

'Better than that, I've got my tape recorder. Let's go and interview them,' Ian replies, always up for an adventure. Ian has a portable quarter-inch recorder and even takes it abroad to make an audio record of his holidays.

Harry and Tony are dubious about whether they'd be allowed into Hendon Hall, but Ian is confident.

'A hotel is a public place; they can't stop us going in there. If you strut around and look as if you think you belong, nobody's going to query.'

They decide to take a chance.

5.22pm

Alf Ramsey refuses to be drawn into the celebrations. 'This is your day. You won the World Cup,' he says to Nobby Stiles and Bobby Moore as they hand him the trophy. Ramsey holds it only briefly.

> *Bobby Charlton said later that it was as if Ramsey was saying 'if at times he had given us hell, had made decisions we didn't like or perhaps agree with, it was really all for us'.*

Sunday Telegraph reporter David Miller watches Ramsey from the press box and is reminded of the time in 1963 when he had given the England manager a lift to Liverpool Street Station. Alf had said, 'It's not my team, you know, it's England's team.'

The players surround Alf Ramsey and are about to hoist him on their shoulders when the Royal Marines Band start to play the national anthem.

Finally the crowd take notice of Michael Hutton and his men performing in the centre of the pitch. Eighty thousand people sing the national anthem as loud as they can.

Close by, Hans Tilkowski, his runners-up medal in his hand, is still in tears and being consoled by Helmut Schön.

Bobby Moore kisses the trophy for the photographers. But they want something else – they want the players to lift their captain up on their shoulders, just as the West Ham team did when they won the FA Cup two years ago. So Geoff Hurst and Ray Wilson lift Moore up, and he raises the trophy with his right hand, putting his left on the back of Ray's neck.

Ray winces in pain. 'There's Geoff, six foot tall, me five foot seven, so I've got Bobby Moore on my shoulders and you can almost see me saying: "For Christ's sake!" That's the look on my face...'

The players are surrounded by television crews and about 30 photographers. 'It's worth only £3000, but it's the supreme prize in soccer,' says Hugh Johns.

Bobby Moore stays up on his team-mates' shoulders for just ten seconds, but it becomes the most famous image of the day.

In 1965, a journalist visited West Ham's training ground and asked manager Ron Greenwood about England's chances in the World Cup. Greenwood looked across the pitch at Bobby Moore.

'We're going to win and that man's the reason why. He can already see in his mind's eye a picture of himself holding up the World Cup and he's calculated what that will mean to him.'

As the photographers and television cameramen capture the scenes of celebration, few notice the man in the suit at the back of most of their shots. It's Bob Geggie keeping an eye on the trophy.

The England players start a lap of honour, taking it in turns to hold the trophy. The German fans are applauding.

In Clarence Grove in Liverpool, ten-year-old Carl Gillwood holds the cardboard Jules Rimet trophy triumphantly above his head, and runs screaming out of the house to join his seven football-mad friends who are also yelling fit to burst. From the bottom of the street, David Lowry hoofs his brand-new brown leather ball in Carl's direction. 'It was perfect for a volley against Mrs Makin's red stone wall,' Carl recalled. 'Although I was very short for my age, my legs were strong and I was known for kicking a ball very hard. Most of the balls that were ever lost over the roofs were normally down to me, but not today – because today I was Geoff Hurst. The ball connected with my deadly right foot so sweetly you could taste the laces.'

The ball leaves Carl's foot, 'like a cannonball at the battle of Waterloo' and straight through the sash window of Number 13, who are in the middle of having dinner.

The boys freeze.

Mr and Mrs Roberts rush outside – Mrs Roberts is holding the ball. She is angry not just because of the broken glass; after travelling through the window, the ball hit a vase containing her uncle Henry's ashes, which are now all over the floor. Mrs Roberts goes back into the house and puts a kitchen knife through David Lowry's new football and throws it back into the street.

The boys are shocked and upset, but also mystified – how come Mr and Mrs Roberts weren't watching the game?

At 73 Longfield Avenue in West End, Hampshire, the bus driver says to his conductor, 'I think we'd better get back on the road.'

Their green double-decker has been parked outside the Halletts' house for over half an hour. The two men thank George and Mark for the use of their television, and make their way to the bus.

At Stonehenge, the people listening to the radio are celebrating by dancing around the stones.

> *Nobby was a truly iconic, heroic figure. He deserved to be feted in song. [It] was a celebration of England's victory. The whole country would have joined in.*
>
> *Bill Oddie*

5.23pm

The England team's lap of honour continues. Nobby Stiles is enjoying his moment with the cup. He is dancing and skipping as he waves it in the air. Bobby Moore runs alongside him and tousles Stiles' hair affectionately. Jack Charlton looks back at Stiles dancing and feels as if he wants to laugh and cry at the same time.

For many people, Nobby Stiles dancing is one of the iconic

moments of the day. Up in the stands, Bill Oddie is particularly struck by his broad but toothless smile as he dances.

The day after the final, Bill Oddie will write a song called 'The Nobby Stiles March', an affectionate tribute to the England player, including the lines:

> *We love Nobby Stiles*
> *We love the way that Nobby smiles.*
> *Tough and ruthless*
> *Rough and toothless.*
> *Nobby Stiles.*

In the middle of the song, Bill Oddie did an impression of Alf Ramsey confessing that he loved Roger Hunt more than he loved Jimmy Greaves. 'The Nobby Stiles March' was to be released on the Polydor label, and Oddie was booked on numerous TV programmes, including an exclusive launch on the Eamonn Andrews Show.

However, Nobby's agent got to hear about it and took out an injunction to prevent the release of the single, out of concern that 'it held his client up to ridicule and undermined his dignity'. Bill Oddie later used the tune and some of the lyrics for a song in tribute to the radio DJ and singer Jimmy Young.

'The Nobby Stiles March' was the second of Bill Oddie's singles that was banned. The BBC had refused to play 'Nothing Better to Do', a song about the Mods and Rockers' weekend fights in Brighton, as it might 'incite people to violence'.

Of all the players, Roger Hunt is perhaps the least emotional. 'I wouldn't say that I felt more excited about winning than I did the previous year when I won the FA Cup with Liverpool.'

5.24pm

The England players complete their lap of honour.

> **The English team was exceptional and worthy of the title. We accepted the outcome the way good sportsmen should do.**
>
> *Uwe Seeler*

5.25pm/6.25pm German Time

In a bar in the small German town of Goch near the Dutch border, 28-year-old RAF accounts clerk Corporal Derek Darbyshire senses there's going to be trouble. The bar is full of British soldiers and other RAF personnel from the nearby base of RAF Laarbruch, as well as many locals. A small black and white television is on in the corner and a radio is broadcasting an English commentary. At the start of the game the atmosphere had been friendly, but as it progressed and as more drink was consumed, the locals have become increasingly irritated.

As the British celebrate their victory with songs and chants, a German declares loudly in English, 'The linesman was Russian and anti-German!'

A Glaswegian soldier shouts back, 'You couldn't beat us in two world wars, so why would you expect to beat us at football!'

A German takes a swing at the Scotsman and he fights back. Others immediately join in and beer starts flying across the room. Corporal Darbyshire stands well back.

5.26pm

On a rainy Manchester golf course, Denis Law and his friend John Hogan have finished their game and are walking away from the 18th hole. Law has lost the game and the £25 bet.

As they walk towards the clubhouse, the Scotsman is faced with a terrible sight. Standing outside are scores of golfers, waiting for Law to finish his game. They all have four fingers held aloft.

Jimmy Armfield and the rest of the England reserves are walking back to the dressing room to wait for the team.

Kenneth Wolstenholme is making his way to the Wembley interview room as quickly as possible. As he goes down the tunnel, he sees Cissie Charlton with a Wembley security man on either side of her. Cissie runs to him and hugs him.

'Kenneth, isn't it wonderful?' Cissie has tears in her eyes.

In Barking, Doss Moore has gone shopping.

5.28pm

PC Don Childs has given up looking for his brand-new 6³/₈" helmet among the crowd. He knows he will be in big trouble back at the station.

In an upstairs flat in Salisbury Road, Leyton, east London, 22-year-old Sandra Rayment is feeling uneasy. She has just enjoyed a thrilling couple of hours watching the final with her father while her mother pottered in the kitchen. But now that joyful feeling has gone.

On Wednesday, her beloved grandfather Jack, who lives

in the downstairs flat, was taken ill and admitted to nearby Whipps Cross Hospital. Jack's been a lifelong smoker and the doctors think he may be suffering from emphysema; on Friday they carried out an operation to ease his condition. Although the nurses reassured Sandra that the operation would help her grandfather, she has a nagging feeling that things aren't right.

Sandra's boyfriend John arrives from his home in Chingford. They plan to go to the hospital later this evening, so Sandra's father can give his father-in-law a shave – but Sandra decides she can't wait that long.

'Can we go up there now? I've got a funny feeling about Granddad.' John agrees to drive her the three miles to Whipps Cross.

Sandra says that, for the four years that her father was away fighting in North Africa, her granddad was her father. Her grandparents have always lived in the flat below. Jack used to have a barber's shop in east London, and he still has a great love of life. His favourite haunts are the Hackney Empire, Collins' Music Hall in Islington and Upton Park to watch his beloved West Ham.

Sandra knows that he would love to find out that England have won and that three West Ham players were the key to their success.

Sandra goes downstairs to her grandparents' flat.

'Nan, are you ready? Do you want to come up with us?' Sandra asks, keen to get going as soon as possible.

Her grandmother Dorothy says she'll come right away and the three of them get into John's Ford Anglia and speed down Salisbury Road.

'You've not done so bad yourself, today.'

5.30pm/6.30pm German Time

In the German town of Goch, the local police are running into the bar to break up the fighting between the locals and the British soldiers and RAF personnel. They start to chase everyone out into the street. There's beer all over the floor. Derek Darbyshire has managed to stay out of trouble; he collects some World Cup Willie beer mats as souvenirs.

Alan Ball finally finds his parents, who have made their way down to the side of the pitch.

'Dad, I want you to have this medal. Thanks for everything you've done for me – there's no way in the world I could have achieved this without you.'

'Thank you, son. That's very kind of you. I'd just like to say, you've not done so bad yourself, today.'

About 5.35pm

The England players are about to go down the tunnel to their dressing room. Bob Geggie isn't far behind.

Suddenly Bobby Moore throws the trophy into the air and catches it.

'You'll get me sacked!' Geggie shouts.

Bobby Moore grins at him.

'Hey, we've just won the World Cup!'

Nearby, one of PC Peter Weston's colleagues nudges him.

'Go on – get the trophy!'

The young constable has no choice – he has to switch trophies now. He walks down the tunnel after the players, opens the boot of the black Wolseley and takes the replica World Cup out of its box. He hides it under his tunic.

As Jack Charlton walks down the tunnel, a man appears alongside him.

'Jack, we need you to give us a urine sample.'

'Not again!' the-centre back exclaims – this would be the fifth time in the tournament.

5.36pm

In the dressing room, Alf Ramsey is having a go at Bobby Charlton about the goal chances he missed.

'What the bloody hell do you think you were doing out there? Shooting when you should have been looking round for other people. We should have had it sewn up!'

Bobby swallows hard and decides not to make a pointed comment about whether Alf had seen Beckenbauer achieve much in the game.

'It's bloody ridiculous. I don't feel anything. I don't, I really don't.' Sitting on a dressing-room bench, George Cohen is finding it all hard to take in.

Outside the dressing room, PC Peter Weston hesitates. He knows that if Jack Charlton is holding the World Cup and he asks him to hand it over, he's going to get a punch on the nose. There's only one way to find out who's got it. Holding the replica trophy with one hand, he opens the door with the other.

The England dressing room is crowded with players and a couple of film cameramen – there is plenty of singing and cheering.

No one takes any notice of the policeman at the door. PC Weston looks around and walks in. He spots the trophy. Nobby Stiles has it. He's sitting on a bench staring at it with a glazed look in his eyes. Weston trusts that a combination of his uniform, an air of authority and speed will do the trick. He pulls the replica out from under his tunic.

'Nobby, thanks very much – I'll have that – and you can have this.' He takes the Jules Rimet trophy from England's Number 4, and walks out before Stiles can say anything.

Now holding the real World Cup under his tunic, Weston walks back to the Wolseley and puts it in the box in the boot.

Peter Weston need not have worried about getting a punch from Jack Charlton. He is in a medical room close to the dressing room, drinking some water. The FIFA doctors are waiting for him to give a urine sample, but it's difficult as he's sweated so much during the game.

Ian Lyons and his friends Harry Klahr and Tony Hurst are walking up the drive to the Hendon Hall Hotel. Ian is carrying his tape recorder. There are a few fans about but not many. They walk into the reception area, which is almost deserted, apart from Hendon Hall staff. They try and look as inconspicuous as possible. They can hear the sound of a wedding reception in one of the nearby rooms.

Robert Mortimer, the bishop of Exeter, is back in front of his television in his palace. It's usual for him to join the confirmation families for tea after the service, but he's giving that a miss today.

5.38pm/9.08pm Iranian Time

In the privacy of the West German dressing room there is plenty of anger and swearing. Some players are just sitting quietly on the benches. Helmut Schön tries to encourage them. 'Men, remember a good second is better than a bad first."

BBC1's *Juke Box Jury* is supposed to be starting now, but has been postponed until the Wembley coverage is over. Waiting in their dressing rooms at Television Centre are the host David Jacobs, and the panelists, racing driver Jackie Stewart, DJ Dave Cash and actress Susan Hampshire.

Two of the records the panel are to review are the Beatles' 'Yellow Submarine' and Tom Jones' latest, 'This and That'.

The BBC World Service has been playing a recording of the 15 minutes of the game that its millions of listeners missed. On their terrace in Tehran, Bill, Gareth and Ian Denley finally discover that England are the world champions, almost half an hour after the final whistle.

Bobby Moore is drinking a bottle of beer with one hand and holding the replica Jules Rimet trophy with the other. In a moment he will fold his dirty kit into a neat pile.

Jack Charlton hands over his urine sample to the FIFA doctors. They have a present for him – a plastic red, white and blue England hat on which they've written 'For one who gave his best for England – the Jimmy Riddle Trophy'.

Nobby Stiles is searching the floor for one of his contact lenses.

About 5.40pm

Bobby Moore comes into the West German dressing room. 'Thanks for a great and unforgettable game,' he says.

They congratulate him on England's victory.

5.45pm

In the interview room at Wembley, Alf Ramsey, still in his blue tracksuit, is asked about his future. A journalist describes him as ' the hottest property in football'.

'Everyone seems interested, but there's another World Cup in Mexico in 1970. It would be interesting to be there,' Ramsey says calmly.

'Do you feel you have been misjudged, that there was any malice towards you?'

'I am not sure there was any malice. Yes, I have been furious with people, but if you carry these troubles on your shoulders, you'll get a stoop.'

On the Wembley pitch, Kenneth Wolstenholme is interviewing Bobby Moore for BBC Television.

'I feel a little ruffled, Ken. I don't really realise what's happened at the moment. We're so overjoyed and so delighted that I don't really think our thoughts are with us just yet, still.'

Kenneth asks whether the team will be celebrating with some drinks.

'As the evening wears on we'll have a few. We just had a drop out of the cup. It's not a very big cup so you don't get too much!'

Jimmy Greaves is on his way to the Hendon Hall Hotel to collect his bags and then head off home to Upminster – he has no intention of joining the celebrations at the banquet. He and his wife Irene and their four children are flying out of the country in the morning for a holiday.

> **If we'd been ten minutes later, it would have all been over.**
>
> **Sandra Rayment**

About 5.55pm

When Sandra Rayment walks into the ward at Whipps Cross Hospital with her boyfriend John and grandmother Dorothy, she can see that her grandfather is in a very bad way. There's an oxygen tank by Jack's bed and he looks grey and very weak.

She can't wait to tell him the news of the final. 'Granddad, England won! They won!' Sandra says.

'Oh, lovely...' Jack says weakly and manages a smile.

Then he puts his head back on the pillow, and closes his eyes. As he breathes, Sandra hears a hideous rattle in his chest. She rushes to find a nurse.

Dorothy is by her husband's side as the nurse pulls the curtains around the bed. Sandra and John wait on the other side of the curtains. After a short while, Dorothy comes out in tears. Sandra knows he's gone.

'Go and see your granddad' is all she can manage to say to Sandra.

'Nan, I don't really want to...'

But Sandra goes to see him one last time.

It's Helmut Schön's turn to face the press in the interview room.

'We worked out the English tactics and were right, because

their danger man Bobby Charlton was blotted out. England won and won well – and we are not annoyed.'

In Morecambe, Brian Bowker is back home after watching the final at his girlfriend's house. His mother Jane gets in after her day's work in the Littlewood's department store canteen.

'I hear England won. That's good news,' she says. 'I've got some more good news for you – you don't have to go into work tomorrow.'

'Really? Why?' Brian asks.

'You've been fired.'

'But I rang in and I explained – and the manageress was fine about it!'

'She was, but I wasn't. They weren't going to fire you – they fully understood you're passionate about football, that it's a big day and all the rest of it, but I think you broke your commitment and should pay the price. I persuaded them to fire you. There you are...' Brian's mother gives him his cards – the written verification of his sacking.

The joint highest scorer in the Scottish League (with 31 goals this season) is finishing off some gardening he began in the morning. Twenty-five-year-old Alex Ferguson, Dunfermline Athletic's star striker, has thoroughly enjoyed watching the final and is delighted that England won.

He looks up and sees his next-door neighbour walking down the street with a can of stout in his hand.

'Alex, have you heard the result? We've won the World Cup! And I'm off to celebrate.'

Ferguson is not impressed.

'Great, but don't invite me, not with just one can of stout...'

He resumes gardening.

Saturday 30th July 1966

6.00pm

Dave Corbett, with Pickles on the front seat of his Triumph, is driving through the streets of south London on his way to the Royal Garden Hotel in Kensington. His agent thinks it'll be a good opportunity for some photos with the England players – all publicity for them and for the film Pickles will appear in.

Along with thousands of others, Gordon Taylor is heading for Wembley Park Tube station. It's looking very unlikely that he'll be on time to meet his fiancée Catherine for the theatre.

Farmers Reg and Philip Hodgskiss are hurrying to their car, which is parked in a Wembley side street. German fans are coming up to them and patting them on the back and saying 'Congratulations!' Philip can't reply as he's lost his voice from shouting and cheering.

The coach carrying the Portuguese team is making slow progress down Wembley Way. The coach stops and one of the players opens a window and points to the England rosette a fan is wearing and then takes off his gold tie-pin; the two men swap souvenirs.

> Q: How did it feel coming off the pitch having scored a hat-trick?'
> A: I didn't know I had – I didn't know the final goal had counted...
>
> Geoff Hurst

About 6.05pm

A solitary figure is walking up the Wembley tunnel, over the greyhound track and onto the pitch. It's Geoff Hurst, and this time he's out of his red strip and in slacks and a shirt.

There are still a few fans in stadium – still singing. There is one vital thing Hurst needs to check – did he really get a hat-trick – did the last goal count? He looks up at the scoreboard. It reads 'England 4 Germany W 2'. He smiles with relief.

A white-coated member of the Wembley ground staff sees him. 'Great, Geoff! How does it feel?'

Hurst waves but doesn't reply.

The England players' wives are on a coach heading to the Royal Garden Hotel. Some of them are wearing rosettes that they bought from fans on the way out of the stadium.

6.15pm

The BBC's coverage of the 1966 World Cup final is drawing to an end. After over six hours of coverage, *Grandstand*'s closing credits are running.

6.20pm/7.20pm German Time

A motorcycle dispatch rider is on his way to London Airport with videotapes of the final destined for those countries in the Middle East which didn't show the game live.

In East Berlin, the Vaal family are sitting in a queue of cars waiting to pass through the checkpoint into No Man's Land and on into West Berlin. They are on their way home from a fortnight's holiday in Denmark. Major George Vaal of the British army is driving his wife Daphne and teenage sons Richard and Nigel.

Their car inches forward, and four Russian guards come out

of their hut by the checkpoint. As they move down the line they are dancing for joy, looking for British cars.

'You won! You won!' they shout at the Vaals, who realise for the first time that England have triumphed in the World Cup. The Russians dislike the West Germans and the English victory has made their day.

A green Second World War jeep is making its way through the Wembley streets. Hanging on the side is 21-year-old Colin Ryan, who is on his way to meet his brother Patrick at the Torch pub on Bridge Road near the stadium. Also in the jeep are three friends – driver and owner Ronnie Wolstenholme (no relation to the BBC commentator), Bobbie Cole and David Newell, plus their girlfriends. It is a tight squeeze. Patrick is a member of the England Supporters Club and so managed to get himself a ticket for the final. He agreed with Colin that if England won he and his friends should join him to celebrate at the Torch.

As they approach the pub, there are so many people milling on the pavement that Colin wonders how he will ever find his brother.

Ronnie parks around the corner and they force their way into the Torch, which is jammed with people drinking and singing. There, standing on a table, wearing an England hat and his Spurs strip is Patrick. Colin and the others try to get to the bar.

Sandra Rayment is leaving Whipps Cross Hospital with her grandmother Dorothy and boyfriend John. It is a lovely warm evening. Everyone they see is happy, buoyed up by England's success. 'It was like a carnival scene. But I just felt as if I was walking in a bubble... totally shocked.'

6.25pm

As the England coach passes Hendon Fire Station for the second time that day, the crews are outside waving, and their engines have sirens blaring and blue lights flashing.

> *I felt about ten feet tall. I was so proud to be English. When we finally left the hotel, what seemed like hours later, we were walking away and it felt like we were a foot off the ground, it was so elevating.*
>
> *Ian Lyons*

About 6.30pm

The England coach pulls up alongside the Hendon Hall Hotel. There are now hundreds of fans on the pavement and on the path leading to the front of the hotel, cheering and banging on the side of the coach. Extra policemen have been drafted in to control the fans.

Ian Lyons and his friends Harry and Tony are waiting beneath the tall portico entrance to the hotel. Harry and Tony have got cold feet but Ian, clutching his microphone and tape recorder, is feeling brazen. He turns to a policeman.

'Now, officer, you make sure none of those people interfere with our work.' Tony and Harry look on aghast. Although the policeman is fooled, a BBC cameraman behind them isn't. He tells them not to get in the way and spoil his shots. The three friends don't budge.

Escorted by the police, the smiling England players are led off the coach and into the courtyard one by one. An immaculate Bobby Moore in jumper and slacks is first. A reporter from ITN asks, 'How do you feel, Bobby?'

'Over the world, over the world...'

Ian Lyons starts recording his own commentary.

'Well done, Bobby... Here comes George Cohen... and all the team, they're all here... and Alf Ramsey...'

Bobby Charlton emerges, carrying his kit bag. A TV reporter spots him.

'How do you feel about things, Jackie?'

'Bobby.'

'Bobby – I'm sorry.'

'You don't have to ask me, really, do you, ay?'

Ian steps forward, holding his microphone out, hoping to capture what Charlton is saying.

'What did you think of the game itself?' says the reporter.

'Very, very hard and tough.'

Ian resumes his commentary: 'Here's George Eastham... Gordon Banks. Well done, Gordon!... Yes, yes, looking a bit tired, Jackie Charlton... Well done! Geoff Hurst, I think... no, Geoff Hurst now... Well done, Geoff!'

The bride and groom who celebrated their wedding at the hotel during the afternoon have been persuaded by some reporters to come out to greet the players. The bride, still in her wedding dress, is kissed by Geoff Hurst.

'Yes, all you team – give her a kiss,' Ian Lyons says. 'You can hear the applause of the crowd.'

People are patting Alan Ball on the back as he walks towards the entrance.

'How do you feel, Alan?' Ian asks, pointing his microphone at him.

'I thought we would win, but you don't know in football to the last whistle, do you?'

'It was a good game...'

'Oh, a fabulous game, fabulous game,' Alan says, and walks into the hotel.

Next to Ian, Tony bursts out laughing – he hadn't realised that Ian had been interviewing a player. 'That little kid? I thought he was the team mascot, or something!'

About 6.40pm

An exhausted Kenneth Wolstenholme is walking through the deserted car park at Wembley Stadium. There are empty bottles of champagne everywhere.

Somebody winds a car window down and calls him over. It's the secretary of the New Zealand FA, who invites Wolstenholme to join a party in his car and have a glass of champagne. He delays his drive home to Surrey for just one glass.

Inside the Hendon Hall Hotel, the banqueting manager Victor Bianchi is pouring a jeroboam of champagne for the squad and their manager. Bobby Moore gives the cork and half a crown to a small boy who has sneaked into the hotel with his grandfather.

Bobby Charlton is chatting to nine-year-old Gary Bradley and his father Geoffrey, whom he met outside the hotel at lunchtime, when they were asking for autographs. 'This is my friend Gary,' Bobby says, introducing him to the other players. Geoffrey has some champagne and Gary has a sip too, quickly followed by some fruit juice.

The players don't have long before they have to change into their FA-supplied Burton suits and get back on the coach for the banquet at the Royal Garden Hotel in Kensington.

With Pickles on a lead, David Corbett is making his way through the crowds in front of the Royal Garden Hotel. The roads were closed off, so Dave parked as close as he could and walked the rest of the way.

He spots his agent George Skinner in front of the main entrance.

'You should have driven up to the front, Dave!'

George Skinner shows his invitation to the doorman, and they walk over to the lifts.

Pickles cocks his leg and urinates against the lift door. Dave is mortified. A member of staff arrives with a cloth and reassuring words.

'That's all right, don't worry, sir.'

About 6.45pm

Ian Lyons is recording his final 'report' on his tape recorder.

'And as I walk away from the Hendon Hall Hotel with Anthony Hurst and Harry Klahr by my side, the wedding party is still going on, there are crowds outside the door, bursting to get in, and lots of people with England rosettes...'

Inside the hotel, the England squad are changing quickly into dark-grey suits and white shirts. Red carnations have been provided for their buttonholes.

7.00pm

It's visiting time at Royal Oldham Hospital. Anita Dunnington has been put in a room by herself as the wards are full up. She's decided on a name for her newborn son. Alice, her mother, arrives to see the baby, with her other daughter Barbara.

'What are you going to call him?' Alice asks.

'I thought Stuart David.'

'Stuart David? You can't call him that! You'll have to call him Geoffrey Stuart after Geoff Hurst. He scored his first goal at 20 past three – exactly when the baby was born.'

Anita doesn't say anything. 'In them days you did as your mother told you, you didn't argue like they do now...'

> **I'd bought a white upright piano. I hadn't written for a time. I'd been ill. I was living in a very 1960s-decorated house. It had orange walls and green furniture. My one-year-old daughter was crawling on the floor and I wrote the opening riff. I remember it vividly. I was wearing a polo-neck sweater.**
>
> **Ray Davies, the Kinks**

7.05pm

The song 'Sunny Afternoon' by the Kinks has been adopted as an unofficial World Cup song by the England supporters. The band had a hunch it would be a perfect song for the World Cup and so were keen to get it released in time. It worked. 'Sunny Afternoon' got to Number one in the charts on 7th July and stayed there for two weeks.

The hit has made the Kinks one of the biggest bands in Britain and this evening they are playing at the 'Bumper Beat BBQ' open-air concert in a field in the picturesque village of Pinhoe outside Exeter.

Fifteen-year-old Charles Lodge and his school friend Trevor Gosling are excited as they have tickets. They enjoy football, but music, fashion and girls are much more their thing. Almost exactly a year ago, Charles saw the Rolling Stones at the ABC in Exeter, which was a fantastic concert, and he's sure that seeing the Kinks on the day England won the World Cup will be equally memorable.

Clutching their six-shilling tickets, the boys are now arriving in Pinhoe after the 15-mile journey from their home town of Sidmouth. At one end of the field is the stage and at the other a licensed bar, hot dog stands and the 'Bumper Beat' barbeque. There will be four support acts tonight: the Variations, the Cordettes, the Codiaks and Trendsetters Ltd.

Charles and Trevor get themselves something to eat and soak up the atmosphere.

The Kinks should be on stage at 10pm. However, lead singer Ray Davies, his brother, lead guitarist Dave Davies, bassist John Dalton, and drummer Mick Avory are still in Ray's home in Fortis Green, north London, celebrating England's win. England's victory, Ray Davies said later, had made life so perfect, 'I wish that I had a machine gun, so that I could kill us all and it would stop there.'

A helicopter is standing by at London's South Bank Heliport to fly them to Pinhoe.

It has been a mixed year for the band. They've had success with both 'Sunny Afternoon' and 'Dedicated Follower of Fashion', which reached Number four in March. But that same month Ray had a breakdown. At one point he ran six miles from Fortis Green to Denmark Street in Soho to punch his publicist. The band toured France and Belgium with a friend taking Ray's place, hoping the audiences wouldn't notice.

In April, Ray slowly recovered, and started writing again.

Anita Dunnington's husband Alan arrives at the maternity ward with his friend Malcolm Taylor. Their eyes are bloodshot and Anita can smell drink on their breath.

'Oh – isn't he ugly!' says Malcolm.

'All babies look ugly when they're born,' Anita retorts. 'Me mum wants me to call him Geoffrey after Geoff Hurst...'

'That's fantastic!' Alan says; as a huge football fan he thinks it's a perfect way to mark the day.

The coach carrying the Soviet squad pulls up in front of the Royal Garden Hotel. The door opens and their most famous player, goalkeeper Lev Yashin, holds aloft a plastic World Cup football as he leads the team off the coach.

On Thursday at Wembley, Portugal beat the Soviet Union 2-1 to finish third. It was Lev Yashin's last international match in England and the Wembley crowd gave him a standing ovation – even the referee applauded him off the field.

There are good-natured boos for the prime minister, Harold Wilson, and chancellor of the exchequer, Jim Callaghan, as they arrive from Downing Street.

Cissie and Bob Charlton are waiting outside the Royal Garden Hotel for the England coach to arrive.

Bobby Charlton was uneasy about the fact that his mother liked the limelight. 'I had a tendency to hold back, almost to seek the shadows.' He never forgot the embarrassment when as a schoolboy player his mother insisted he give a fan an autograph, even though he didn't want to.

The England coach is making slow progress through the streets of London, even though it has a motorcycle escort, because there are so many people spilling off the pavements to see them and the numbers are increasing the closer they get to Kensington. As they pass one pub, about 40 customers outside raise their glasses to the victorious team. A girl in a bright-red mini-skirt dances on top of a car. It seems to Bobby Charlton that there is a face in every house window. He says to Ray Wilson sitting next to him, 'What would we have done if we had lost?'

The driver slows the coach – there is a man in the middle of the road waving his arms in the air. He runs alongside and shouts through a window, 'I love you all! I love you all!'

Alf Ramsey later described the journey to the Royal Garden Hotel as something he would never forget. 'That meant as much to me as winning the match, the fact that our team had given so much happiness.'

7.25pm

The England coach finally arrives at the Royal Garden Hotel. The vast crowd are chanting 'Eng-land! Eng-land!' Many of them have come straight from Wembley.

A hotel doorman stands on each side of the coach steps as the players alight. Bobby Moore is first off and he walks round the side of the coach to wave to the crowd.

There's not a day that goes by when I don't think back to what it felt like to lift the World Cup.

Jack Charlton

7.27pm

The entire England squad is being led onto a long balcony overlooking Kensington High Street. The crowd yell enthusiastically as the players emerge. People break through the barrier of police who are lining the pavement and almost completely block the street.

Bobby Charlton looks down at the crowd and then at Alf Ramsey. He sees him smile genuinely for the first time; he thinks he looks like a grateful little boy rather than a world-weary manager.

The crowds are chanting 'Ram-sey! Ramsey!'

Guests in hotel rooms above throw down torn-up paper in a mock tickertape celebration.

The players pull their red carnations from their buttonholes and throw them into the crowd. Then they pass the cup along the line right to left and the crowd cheer as each time it's thrust into the air.

Dave Corbett and Pickles have followed the England players onto the balcony. Bobby Moore spots Pickles and calls Dave over. The England captain picks the dog up and lifts him into the air. The crowd below clap and cheer, loving the fact that, moments after lifting the Jules Rimet trophy, Moore is holding the dog that found it. Dave can see that Pickles, as usual, is loving the attention.

The real World Cup is, of course, in the boot of PC Peter Weston's police car, parked nearby. He is watching the balcony celebrations from the street, relieved that the tough part of his job is over.

He wonders if the England players realise that the trophy they are passing around isn't the real thing and if Nobby Stiles said anything to them.

Soon PC Peter Weston and his colleagues will drive the short

distance to the FA's offices in Lancaster Gate and hand the trophy
over. Meanwhile, he enjoys the euphoria of the moment.

**The wives were not happy people, I'll tell you that! I bet
their husbands took a whacking that night!**

Dave Corbett

7.30pm

In a room in the basement of the Royal Garden Hotel, a buffet
has been laid out. In the room is Dave Corbett and Pickles,
their agent George Skinner and all the England wives and girlfriends dressed in their best outfits.

The wives are not happy and are saying to Dave, 'There's
people up there with nothing to do with football – and we're
down here with a little buffet!'

Meeting and stroking Pickles is little consolation.

About 7.40pm

In a reception room in the Royal Garden Hotel to which the
press has been invited, Harold Wilson is chatting to Bobby and
Jack Charlton's mother Cissie.

'I wish you'd had more children when the match was in the
balance!' the prime minister says.

'So do I – I could have done with eleven!' Cissie laughs.

Wilson says to the watching reporters, 'I said before the game
it would be 2-1 and I was only a minute out!'

A reporter asks Bobby Moore where the match ball is.

'One of the Germans nicked it,' he replies.

'It's in our bus,' a German player whispers to the reporter.

'Where's your friend?' Alf Ramsey asks Bobby Moore, referring to Jimmy Greaves.

Moore reassures him that Jimmy isn't bitter.

'It's just he'd rather be away from it all.'

> **As we sat at our tables everyone in our team was disappointed that we had lost – due to a dubious decision. But it was over. We accepted it as it was.**
>
> **Siggi Held**

8.00pm

In the Royal Garden Hotel's banqueting hall, the official dinner for all the players and officials of the four semi-finalists, FIFA and FA dignitaries and the World Cup organising committee is about to begin.

They are being served melon frappé.

The West German team has received a telegram from the chancellor, Dr Ludwig Erhard, who had watched the final from his holiday bungalow in Bavaria. He told them that he applauds their efforts in a 'great game' and awards them the Silver Laurel – the highest award he can give for achievement in sport.

They are ignoring Dienst and Bakhramov. They still resent their decision about England's third goal. Uwe Seeler wrote later: 'I still maintain that Dienst was a coward. The ball could not have been behind the goal line, purely on the basis of physical laws. Because then Wolfgang Weber would not have been able to propel it with a header to the corner.'

A bell rings in the maternity ward at Royal Oldham Hospital. Visiting time is over.

Alan says goodbye to his baby son and to Anita.

'I'm going back out with Malcolm to wet the baby's head...' he says.

'You're so drunk it looks like you've already drowned him before you got here,' Anita thinks.

The head groundsman at Wembley, Percy Young, and his staff are leaving the stadium. For the past two hours they've been spreading fresh seed and applying new turf to heal the scars on the pitch, which has endured nine matches in the past month.

8.15pm

The players' wives have been escorted upstairs to the hotel restaurant, the Chophouse. They are seated at long tables decorated with the flags of the 16 countries that have taken part in the tournament. On the wall is a screen showing the banquet downstairs on closed-circuit television.

The women's mood has not been improved by the gift they've each received from the FA – a pair of scissors.

Nobby Stiles is furious that his wife Kay isn't allowed to the banquet. She gave birth while he was at Lilleshall for the pre-tournament training and he just about accepted it was impossible for him to leave to see his new baby, but it disgusts him that Kay is excluded from the party now.

> George Cohen said later, 'Our wives were upstairs in a burger bar, which is just about as bad manners as you could get. We'd been away from our wives for ages, and even Nobby Stiles can look attractive after six and a half weeks.'

The secretary of the FA, Denis Follows, stands up and introduces Alf Ramsey as 'a great man'.

Alf stands up, waits for the applause to die down and says, 'There are no great men – only men.'

Crowds have started to gather in Trafalgar Square and some, draped in flags, are dancing in the fountains. Many of the fans who've made their way to central London are discovering that if they go into a pub and show the barman a match ticket or a match programme, they get free beer.

8.30pm

At the Chequers pub in Wembley, the police have been called as the fans have been dancing so energetically that the landlord is worried the floor is about to give way, and he can't get them to stop.

Along the road, Colin and Patrick Ryan have been celebrating with their friends in the Torch pub. Now they and seven others are squeezed into Ronnie Wolstenholme's jeep and are slowly heading to Trafalgar Square.

All of them, including Ronnie, are a little worse for wear. At their feet and on their laps are large cans of Watney's Party Seven beer.

9.00pm

At Earls Court, the Royal Tournament is drawing to a close. Field Marshal Montgomery of Alamein is standing up, taking the salute as the Bands and Bugles of the Light Infantry Brigade march past.

Graham and Sally Saunders and their friends are only about 20 feet away from Monty. England's victory has given the evening a special magic.

Suddenly, the bands start playing their version of the Lonnie Donegan song 'World Cup Willie' and the audience stand up and burst into spontaneous applause.

Father and son Reg and Philip Hodgskiss arrive at their Staffordshire farm. Philip still has no voice after shouting so much at Wembley.

Their cows should have been milked two hours ago. It's still light, and walking into the field, they can see that the cows are looking surprisingly content. Reg and Philip soon discover why – the milking parlour door is open. The cows have broken into the parlour and eaten all the feed.

9.15pm

Colin and Patrick Ryan and their friends in Ronnie Wolstenholme's jeep are stuck on the Edgware Road. Most of the roads into the West End are lined with slow-moving cars honking their horns in celebration. It's been slow progress in the jeep through Hendon and Cricklewood Broadway, but no one seems too bothered.

Police from Paddington Green Police Station are busy directing traffic on the Edgware Road as best they can. Ronnie drives slowly past a couple of officers standing in the middle of the road.

'Any chance of a drink?' the policemen ask. Colin hands them a can of Party Seven.

Sir Stanley Rous hands over a cheque for £1000 to Eusébio for scoring nine goals – the highest of any player in the competition.

The Russian goalkeeper Lev Yashin receives an award as the tournament's best goalkeeper. All the England players turn to look at Gordon Banks – who is stunned. 'I found it hard to accept, as they hadn't even reached the final.'

The crowd outside the Royal Garden Hotel are singing 'You'll Never Walk Alone' and 'God Save Our Gracious Team'. A policeman tries to disperse them with a megaphone announcement that the players won't be leaving the hotel until after midnight (they are in fact all staying the night there). The crowd ignore him and carrying on singing.

The Goat, the pub opposite the hotel, is providing a non-stop supply of drinks.

9.30pm

In the banqueting room, the celebratory meal is almost over. The players and officials have enjoyed *entrecôte sauté marchand de vin* followed by a *bombe glacée* World Cup for dessert.

The England players are bored with the speeches and the formality. Geoff Hurst exchanges some nods with the German players seated at a nearby table. Bobby and Tina Moore plan to go to the Playboy Club and Bobby has invited the other players. 'There's something about that that might just attract me,' Jimmy Armfield says.

In Crawley, newly-weds Joe and Cathy Matos are being shown their room in the pub. They are staying not in a wooden beamed suite as she'd hoped but in a modern annexe at the back. This is not a good start to their honeymoon.

About 9.45pm

The West German squad is leaving the Royal Garden Hotel.

Helmut Haller is carrying the match ball signed by about 30 players, including his captain Uwe Seeler, Bobby Moore and Portugal's Eusébio.

Before he leaves, Uwe Seeler, feeling more conciliatory, apologises to linesman Tofik Bakhramov for the behaviour of some of his players after England's disputed goal.

10.00pm

At the 'Bumper Beat BBQ' open-air concert at Pinhoe outside Exeter, the support acts have stretched out their sets for as long as they can. But there's still no sign of the Kinks, whose helicopter should have landed in a field close by two hours ago.

Charles Lodge and Trevor Gosling and the rest of the 2000-strong crowd are getting impatient. Word has got around that the power will be cut at midnight, so the Kinks haven't got long. There's been an announcement on stage apologising for the delay, together with a reassurance that the Kinks are on their way. The barbeque and licensed bar are doing a roaring trade.

Graham and Sally Saunders and their friends Alan and Sandra Morris have finished a meal in a Golden Egg restaurant near Earls Court and are making their way towards their car. The roads are solid with traffic – people are sitting half in and half out of their cars and banging on the roofs in celebration. The four friends decide to delay their trip home to Birmingham and join in the fun.

> **They looked like a team of models.**
>
> **Hilary McMahon**

10.15pm

Eric McMahon, businessman and former mayor of Wrexham, had always wanted to have sons so he could teach them to play football. Instead, he and his wife Phyllis had three girls – 21-year-old Hilary, Valerie, 19, and Janet, 16. Tonight they are staying at the Cumberland Hotel in the West End. They'd been travelling this afternoon so missed the final, and Eric insisted they watch the highlights of the game on *Match of the Day*. None of the hotel rooms have a television, so the family are filing into the television lounge and taking their seats on gilded chairs usually used by the hotel for wedding receptions.

The girls don't mind watching the final; their father is a director at Wrexham Town, so they've spent many a Saturday afternoon in the directors' box at the Racecourse Ground. Hilary in particular is a fan of the game. Over the years, she's met many star players, including Bobby Charlton: 'a gentleman', Jack Charlton: 'a yob', and managers such as Matt Busby of Manchester United and Brian Clough of Hartlepool: 'He mesmerized every lady in the room with his brilliant shining eyes.'

In the Chophouse a few floors above the official banquet, a *Sunday Mirror* reporter has brought first editions of tomorrow's paper for the players' wives. The headline reads 'GOLDEN GLORY!' A *Sunday Mirror* photographer gets a shot of them reading the paper seated either side of a long table.

At the Royal Garden Hotel, the secretary of state for economic affairs, George Brown, is dancing on a table. He is a lifelong West Ham fan and is singing their anthem 'I'm Forever Blowing Bubbles'. Earlier, when he was more sober, Brown had told reporters, 'It was a good job Ramsey picked three West Ham men!'

Brown is a notorious drinker, and his behaviour is often erratic. In April 1965, when his official car broke down, he stopped a passing Mini and demanded to be driven to London for an important meeting. On arriving at Westminster, Brown dashed into his office, leaving a crucial economic planning document on the back seat. It was the only copy. Fortunately for the minister, the young Mini driver returned the document a few hours later.

10.20pm

On BBC1 David Coleman is introducing a special edition of *Match of the Day* showing highlights of the World Cup final.

A cake shaped and decorated like a football pitch is presented to the England team by two chefs from the Royal Garden Hotel kitchen. It even has an orange football in the middle. Bobby Moore cuts the cake along the halfway line.

Lord Harewood, president of the FA, says to the players, knowing Harold Wilson's love of publicity, 'The cake has been prepared to remind you of Wembley. After you have cut it would you mind going out again to the crowd? To lend you a little moral support the prime minister's prepared to take you there...'

Alf Ramsey picks up the cup rather nervously but Harold Wilson takes him by the arm and says, 'It's only once in a lifetime, you know.'

By now the squad have been reunited with their wives. The prime minister and Alf Ramsey hold the trophy with both hands and they all walk out onto the balcony once more, and wave to the crowd still filling Kensington High Street.

10.22pm

In the Cumberland Hotel television lounge, the McMahon family are settling into *Match of the Day*. Hilary becomes aware of some movement behind her and turns round. A group of young men arrive silently, immaculately dressed in powder-blue suits, with perfect hair and pink faces, 'as if they'd just been washed', Hilary thinks.

Her father turns round too.

'That's the West German team!' he whispers.

'Oh, gosh!' Hilary says to herself.

About 10.50pm

The England squad haven't stayed up this late for two months. They are keen to get on and have some fun after the evening's formalities. Bobby Moore has a word with Alf Ramsey. That does the trick.

'Thank you for everything, gentlemen, now off you go and have a good time. Most certainly, you deserve it,' he says.

'See you soon, Alf,' says Geoff Hurst.

'Perhaps, Geoffrey, perhaps,' Ramsey replies. Hurst reckons he's trying to keep his match-winner's feet on the ground.

Jimmy Greaves is getting drunk at home in Upminster.

About 10.55pm

In the Cumberland Hotel television lounge, the McMahon family have just seen Martin Peters score to put England in the lead for the first time. There is some polite clapping from the English guests. The West German squad sits in silence.

11.00pm

At the Talk of the Town theatre in the West End, American singer Johnny Mathis takes to the stage to much applause. Dressed in a slim dark suit, the first of three outfits he'll wear in his hour-long set, he launches his late-night cabaret with the accidentally appropriate 'On a Wonderful Day Like Today': 'On an evening like this, I could kiss everybody...'

In the audience are Gordon Taylor of Bolton Wanderers and his fiancée Catherine. As he feared, he didn't get back from Wembley in time for the musical *The Owl and the Pussycat* at the Criterion Theatre. But Gordon and Catherine are delighted that they are still getting to see one of their favourite singers.

Over the sound of Johnny Mathis and his band they can hear the noise of hundreds of car horns as people celebrate the World Cup victory along the Charing Cross Road.

Watching England's victory on *Match of the Day* is not proving to be as much fun as the McMahon family had hoped. It's hard to whoop and cheer when the defeated West German squad is seated behind you. Every now and then Hilary McMahon steals a glance at them. They remain stony-faced.

'What's wrong with you?' We're only ten hours late!'

About 11.15pm

Jack Charlton is walking down the stairs and into the foyer of the Royal Garden Hotel. He bumps into an old friend, the football reporter James Mossop, who's just filed his copy for the *Sunday Express*. The other players are going out on the town with their wives, but Pat Charlton is at home, about to give birth. Mossop says that he's off to catch the train back to Manchester.

'No you're not, we're going out.'

'But I've only got 15 quid...' Mossop says.

'Don't worry – I've got 100!'

The two men try to leave the hotel by the front entrance, but there are too many people on Kensington High Street. Charlton asks a waiter if he could help them escape. He shows them to a side door and they slip out around the back of the crowd. There's a black cab waiting to get past the crush of people, so they seize the opportunity to clamber in. Only then do they realise that there's someone already in it – a professional violinist on his way back from a concert at the Wigmore Hall. He has the unique privilege of finding out that England have won the World Cup from one of the England team.

Roger Hunt has decided to stay in the hotel with squad member and fellow Liverpool player Gerry Byrne and their wives. Gordon and Ursula Banks are drinking with George and Daphne Cohen. Banks is feeling disappointed that they aren't all socialising as a team.

The Kinks' helicopter has arrived at Pinhoe. The band, clearly drunk, stagger backstage. The promoter of the Bumper Beat BBQ kicks Ray Davies up the backside.

'What's wrong with you?' Davies yells at him. 'We're only ten hours late!'

11.20pm

The distinctive *Match of the Day* theme tune is playing in the television lounge of the Cumberland Hotel as the credits roll. The McMahon family watch the West German squad get up as one, and file out.

Martin Peters is too exhausted to join the other players out on the town. He and his wife Kathy are in their room at the Royal Garden Hotel drinking champagne and staring at his winner's medal, 'like two kids', Kathy said later.

About 11.30pm

Bobby and Tina Moore are leaving the Royal Garden Hotel to go to the Playboy Club on Park Lane, where later they'll be joined by some of the other players. The club only opened on 1st July, and keen for publicity, has invited them to celebrate there.

There are still so many people outside applauding and cheering that Bobby is speechless. As they walk to a taxi, people reach out to shake his hand and touch him.

John Janes, who spent the afternoon watching the final in a warden's house in Parkhouse Prison, emerges from a pub in Ryde to find that someone has written WEST HAM WON THE WORLD CUP in lipstick on the bonnet of his Ford Zephyr.

About 11.45pm

Nobby and Kay Stiles, Alan Ball and his girlfriend Lesley Newton, and John and Sandra Connelly are getting out of a black cab in front of the Playboy Club. The crowd outside cheer when they see them.

The players are then told by a doorman that they'll have to wait for a photographer to arrive before they can go in. 'We want to take a picture when all the team get here.'

Nobby Stiles swears at him and they all decide to leave.

The rooms in the Playboy Club are just like those in the Playboy Mansion, home of the club's founder, Hugh Hefner. There's a penthouse, a library/VIP room and a living room, all looked after by the Playboy Bunnies. The Bunnies wear tights, high heels, a basque with a fluffy white tail on the back, and rabbit ears on their heads. Part of the Bunny Girls' two-week training is to learn the 'Bunny Dip' – arching the back to avoid exposing too much cleavage when placing drinks on a table. To make sure the girls don't date clients, private detectives are sometimes employed by the club to test the girls by offering them money or theatre tickets for their phone number or last name.

Just before the London club opened, 400,000 people were sent membership packs – including a former archbishop of Canterbury – and 20,000 people responded by paying the eight-guinea membership fee.

11.45pm

At the 'Bumper Beat BBQ', the compere finally introduces the Kinks, who lurch on stage. Ray Davies grabs a microphone and apologises for being late. 'We were celebrating England's win...'

They launch into their opening song. Fifteen-year-old Charles Lodge and his school friend Trevor Gosling look at their watches – the band haven't got long.

The German team is now in the West End – on a pub crawl. Uwe Seeler is delighted at people's reaction. 'Complete strangers, Englishmen, patted us on the back and apologised to us. It was a faint but beautiful consolation.'

The Kinks would have been the perfect culmination to a perfect day.

Charles Lodge

Midnight

The Kinks are in the middle of their third song. The amps suddenly go dead. The licence granted to the Pinhoe festival allowed music until midnight. For a moment, Ray Davies carries on singing, then the band abruptly walk off stage. If there was an apology no one can hear it, as the mics have no power. The crowd start to boo.

Graham and Sally Saunders and Alan and Sandra Morris are partying in Trafalgar Square. People are sitting on the lions and dancing in the illuminated fountains. There is a conga line stretching down the Mall.

There are endless chants of 'We won the cup! We won the cup! Ee Ai Adio, we won the Cup!' and 'When the Reds go marching in'.

'It was a carnival of excitement – just like Rio,' Graham recalled.

Geoff Hurst, Nobby Stiles, Alan Ball and John Connelly and their wives and partners have moved on to Danny La Rue's – a club in Hanover Square, one of the most successful nightclubs in London, named after its owner, the female impersonator Danny La Rue. Noel Coward, Judy Garland and Diana Dors all love coming here. Famously, when it opened in 1964, the Beatles were guests, but had to stand, as there wasn't a free table.

Tonight, England's World Cup winners do have tables and complimentary jugs of beer and Bacardi. The players are happy to be silent for much of the time, occasionally turning to each other to say, 'We did it, we won the World Cup!"

James Mossop and Jack Charlton are at the Astor Club in Mayfair. Charlton hasn't had to touch his £100 as champagne and whisky are being provided free of charge.

About 11.30pm, 30th July 1966. Bobby Moore emerges from the
Royal Garden Hotel and is greeted by cheering fans.

Sunday 31st July 1966

00.15am

The Kinks' helicopter takes off from Pinhoe. They'd marched off the stage without speaking to anyone.

With no buses to Sidmouth at this time of night, Charles Lodge and his friend Trevor Gosling have no option but to hitchhike home.

In the West End, the early editions of the Sunday papers are on sale at newsstands.

The *News of the World* headline is 'THE WORLD BEATERS!' 'England are the Soccer champions of the world! Shout it from the twin towers of Wembley Stadium. From the Houses of Parliament. And shout it across the Rhine. By courage, guts and fighting spirit they slammed West Germany 4-2 after a half-hour of extra time...'

The *Sunday Express* contains an article by former Northern Ireland captain Danny Blanchflower. Although it was entitled 'Now I Must Pay Tribute to Alf Ramsey', Blanchflower was less than enthusiastic. England won 'because more than anything else, they had home advantage'. West Germany were better in the first half and generally 'England favoured defensive methods rather than attacking ones'.

The paper also contains a special four-page 'World Cup Souvenir' supplement, written from the imagined perspective of 1986 and looking back on 'The Day It Happened'. Nobby Stiles, as a grandfather, reminisces about 'The greatest day of my life'. There is also a full page on 'That Swinging Summer' that accurately predicts the significance of the team's victory: 'And so it was, as every middle-aged ex-mod or ex-dolly will cheerfully confirm, either by coincidence or divine planning, England's World Cup triumph came smack on time to crown an era.'

About 00.30am

A man named Lenny approaches Jack Charlton and James Mossop's table at the Astor Club and asks if they'd like to join him and his friends.

At the Playboy Club, Bobby and Tina Moore and their guests are partying with Kenny Lynch, an old friend of Bobby's who is 'running the music', as Lynch calls it. The maitre d' comes to Kenny and says, 'Burt Bacharach is downstairs with Hal David; would you mind if they join you?'

About 1.00am

At Danny La Rue's nightclub, the house band is playing 'When the Saints Go Marching In' in honour of the England players in the audience. The club didn't know that they were coming, but has managed to speedily make a special cake in the shape of the World Cup with 'World Cup Winners' written on it.

As usual on a Saturday night, Ronnie Corbett and Danny La

Rue are providing the cabaret. Their most popular routine is a parody of Margot Fonteyn and Rudolph Nureyev – Danny is Margot Bunting and Ronnie is Rudolph Nearenough.

Ronnie is beginning to make a name for himself on television; he's appeared this year in 13 episodes of the BBC's Frost Report *with John Cleese and Ronnie Barker. Danny describes Ronnie as 'Cary Grant on his knees'.*

Bobby Moore is on stage at the Playboy Club singing Stevie Wonder songs.

Moore's usual party trick when in a club is to stand innocently behind the bar, chatting and drinking. Only those around the back can see that he has his trousers around his ankles.

2.00am

On the A40 not far from Oxford, the rain is horizontal. The windscreen wipers on Graham Saunders' maroon Mini can barely cope with the deluge. His wife and their friends have been partying in Trafalgar Square after seeing the Royal Tournament. As the car begins a slow climb up a steep hill, the engine starts to misfire. Graham tells his passengers that he knows what's wrong. The Mini's transverse engine has the distributor at the front and rainwater is getting into it. He has an idea and pulls over.

Jack Charlton is now very drunk. He and journalist James Mossop are in Leytonstone, east London. They have gone back to the home of Lenny, the man they met in the Astor Club, and carried on drinking.

Alf Ramsey arrives at the Hendon Hall Hotel. His wife Vickie decided to avoid the celebrations at the Royal Garden Hotel and has been waiting for him here since the match ended.

2.15am

Graham Saunders' Mini is reversing up the hill in the pouring rain; it's the only way he can think of to keep water out of the engine. Sally, Sandra and Alan are keeping an eye out for other cars – thankfully the A40 is empty.

Graham's plan seems to be working. They should be home in Kings Heath in about an hour.

3.00am

Black cabs containing the Hursts, the Stiles, the Connellys and Alan Ball and his girlfriend arrive back at the Royal Garden Hotel. At the end of the evening they had tried to pay for their food and drink at Danny La Rue's but his maître d' Mr Lovis told them, 'Danny told me that on no account should I take a penny from you. He's just delighted you came to celebrate in his place. He's so proud of you, so proud of how you played, and so proud that you've come to his club.'

> *Many years later, Nobby Stiles thanked Danny La Rue for his generosity. 'You have nothing to thank me for – it was the best night we ever had in the club.'*

4.00am

Jack Charlton and James Mossop are fast asleep on Lenny's settee.

Alf and Vickie Ramsey have been up drinking and chatting for the past two hours. They are finally going to bed.

> *'We could not stop talking. I don't know what I thought as I lay in bed that night. I know I didn't sleep much. I can't remember my thoughts – they were just a jumble. I kept wondering if it were really true and if we had really done it,' Alf Ramsey recalled.*

5.30am

Joe and Cathy Matos' wedding night has been spoiled by a hotel room utterly lacking in character and romance. Joe loses his temper and says that he's had enough of Cathy's moaning – they are leaving right away for London to search for a nicer hotel.

'Where have you been? I have been up to your room this morning and the bed has not been slept in!'

9.00am

In Leytonstone, a bleary-eyed Jack Charlton is having breakfast in the garden with James Mossop and their new friend Lenny.

A woman pops her head over the wall.

'Hello, Jackie!' she says.

Jack can't believe it – it's Mrs Mather, one of his parents' neighbours from Ashington who happens to be on holiday in London.

'How are you going, Jackie?' she asks him dubiously.

Joe and Cathy Matos are driving along Kensington High Street. They spot the Royal Garden Hotel. Cathy thinks it looks perfect – if expensive. Joe drives his Alfa Romeo up to the door. It still has 'Just Married' written all over it.

About 10.30am

At Wembley, a football match is taking place. After big events at the stadium, locals are taken on to help clean up; they all have other jobs and are known as the 'casuals'. Because of the amount of work generated by the World Cup, people with no other job have also been taken on, and dubbed the 'student crew'. The pay is good – both the casuals and the students have been making £30 a week. There are perks – when clearing the terraces they often find jewellery, money and cameras.

As a 'thank you' on their last day, the Wembley owners have laid on beer and sandwiches and are allowing the casuals and the students to play each other on the hallowed turf that still bears the scars of yesterday's final. The game is about 20-a-side, and the players are finding the soft surface exhausting.

On the morning of the final, a reporter said to Percy Young the groundsman, 'You've got a big game on today...'
'Yes, but an even bigger one tomorrow!'

11.00am

Jack Charlton is finally arriving back at the Royal Garden Hotel. Waiting for him in the foyer is Cissie, his mother.

'Where have you been? I have been up to your room this morning and the bed has not been slept in!'

'No need to have worried,' he says, and produces a card from

278

his pocket on which is written: 'This body to be returned to Room 508 Royal Garden Hotel.'

Cathy Matos is extremely happy with their choice of hotel. Every corridor seems to be full of 'beautiful people' – attractive footballers and their wives. Joe is less happy. He thinks their room is expensive at £10 a night and his new bride is getting too much attention from other men. He decides that what might cheer him up is a visit this evening to the Playboy Club.

Midday

The West German captain Uwe Seeler sportingly poses for photographs at the top of the steps of the aircraft taking the squad to Frankfurt, shaking hands with a dwarf in a football strip wearing a World Cup Willie lion's head.

> **If you had made that game into a film, people would say 'that's rubbish' and not believed it.**
>
> **Ray Wilson**

3.00pm

'The West German attack had bite and purpose – on they came again. An English defensive lapse gave the ball to Haller – and that was it! One down after 12 minutes spurred the English attack – no time for lethargy or half measures, they swept into German territory...'

Two days after their visit to the Hendon Odeon to see *Those Magnificent Men in Their Flying Machines*, the England squad are once more at the cinema – but this time *they* are the stars on the screen. The players are sitting in Elstree Film Studios, their faces illuminated by colour footage of the World Cup final, shot by Pathé News.

For Nobby Stiles, the film is filling in the gaps of what he can't remember. 'It was if I was seeing it for the first time.'

Alf Ramsey notices that the elderly usherette who showed them to their seats is standing to one side, as there is nowhere for her to sit. He gets up and takes her by the hand and gives her his seat.

The commentary continues: '... Into his gallant team the England manager Alf Ramsey instilled sportsmanship first and foremost. How well they applied his teaching. May we, in 1970, be represented by a team of sportsmen as good as these winners of the World Cup.'

Ramsey watches the rest of the film standing up.

5.17pm, 30th July 1966. Jack Charlton sinks to his knees as Geoff Hurst and Martin Peters celebrate.

After July 1966...

Alan Ball

The day after the World Cup final, Alan Ball drove home with Lesley in his red Ford Zephyr, stopping off at Knutsford service station to eat egg and chips. He had his World Cup winner's medal in his pocket.

Two weeks later, Blackpool sold him to Everton for £110,000. He and Lesley married in May 1967. Ball went on to play for Arsenal and Southampton and in the North American Soccer League.

He won 72 caps for England and was briefly captain when Don Revie was in charge – it was, he said 'even better than winning the World Cup in 1966'. Ball had mixed fortunes as a manager of a number of clubs, including Southampton and Manchester City.

Lesley died in 2004 after a long battle with cancer. She had prepared him for her death. 'She said, "I want everything shared between our three kids." And she asked me to sell my World Cup medal because she said you can't split that in three.'

In April 2007, Alan Ball suffered a heart attack while attempting to extinguish a bonfire in his garden. The surviving members of the England team came to his funeral at Winchester Cathedral. Nobby Stiles told the congregation: 'My most abiding memory of Alan is in the World Cup final. I think all the lads would agree he was the best player on the pitch by far. He covered every blade of grass.'

Gordon Banks

For six years after the Wembley final, Gordon Banks was the finest goalkeeper in the world. When England defended their crown in Mexico in 1970, there was no question who would be between the posts. Banks' save from Pelé's header when England played Brazil in the group stage is legendary. It looked unstoppable and Pelé was already shouting 'Goal!' when Banks got a hand to it. 'I'm picking myself off the floor and you can see me laughing because Bobby Moore has just said, "You're getting old, Banksy. You used to hold onto them!"'

Gordon Banks was taken ill just before the crucial quarter-final against West Germany. 'Of all the players to lose – it had to be him,' Alf Ramsey said. (Banks doesn't completely rule out the theory that his food was tampered with.)

England were 2-0 up after 50 minutes. Alan Ball shouted, 'Goodnight, God bless, see you in Munich!' to the West Germans after the second goal went in. Minutes later, Banks' replacement Peter Bonetti failed to stop a shot by Franz Beckenbauer. 2-1. Then Alf Ramsey made a disastrous decision – he took Bobby Charlton and Martin Peters off to save their energy for the semi-final. Beckenbauer and West Germany took control. Uwe Seeler equalised just before full time. It was 2-2, extra time and 1966 once more.

Alf Ramsey tried to inspire his troops as he had at Wembley. 'You did it in 1966, you can do it again.'

'Yeah, but it wasn't 100 degrees in the shade,' striker Alan Mullery said. England lost 3-2. Gordon Banks was too ill to attend the game and watched it unfold on television.

In 1972, Gordon Banks was voted Footballer of the Year. In

October, he was involved in a car accident and lost his right eye. Although he went on to have a successful spell in the United States, his playing career never recovered.

Banks managed Telford United for the 1979–80 season until he was sacked. The club owed him money and said his contract terms could only be satisfied if he worked for them in a different capacity. They offered Banks a job as a raffle-ticket seller in a kiosk the club leased at a local supermarket. He accepted 'out of sheer bloody-mindedness'. After six weeks, Telford bowed to anger from the public that a 1966 hero should be treated so shabbily, and he finally received 50% of what he was owed. Banks went on to work for the pools panel for many years.

In 2001, he sold his World Cup winner's medal for £124,750. Three years later, Pelé named Gordon Banks as one of the world's greatest living footballers.

Franz Beckenbauer

Beckenbauer became one of the most successful footballers of all time. With Bayern Munich he won four Bundesliga titles, four German Cup finals, three European Cup finals and the Cup Winners' Cup. As captain of West Germany, he won the 1972 European Championship and the 1974 World Cup.

But 'The Kaiser' was never universally liked in West Germany. On returning home after playing for three years in the United States, he said, 'As soon as I heard the catcalls, I knew I was home.'

He and Bobby Charlton became good friends. Charlton once asked him if he felt England deserved to win the World Cup. 'Yes, I have to say that England were the best team. I had the sense when the match happened and I still feel it now, that you wanted to win it more... deep down, we were just glad to be there.'

In 1984, Beckenbauer became the manager of West Germany, guiding them to victory in the 1990 World Cup. He became a member of FIFA's executive committee. In March 2016, FIFA announced that its ethics committee was investigating his part in the bidding process for hosting the 2006 World Cup in Germany.

Bobby Charlton

Bobby Charlton once said about the 1966 victory, 'I learned quickly enough that not all of the guilt of surviving Munich... could be banished by one night of great triumph.'

In 1968, as captain of Manchester United, he walked up the 39 steps to Wembley's royal box to collect the European Cup – the first Englishman to do so. He had scored twice in United's 4-1 victory over Benfica. It was a bittersweet experience as it was ten years since the Munich air disaster. 'I felt it was a tribute to those who died at Munich. We might have won in 1958 instead of 1968 – but they never got the chance... so the feeling was to put that right.'

Bobby Charlton never played for England again after being substituted in the 1970 World Cup match against West Germany. In 1973, he played his 606th and last league game for United. By coincidence, it was the same day that his brother Jack played his last game for Leeds. The brothers have had a fractious relationship over the past 50 years, but now, Bobby says, 'Jack and I have rebuilt our relationship in a way that works for both of us.'

Charlton was the player-manager of Preston North End for the 1974–75 season, but after a dispute with the club's board, he resigned. Since then he has been involved in a number of businesses, from travel to soccer schools and has worked as a pundit for BBC television. He has campaigned for cancer and landmine charities. Bobby Charlton was knighted in 1994. 'I still can't walk past a ball without wanting to kick it,' he once said.

Over the years he has got used to the admiration in which he's held. 'We got reasonable results for England and Manchester United, and when I used to shoot from 20 or 30 yards, it was what they loved to see... '

Jack Charlton

After 1966, Jack remained in the England squad, but played only once in the 1970 World Cup in Mexico. On the flight home, he wanted to find out whether Alf Ramsey thought he had a future as an England player. There was an empty seat next to the manager. Ramsey lowered his newspaper.

'What is it, Jack?'

'I've enjoyed playing for England, but I'm well into my thirties, so I think it would be wise if I called it a day.'

'I totally agree.'

Ramsey then lifted up his paper and carried on reading.

Of all the 1966 players who went into management, Jack Charlton was the most successful. His style was compared to Alf Ramsey's. While he was in charge of the Republic of Ireland team they qualified for a European Championship and two World Cups – reaching the quarter-finals in 1990.

When Charlton took the Republic of Ireland team to meet Pope John Paul II on the eve of the 1990 World Cup, his Holiness said, 'I know who you are: you're the Boss.'

George Cohen

In early 1968, George Cohen's football career was ended by an injury in a Liverpool v Fulham game at Anfield – 'I was screaming in pain before I hit the ground.' After a few years coaching Fulham's youth team, Cohen became a successful property developer.

In 1976, after one of his regular four-mile runs, he felt 'suddenly exhausted'. It was the start of a long battle against bowel cancer that didn't end until he was given the all-clear in 1990.

In 2000, George Cohen was awarded an MBE, along with Nobby Stiles, Roger Hunt, Ray Wilson and Alan Ball. Fulham announced in 2016 that they had commissioned a statue of the World Cup winner who had played for them 459 times.

Lothar Emmerich

'Emma' Emmerich never played for West Germany again. He continued to be a highly effective striker for Borussia Dortmund – when he left the club in 1969 he had scored 115 goals in 183 appearances.

In January 2003, he was diagnosed with lung cancer and died that August.

Helmut Haller

In 1968, Haller left Bologna for Juventus. After five years, he returned to his home town and the newly created club of FC Augsburg. Haller was extremely popular and attracted large crowds who would chant 'Haller-Haller-Haller-lujah!'

After a campaign by the *Daily Mirror* ('Geoff wants his ball back!'), Helmut Haller agreed to part with the match ball for £80,000. *Mirror* photographer Kent Gavin, who'd struggled to get good pictures of the 1966 final from the stands, was on hand to capture the moment Hurst and Haller shook hands and the famous orange ball was handed over. It's now with the National Football Museum in Manchester.

Helmut Haller died in October 2012, aged 73.

Siggi Held

Siggi Held continued playing in the Bundesliga until 1979. As a manager he looked after both club and national teams, including Dynamo Dresden, Thailand and Malta.

Horst-Dieter Höttges

'Iron Foot' Höttges was a key member of Helmut Schön's squad until 1974. He played for his club Werder Bremen a record 423 times.

Roger Hunt

Liverpool manager Bill Shankly brought Roger Hunt down to earth when he returned for pre-season training: 'Well done, son, but we've got more important things now!' However, at the 1966 Charity Shield, Hunt and Everton's Ray Wilson did have the satisfaction of doing a lap of honour around Wembley with the World Cup.

The prospect of another World Cup didn't appeal to Hunt: 'I didn't want to be the one up front at the age of 32, with all the load and the responsibility of carrying the burden *again*.' In 1969 he told Alf Ramsey that he didn't want to be considered for Mexico. In December, out of favour with Shankly, he left Liverpool for Second Division Bolton Wanderers, but found it hard to get used to empty terraces.

At his testimonial to mark his retirement at the age of 34, fans were locked out of Anfield, such was the demand for tickets. They idolised 'Sir Roger'. His 245 league goals for Liverpool are unlikely to be bettered. Roger Hunt left football behind and joined Hunt Brothers, the family's haulage firm.

Geoff Hurst

Just over 24 hours after Geoff Hurst scored his hat-trick on Wembley's turf, he was back at home cutting his own grass.

After the World Cup, he became an even better player, and a highly valued one. Matt Busby sent Ron Greenwood at West Ham a telegram offering £200,000 for the forward. The reply came back: 'No. Greenwood.'

By 1970, Hurst wanted to leave the club and went to see Greenwood just as Martin Peters was leaving the manager's office. Greenwood was pale – Peters had asked for a transfer. 'I thought Ron was near to tears about Martin. There's no way I could make it two in a day.' It was two years before Hurst departed for Stoke.

When he retired as a player in 1976, Hurst was determined to succeed as a manager. 'That hat-trick gave me a great start in life, but it is not going to be the one thing I'm remembered for.' Hurst managed Telford and then for two seasons Second Division Chelsea. When he left football, Hurst embarked on a successful career in insurance.

He was awarded an MBE in 1975 and knighted in 1998.

Bobby Moore

On the day after the final, Alf Ramsey got the players together and told them that the FA was giving the squad £22,000. He proposed each of them should get £500, and the rest of the money should be divided up between those who had played in the finals. Bobby Moore said immediately, 'Look, Alf, there are 22 of us in the squad – it looks pretty straightforward to me – £1000 a man.' They all agreed that this was the fairest solution.

It was the captain who got most of the adulation after England's victory. He won the 1966 BBC Sports Personality of the Year (Geoff Hurst was third after a New Zealand speedway rider) and in 1967, he was awarded an OBE. As the Queen handed Moore the OBE she told him she had 'enjoyed the final very much'.

Moore retired in 1977 after playing a match for Fulham against Blackburn – it was his 1000th league appearance. He found it hard to get a job in top-flight football. After Don Revie left the England manager's job in 1977, the former captain wrote to the FA: 'I have gained considerable experience in assisting with coaching both with my clubs in England and abroad during the latter stages of my playing career. I know you are aware of [...] how proud I was of my years with the England team.' He received no reply.

Moore had unsuccessful spells as the manager of Southend United, Eastern AA in Hong Kong and at Oxford United. His managerial career was not without its small triumphs. After Oxford beat Slough the Premier Division leaders in the Isthmian League, he said, 'It was an indication of the progress we'd made and I came into the dressing room with the old fists raised in triumph.'

In 1991, Bobby Moore was diagnosed with bowel cancer. Although he never disclosed to his friends he was ill, it was clear to them how poorly he was. Harry Redknapp burst into tears when he saw his friend. At the unveiling of a statue of Bobby Charlton, George and Daphne Cohen saw Moore and could tell immediately he was sick. 'His eyes have the same life-less look yours did,' Daphne said to her husband. Doss Moore died in 1990 not knowing how ill her son was.

Bobby Moore's earlier battle with cancer was a secret until

after his death on 24th February 1993, aged 51. Tina, who had divorced him in 1986, told the *Mail on Sunday* about his testicular cancer the day before his thanksgiving service at Westminster Abbey. 'I feel it can do nothing but enhance his memory,' she said.

Just before Bobby Moore died, he made a pilgrimage to the Royal Garden Hotel and to Wembley Stadium.

Wolfgang Overath

After winning a World Cup runners-up medal in 1966, Overath went on to win a third-place medal in 1970 and a winner's medal in 1974. He played in every game in each of those World Cups.

In July 1974, a party was held at Munich's Hilton Hotel for the victorious World Cup team. To their disgust, their wives were not invited by the *Deutscher Fußball-Bund* (DFB) and most of the players, including Overath, walked out. Overath and team-mates Gerd Müller and Jürgen Grabowski retired from international football in protest. Goalkeeper Sepp Maier said, 'Germans can organise a World Cup perfectly and crush the strongest opposition through unflagging discipline – but we don't have the faintest idea about holding a party.'

Martin Peters

Frustrated by the lack of West Ham success in the late 1960s, Martin Peters joined Spurs in 1970 for the then record sum of £200,000 (he received £10,000). With Spurs he won the League Cup in 1971 and 1973 and the UEFA Cup in 1972. Martin Peters' ability to appear as if from nowhere earned him the nickname 'The Ghost'; Alf Ramsey told a reporter, 'Martin Peters is a player ten years ahead of his time.'

In 1973, Peters captained Ramsey's England side that drew with Poland and so failed to qualify for the 1974 World Cup finals. 'Three weeks before we'd played Austria at home and won 7-0, and everything went right, but on that night everything went wrong.'

After leaving football, Martin Peters worked in the insurance business until his retirement in 2001. In 2016, his family announced that he was suffering from Alzheimer's.

Alf Ramsey

In May 1974, the FA sacked Alf Ramsey. He was given a golden handshake of £8000 and a pension of £1200 a year. His successor Don Revie was given a salary of £25,000 a year. Ramsey said he 'died a thousand deaths' in the weeks after his dismissal.

Although under Alf Ramsey's leadership England lost only 17 times in 113 games, the years after the 1966 victory were seen as a disappointment. In 1968, England came third in the European Championships, and two years later, they were losing quarter-finalists to West Germany. After being knocked out of the 1970 World Cup, they failed to qualify for the 1974 finals in West Germany.

Ramsey was offered work abroad, but said he wanted to continue to work with English footballers. In 1976, he joined the board of Birmingham City and the following year was offered the job of manager. He resigned in February after the board overturned his decision to allow their star player Trevor Francis to leave the club (Ramsey believed Francis lacked commitment).

Alf Ramsey retired to Suffolk. Occasionally the FA would send him tickets for games; he would swap the tickets with a spectator to avoid sitting near anyone from the FA.

In 1977, he went to watch Brighton and Hove Albion play.

The board were delighted to have Ramsey at the ground and asked him if he would do the half-time lottery draw. He was cheered by the entire crowd as he walked out onto the pitch. The reaction was a revelation. 'I never knew I was loved like this,' he said to a friend afterwards.

Alf Ramsey was knighted in 1967. He died on 28th April 1999. George Cohen spoke at his funeral and ended by saying: 'I feel we are here to celebrate not only the life of a great football manager but a great Englishman. One who, should he be looking down now, is probably thinking, "Yes, George, I think we've had enough of that."'

Karl-Heinz Schnellinger

The 1966 World Cup was the last final Schnellinger lost for many years. With AC Milan he won the 1968 Cup Winners' Cup (defeating Uwe Seeler's Hamburg), the 1969 European Cup and the 1972 Coppa Italia.

Helmut Schön

Under Schön, West Germany became a hugely successful team. They were European Champions in 1972 and runners-up in 1976. The team came third in the 1970 World Cup, and were winners in 1974. After 14 years in charge, 'The Tall One' decided to retire after defending West Germany's title at the 1978 World Cup in Argentina. It wasn't the ending he had hoped for – they were knocked out in the quarter-finals.

Helmut Schön died in February 1996, aged 80.

Willi Schulz

After 1966, he acquired the nickname 'World Cup Willi'. In

Mexico in 1970, he came on as a substitute for Horst-Dieter Höttges in the game against England.

After retiring from football, he worked in insurance and ran a slot-machine business.

Uwe Seeler

Defeat at Wembley did not diminish Seeler's popularity. The day after the final, 12,000 fans greeted the West German squad at Frankfurt Airport. The players were then driven into the city in open cars as supporters chanted *'Uwe Uwe!'* Banners were held up declaring: 'We welcome the real World Champions!' The mayor of Frankfurt's speech was interrupted by chants of 'Wangle! Wangle!' – a protest against England's third goal.

'Uns Uwe' ('Our Uwe') played a total of 72 times for West Germany, scoring 43 goals. He became Adidas's head representative for the north of the country.

Outside the Hamburg SV stadium is a giant monument depicting Seeler's naked right foot.

Nobby Stiles

During his week off after the World Cup and before the new season started, Nobby Stiles vowed to put his hard-man image behind him and bet a Manchester United team-mate that he wouldn't be cautioned before Christmas. He lost his money within a few days.

After a successful career with United spanning 14 years, including winning the European Cup in 1968, Stiles left Manchester United to join Jack Charlton's Middlesbrough. 'It's like cutting off my arm,' he said at the time. He was unhappy at Middlesbrough and accepted Bobby Charlton's invitation to join Preston where he was now manager. Preston was Stiles' last club as a player.

Alex Ferguson invited Stiles to be a youth coach at Manchester United, and he helped develop the talents of Ryan Giggs, Paul Scholes and David Beckham.

In June 2002, Nobby Stiles suffered a heart attack. As he recovered, he watched the World Cup finals on television from his hospital bed. In 2012, Nobby was diagnosed with Alzheimer's.

Hans Tilkowski

Even before the World Cup was over, fan mail was being delivered to his home 'in a container resembling a laundry basket'. Despite his popularity, he lost his position as West Germany's goalkeeper to Sepp Maier the following year. Tilkowski retired in 1970.

Wolfgang Weber

The defender who got West Germany's last-minute equaliser scored only one other goal for West Germany, despite representing his country for another eight years. When he retired he worked for Adidas.

Ray Wilson

Wilson stayed at Everton for two more years, before being given a free transfer to Oldham Athletic. In 1971, he was appointed caretaker manager at Bradford City and held the post for three months, before retiring from football altogether.

To make up for the lack of wages during the summer, Ray had started helping out at his father-in-law's West Yorkshire undertaking business and then, having sat the necessary exams, took it over. He was awarded a distinction in his embalming exam.

Although he no longer went to football matches, he used to watch recordings of the 1966 final. 'It moves me more now than it did then. It has got more important. I do find it much more difficult to sit and watch it on the television and see me standing there, and the Queen, and I'm thinking – how the hell did you do that?'

Ray Wilson was the first of the 1966 team to be diagnosed with Alzheimer's. In 2016, the FA asked FIFA to investigate whether professional footballers are more likely to suffer from forms of dementia. Heading heavy leather footballs has been cited as a cause.

They think it's all over...
The 1966 World Cup final teams did meet once again – in very different circumstances.

On 11th May 1985, debris caught fire underneath a stand at Bradford City's Valley Parade ground. Fifty-six spectators died in the inferno. The stand had been due to be demolished two days later.

The World Cup final players were contacted soon after to see if they would replay the 1966 fixture to raise money for the victims' families.

Watched by 19,000 people at Leeds United's Elland Road ground, the two teams trotted out to a standing ovation as Kenneth Wolstenholme called out their names. This rematch was one of the first games to be affected by the Popplewell Inquiry, which recommended changes to make football grounds safer, so no drink was allowed and no bars were open.

Playing was a struggle for some. Ray Wilson had a plastic

kneecap and a hand in plaster and George Cohen, who was battling cancer, only managed to play for a few minutes. Gordon Banks had an artificial hip and was blind in one eye but still produced some magnificent saves.

The final score was 6-4 to England. Geoff Hurst once more produced a hat-trick. Bobby Moore was presented with a mocked-up Jules Rimet trophy and the two teams did a lap of honour together. Over £50,000 was raised.

Even if they had wanted to reunite the 1966 team with the real Jules Rimet trophy, it would have been impossible. When in 1970 Brazil won the World Cup for the third time, they were given the trophy in perpetuity. In 1983, it was stolen and has never been recovered. The replica was returned to George Bird, the silversmith who made it, and he kept it hidden under his bed for 25 years. It is now in the National Football Museum.

Brian James, who had reported on the 1966 final, was at Elland Road for the reunion. He wrote: 'It is impossible to overestimate the impact these 11 men made on England's view of itself back in 1966. For a month they were the centre of the nation's life. Because of their manners as well as their skills, because of the way they achieved great triumph and then lived the remainder of their sporting lives without disgrace, it is very easy for us to believe them to be the last of the real heroes.'

Acknowledgements

This book was written in part to accompany a BBC Radio 2 '1966 World Cup Minute by Minute' broadcast marking the game's 50th anniversary. My thanks to the talented TBI Media team, especially Mark Sharman whose idea it was in the first place and to Phil Critchlow who has been a good friend to me and the Minute by Minute series. Much thanks also to Bob Shennan the controller of Radio 2 and Robert Gallagher its commissioning editor.

Many of the stories in this book originated from a request I made on air on Jeremy Vine's Radio 2 show. Special thanks to Jeremy and his editor Phil Jones for making it possible. It was a great joy to speak to so many people with such varied memories of that extraordinary day. Carl Gillwood in particular deserves credit for taking the trouble to write his account for me with such flair.

Kevin Moore, Kevin Haygarth and David Pearson at the National Football Museum provided many useful contacts and more importantly let me hold the 1966 match ball and the replica Jules Rimet trophy. Thanks also to Dave Corbett, Dave Davies, Mark Anderson at the Royal Garden Hotel, and Tony Jameson-Allen at the charity Sporting Memories.

Keely Allan, Alan Ball's daughter shared with me a speech her father made, in which he talked about his life. He was fine orator as well as a gifted footballer.

In my quest to reflect the stories of the West German fans and players I was helped by Uli Hesse, Raphael Honigstein, Günther Simmermacher, Gregor Schnittker, Stefan Erhardt, and the team at Zeitspiel magazine. Special thanks to Christoph Wagner for his knowledge, translations and for conducting the interview with Siggi Held on my behalf.

Thanks also to Rebecca Nicolson, Aurea Carpenter, Klara Zak and Paul Bougourd at Short Books for their help and support, and to my editor Emma Craigie who, like Bobby Moore, was always calm and could spot where I was going wrong.

I've loved stepping into the world of 1966 and I shall miss it. But I know my ever-patient wife Hannah and son Charlie will be glad that I've hung up my England scarf and put away my rattle and rosette – for now.

Bibliography

Armfield, Jimmy, *Right Back to the Beginning* (Headline, 2004)

Ball, Alan, *Playing Extra Time* (Pan, 2004)

Banks, Gordon, *Banksy* (Michael Joseph, 2002)

Barclay, Patrick and Powell, Kenneth, *Wembley Stadium: Venue of Legends* (Prestel, 2007)

Barwick, Brian, *Watching the Match* (Andre Deutsch, 2013)

Best, George, *Blessed* (Ebury, 2002)

Best, George, *Hard Tackles and Dirty Baths* (Ebury, 2005)

Bowler, David, *Winning Isn't Everything* (Orion, 1998)

Charlton, Sir Bobby, *My Manchester United Years* (Headline, 2007)

Charlton, Sir Bobby, *My England Years* (Headline, 2008)

Charlton, Jack, *The Autobiography* (Corgi, 1996)

Cheeseman, Doug and Robinson, Peter, *1966 Uncovered* (Mitchell Beazley, 2006)

Clay, Catrine, *Trautmann's Journey* (Yellow Jersey Press, 2011)

Cleese, John, *So, Anyway* (Arrow Books, 2014)

Cohen, George, *My Autobiography* (Headline, 2003)

Corbett, Ronnie, *High Hopes* (Ebury Press, 2000)

Dickinson, Matt, *Bobby Moore: The Man in Full* (Yellow Jersey Press, 2014)

Downing, David, *The Best of Enemies: England v Germany* (Bloomsbury, 2000)

Fulbrook, Mary, *History of Germany 1918–2000* (Blackwell, 1991)

Greaves, Jimmy, *Greavsie: The Autobiography* (Time Warner Books, 2003)

Hasted, Nick, *The Kinks: You Really Got Me* (Omnibus Press, 2011)

Held, Siggi, *Rund um den Ball* (Gerhard Hess Verlag, 2013)

Hesse-Lichtenberger, Ulrich, *Tor! The Story of German Football* (WSC Books, 2002)

Hunt, Chris, *World Cup Stories* (Interact, 2015)

Hurst, Geoff, *1966 and All That* (Headline, 2001)

Hurst, Geoff, *World Champions* (Headline, 2006)

Hutchinson, Roger, *'66* (Mainstream, 1995)

Kelner, Martin, *Sit Down and Cheer* (Bloomsbury, 2012)

Körner, Torsten, *Franz Beckenbauer: Der Freie Mann* (Fischer Taschenbuch, 2005)

La Rue, Danny, *From Drags to Riches* (Viking, 1987)

Law, Dennis, *The King* (Bantam Press, 2003)

Massarella, Louis and Moynihan, Leo eds, *Match of My Life* (Know the Score Books, 2006)

McIllvanney, Hugh, *World Cup '66* (Eyre & Spottiswoode, 1966)

McKinstry, Leo, *Jack and Bobby* (Collins Willow, 2002)

McKinstry, Leo, *Sir Alf* (Harper Sport, 2006)

Miller, David, *England's Last Glory* (Pavilion, 1986)

Moore, Brian, *The Final Score* (Hodder & Stoughton, 1999)

Moore, Kevin, *Museums and Popular Culture* (Leicester University Press, 1997)

Moore, Tina, *Bobby Moore* (Harper Sport, 2006)

Morris, Jim, *Gordon Banks: A Biography* (Amberley, 2013)

Oddie, Bill, *One Flew Into The Cuckoo's Egg* (Hodder, 2009)

Peel, John, *Margrave of the Marshes* (Bantam Press, 2005)

Peters, Martin, *The Ghost of '66* (Orion, 2006)

Powell, Jeff, *Bobby Moore: The Life and Times of a Sporting Hero* (Robson Books, 1998)

Ramsey, Alf, *Talking Football* (Stanley Paul, 1952)

Rowlinson, John, *Boys of '66* (Virgin Books, 2016)

Sandbrook, Dominic, *White Heat* (Little, Brown, 2006)

Savage, Jon, *1966* (Faber and Faber, 2015)

Seeler, Uwe, *Danke, Fussball!* (Rowohlt Taschenbuch Verlag, 2003)

Shiel, Norman, *Voices of '66* (Tempus, 2006)

Smit, Barbara, *Pitch Invasion* (Allen Lane, 2006)

Stiles, Nobby, *After the Ball* (Hodder & Stoughton, 2003)

Summerbee, Mike, *The Autobiography* (Century, 2008)

Talbot, Bruce and Weaver, Paul, *1966: The Good, the Bad and the Football* (Sutton Publishing, 2006)

Thomson, David, *4-2* (Bloomsbury, 1996)

Tilkowski, Hans, *Und Ewig Fällt Das Wembley-Tor* (Verlag Die Werkstatt, 2006)

Tyler, Martin, *Boys of '66* (Hamlyn, 1981)

Wilson, AN, *Our Times: The Age of Elizabeth II* (Hutchinson, 2008)

Wilson, Jonathan, *Inverting the Pyramid* (Orion, 2008)

Winstone, Ray, *Young Winstone* (Canongate, 2015)

Wolstenholme, Kenneth, *The Boys' Book of the World Cup* (World Distributors, 1966)

Wolstenholme, Kenneth, *They Think It's All Over* (Robson Books, 1996)

Wright, Chris, *No More Worlds to Conquer* (The Friday Project, 2015)

The Football Book (Dorling Kindersley, 2009)

Royal Garden Hotel: Fifty Years (TriNorth Limited, 2015)

World Championship Programme 1966 (Football Association, 1966)

Other sources:

1966 World Cup Final, Pathé News

Ball, Alan, After Dinner Speaker, *Vimeo*, https://vimeo.com/8691291

Cattani, Derek, 'When the World Cup came to London', *Time Out London*, http://www.timeout.com/london/things-to-do/when-the-world-cup-came-to-london, 6th June 2006

Corbett, James, 'The Last Days of Bobby Moore', *Observer Sport Monthly*, http://www.theguardian.com/observer/osm/story/0,,1541919,00.html, 7th August 2005

'Goodies Solo Records', *The Goodies Illustrated Guide*, http://www.the
goodies.info/records_solo

Hattenstone, Simon, 'The Best of Times', *Guardian Online*, http://www.
theguardian.com/football/2006/apr/08/newsstory.sport, 8th April 2006

Hendon Times, 29th July 1966

Jackson, Jamie, 'A Twist in the Tale', *Observer Online*, http://www.
theguardian.com/football/2006/apr/23/newsstory.sport1, 23rd April
2006

Ladyman, Ian, 'Gordon Banks', *Mail Online*, http://www.dailymail.co.uk/
sport/football/article-3412772/Gordon-Banks-England-good-Brazil-
1970-come-one-got-poisoned-Pele-save-good-better-one.html, 23 January
2016

'The Official Website for Sir Geoff Hurst', http://www.geoffhurst.com

Parry, Haydn, 'Glad All Over', *WSC Online*, http://www.wsc.co.uk/
the-archive/919-World-Cup/3528-glad-all-over, December 2000

Penner, Barbara, 'How the London Playboy Club Bankrolled Hef's Empire',
The Architectural Review, http://www.architectural-review.com/today/
how-the-london-playboy-club-bankrolled-hefs-empire/8680952.
fullarticle, 7th April 2015

Pesti, Peter, '1966 World Cup ball (Slazenger Challenge)', *Worldcupballs.info*
http://worldcupballs.info/world-cup-balls/1966-england/1966-world-
cup-ball-slazenger-challenge.html

Those Magnificent Men in Their Flying Machines (20th Century Fox, 1965)

Total Football Magazine, August 1996

Wagner, Christoph, *Crossing the Line: The English Press and Anglo-German
Football* (De Montfort University Thesis, 2014)

The World Cup Final, BBC Worldwide, 2006

Index

Also Available in the Minute by Minute Series